indivisible by two

Nancy L. Segal

indivisible by two
Lives of Extraordinary Twins

Harvard University Press

Cambridge, Massachusetts, & London, England   2005

Library of Congress Cataloging-in-Publication Data

Segal, Nancy L., 1951–
    Indivisible by two : lives of extraordinary twins / Nancy L. Segal.
        p.   cm.
    Includes bibliographical references.
    ISBN 0-674-01933-4 (alk. paper)
    1. Twins—Case studies.   2. Twins—Psychology.   3. Multiple birth.
    I. Title.
HQ777.35.S44   2005
155.44'4–dc22   2005045979

For the lucky few who are indivisible by 2 or 3 or 4 . . .

Contents

Introduction

To many people, twins seem extraordinary, sometimes even strange. Their lives are hard to imagine, even though they are just being themselves. Maybe it's the unplanned joining of humanity and science that makes twins alluring—each pair tells us something about ourselves or about someone we know in a new, romantic, or funny way. I love being with twins and I love telling their stories.

Thinking about twins (partly because I am a fraternal twin myself; my sister Anne is seven minutes younger than I am) has absorbed me for much of my adult life. When I was fresh out of graduate school in 1982, I became a post-doctoral fellow at the University of Minnesota, where I studied twins who were reared apart. The real-life science was better than the reports I had read in journals or newspapers because the findings were in front of me, evident in whatever the twins said and did. I understood completely that identical twins are more alike than any other pair of people, even when they are separated at birth. But their similarity isn't complete, despite the fact that they have identical genes. I decided to find out why.

In my first book, *Entwined Lives,* I took a close look at how twins are used in research and what they tell us about human behavior in general. I also examined different kinds of twins. Many people talk about twins as though there is only one kind, but there are two—identical and fraternal—and both have lots of intriguing variations.

✳ No one knows what causes a fertilized egg (or zygote) to split within the first two weeks after conception, but this happens naturally in about 1 out of every 250 births. The result is two individuals with the same genes. Actually, the preferred term for identical twins is *monozygotic,* or MZ, because identical twins are never really identical. Differences between them can happen for genetic reasons, environmental reasons, or both—and the differences can occur before or after birth. If one female twin loses one of her two X chromosomes soon after conception, she will have Turner's syndrome (XO), whereas her sister might be normal (XX). And if twins get assigned to different classes at school, they may show differences in some interests and abilities.

Fraternal twins result when a woman simultaneously releases two eggs that are both fertilized. These twins share half their genes, on average: the same amount shared by ordinary brothers and sisters. Fraternal twin pairs can consist of two females, two males, or one of each. The preferred term for these twins is *dizygotic,* or DZ, not just because the twins started out as two zygotes, but because the word "fraternal" has a male connotation and neglects the female fraternals out there. Like most other siblings, fraternal twins can be similar in some ways and different in others. Amazingly, some fraternal twins have the same mother but different fathers—this can happen if a woman releasing two eggs has intercourse with different men in a short space of time.

✳ Twins love being in studies and researchers love having them. The logic behind twin studies, first discussed in 1875, is simple and elegant: If pairs of identical twins show greater resemblance in verbal reasoning, heart rate, or running speed than pairs of fraternal twins, then genes probably influence those traits. Some critics have attributed identical twins' greater similarity to the way their parents raised them, arguing that if twins get the same treatment they will end up the same. But identical twins usually turn out quite a lot alike whether or not their parents treated them alike.

Twin research has given us virtually irrefutable evidence that genes affect most of our behaviors. But the degree of genetic influence isn't the same for all traits: It's about 50 to 70 percent for general intelligence, 50 percent for extraversion, and 30 percent for job satisfaction. This means that if I measured extraversion among a group of people, I would find that half the differences among them were linked to their genes and half were linked to their environments. But this all works differently for individual people—an unusual life experience like being raised on an exotic island or contracting a rare disease can make these percentages irrelevant because its effects can be so powerful.

I refer to twins in the conventional way, as identical or fraternal, in the chapters that follow. But it is important to know the limitations of these terms—none of the identical twins I describe are exact duplicates, and the one (possibly) fraternal pair is female, not male. I wanted to write about these particular pairs because they had such thought-provoking stories to tell.

Most people say that twins are naturally interesting, but there is more to the story. Identical twins' matched bodies and minds challenge our beliefs in individual uniqueness. And the "power of two" can be intimidating—even mothers and fathers have felt left out of whatever their twins are up to. Twins are born into an intimate relationship that most people envy. But the differences between identical twins are more interesting to researchers than their similarities. If we know why only one twin is infertile, gay, or overweight then we can better understand what happens—inside and outside the womb—to affect these traits.

Both in Minnesota and in California, where I have lived since 1991, I have conducted twin studies in the hopes of shedding some light on such nature-nurture questions. But laboratory studies miss the vitality of twins' lives—and maybe some important reasons twins differ. So I decided to hang around with some twins, triplets, and quads and become part of their lives for a while. My three-part background as researcher, author, and twin turned out to be a great recipe for trust and candor on the part of the twins and their families. I have been teased for dressing more like a California teenager than a respectable professor of psychology, but maybe the sight of a slim woman in a T-shirt, jeans, and silver sneakers, scribbling down notes, helped put people at ease. Listening to young quadruplets' bedtime stories, shopping with identical women married to identical men, drinking coffee with a transsexual twin's mother, and dining with triplets, two straight and one gay, were extraordinary experiences. Their stories really came out during these times, in casual remarks and spontaneous reactions. I started to know the twins not just as likable research subjects but as people whom I increasingly admired. They taught me a lot about human behavior without trying to, and I feel happier and maybe even smarter for having known them.

The ten twin pairs, one triplet set, and one quadruplet set I write about fall into four categories: I. Separated at Birth, II. Variations on Common Themes, III. Extraordinary Circumstances, and IV. Everyday Wonders.

Part I: Separated at Birth. When identical twins raised apart both become firemen, both watch weird movies, or both like to sneeze loudly in elevators, it probably has something to do with their shared genes. There are no genes for fighting fires, watching films, or goofing around, but these behaviors are probably influenced, in some way, by our basic personalities and temperaments.

When the fireman twins, Mark and Gerry, met by chance at age thirty-one, neither one knew that the other existed. But their voices, physical build, interests, and occupations were practically matched, and they had no trouble becoming friends. The Canadian twins, Brent and George, met when they were twenty, when one twin was mistaken for the other in a university lounge. Their tastes for unusual games, books, music, and sports statistics drew them together, at least in the beginning. But Jack and Oskar may be the best example of twins whose lives seem more like fiction than reality. They were raised apart as Trinidadian Jew and German Catholic, just as Hitler was coming to power. When they met briefly in their twenties, each one knew that he might have grown up as the other. The twins didn't meet again until they were adults, but this time they tried to get along, as they would repeatedly over the rest of their lives. If they hadn't been identical twins and hadn't been so fascinated by their similar habits and quirks, they may not have tried so hard to reach across the cultural gulf between them.

Part II: Variations on Common Themes. Differences between identical twins can be slight or extreme. Many differences are understandable, but some remain very curious.

I was intrigued and disturbed by the silent sisters Mira and Melanie, whose shyness stopped them from talking to people outside their family. Both twins had a rare social anxiety disorder—selective mutism—and even though they were reared together, one twin was more severely affected than her sister. I also visited identical triplet brothers, two straight and one gay. Owen, Tom, and Frank were remarkable variations of the same DNA. Their mother insisted that she treated them all exactly the same, so how could they have turned out so differently? Agnes and Audrey were an even rarer pair—identical twin sisters, one who felt like a man and one who felt like a woman. Today, Agnes no longer exists. She has become a man named Andru.

Part III: Extraordinary Circumstances. Some of the twins' stories have been very painful but nonetheless inspiring. Despite their losses and injustices, the twins survived not only physically but spiritually.

Stepha and Annetta were forced participants in Josef Mengele's horrific experiments on twins and dwarfs at Auschwitz. They were among the few who survived, although they lost many relatives. As a Jewish twin, I have thought about the protective effects of time and place: had my twin sister, Anne, and I been born earlier and elsewhere, we might have been two of Mengele's subjects.

Linda lost her twin sister, Brenda, in the World Trade Center attack, when they were forty. "Twin Towers" was once a popular metaphor for unusually tall or strong twins, but it brings a different image to mind now. Another twin survivor said of September 11, "When the first tower collapsed, the remaining one was just a burnt-out shell. And burnt-out shells do not stand up alone for long."

Two Canadian couples, Allyson and Kirk and Lynette and Mike, separately adopted abandoned infant twins from China. Once they learned that their girls, Lily and Gillian, were twins, they worked hard to bring them together often. So even though the twins are growing up in different families, their story promises a happy conclusion.

Part IV: Everyday Wonders. Unusual relationships emerge naturally in families with twins. Twins turn ordinary families into strange coalitions just by getting married—and they make genetic calculations tricky. For example, identical twins are the "parents" of their nieces and nephews because identical twins are genetically interchangeable; DNA tests could never identify the real mom or dad. And when identical twins marry identical twins, their relationships become even closer.

Identical twins Tracy and Marcy did almost everything together. But when it was time to have children, Marcy was successful and Tracy wasn't. The twins' same genes let Tracy become a biological mother to her daughter, Ella, even though she didn't give birth to her. Identical twins Craig and Mark married identical twins Diane and Darlene. The two married couples are wonderfully close—but at the same time, each swears that they could never have married their twin's spouse.

We come last to the Quad Boys, four four-year-old brothers, two sets of identical twins. Watching them gives anyone an education in behavioral development, family relations, and parenting challenges.

I cannot fully explain the differences between these twins, triplets, and quads. But I can make some educated guesses about aspects of their environments that could have sent them in their different directions. I admire those who struggled knowing that each one could have turned out differently, if only . . .

This book is not just for twins and their families, but for anyone puzzled and fascinated by the tiny twists and great puzzles behind individuals' similarities and differences. My goal for this book is to bring humanity and science together—to do for twin studies what Oliver Sacks did for clinical studies: "Restore the human subject at the center."[1] Here are the stories.

I

SEPARATED AT BIRTH

Twins reared apart are literary tricks and scientific dreams. Writers use them to explore identity and duality, or to create hilarity and absurdity, as Shakespeare did in his play *Twelfth Night*.[1] These stories engage us because they capture the everyday conflicts and mishaps that can occur when two people look alike. Most people aren't twins— but since seemingly unexplained events affect us all, reared-apart twins' tales are meaningful and amusing. Researchers, myself included, relish such stories because they tell us how, and how much, genes and environments affect human growth and development.

The first literary mention of separated twins comes from the Roman comic dramatist Plautus (254–184 B.C.). His play *Menaechmi (The Twin Brothers)* captures the confusion and frustration that can result when identical twins are mistaken for each other.[2] Seven-year-old Menaechmus was separated from his identical twin brother, Sosicles, when they were traveling with their father. Sosicles eventually set out to find his missing twin. When he encountered his brother's courtesan, she mistook him for Menaechmus, leading to false identities and misunderstandings.

Separated twins did not appear in the scientific literature until 1922, when Paul Popenoe published an account of identical twins Bessie and Jessie.[3] The twins were placed with different families when they were eight months old and didn't meet again until they were eighteen. Both twins were avid readers and had impressive administrative skills. They were also very attached to each other; Jessie wrote, "We have never had a disagreement . . . I am fond of my older sister and two brothers, yet they have never seemed as close to me as Bess."

I studied approximately 70 of the 135 reared-apart twin pairs who participated in the Minnesota Study of Twins Reared Apart.[4] The project, headed by Thomas J. Bouchard, Jr., had its own special jargon. *MZTs* were monozygotic (identical) twins raised together; *MZAs* were identical twins raised apart. *Twin Weeks* were seven-day twin assessments that began on Sunday and ended the next Saturday. *Scheduled Inventories* were booklets containing the 15,000 questions twins completed during a *Twin Week*. Bouchard's *Glamorous Entourage* was the most recent group of research associates, of which Kimerly J. Wilcox and I were the sole members.

We found the reared-apart twins in many ways, including referrals from colleagues, reunion registries, and the media.[5] Some pairs acquired appropriate nicknames once we got to know them: Barbara and Daphne were the *Giggle Twins* whose spontaneous laughter was irresistible. Mark and Gerry were the *Fireman Twins* whose voluntary service defined their lives. Jim Lewis and Jim Springer were the *Jim Twins* whose meeting launched the Minnesota Study in March 1979.

Our mission was to gather enormous amounts of information from the reared-apart twins during their visits to the university. We accompanied the pairs to heart exams, dental check-ups, and chest X-rays. We administered ability tests, stress tests, and personality questionnaires. We sat with the twins at lunch and were riveted by their stories of separation and reunion. And we watched them close up and from a distance, attentive to each pair's similarities and differences.

I loved the Minnesota study. It provided me with an opportunity to look beyond the published data to the experiences of people meeting their genetic duplicates and half-duplicates for the first time. I shared in their discovery of a past they never knew and their glimpse of a future they never expected. I smiled when they played at being the twin children they never were. And I sensed their bitterness over events that caused their separation. There were lots of stories.

Sixty-four-year-old Scottish twins Caroline and Margaret recognized each other when Margaret visited a church where Caroline worked. Caroline, hearing a knock at the door, came outside and found her identical twin sister standing before her. Having never married, the twins left their solitary lives for a happier life together. Mistaken identity reunited nineteen-year-old identical male triplets Bob, Dave, and Eddy. Eddy had attended a small college in New York, but he left after one semester. When Bob enrolled the following semester, Eddy's best friend saw the resemblance between the two and brought them together. Pictures of the reunited "twins" appeared in newspapers around the world. A few days later, Dave's friend showed him the story and they were a threesome. The triplets later owned and operated Triplets, a steakhouse in lower Manhattan.[6]

As children, Bob, Dave, and Eddy, along with their families, had been unwitting participants in the psychiatrist Peter Neubauer's 1960s study of young multiples who had been intentionally separated.[7] The twin subjects came from the Louise Wise Adoption Agency, in New York. The Columbia University psychiatrist Viola Bernard advised the agency to separate twins in order to give each child a special place in the family; this gave Neubauer the first opportunity ever to study reared-apart twins growing up.[8] For purposes of the research, twins and triplets were placed in families that matched in certain ways—for example, Bob, Dave, and Eddy were each raised by middle-class Jewish families, and each triplet had an adopted sister who was older by two years.

Research teams studied the reared-apart twins in their respective homes about one week apart—but the twins' parents had no idea that their children were part of a separated set. Dr. Lawrence Perlman assisted on the project between 1968 and 1969. He recalls worrying that "the twins would run into each other some day."[9] He also called the data an eye-opener: "At that time people thought that behavior was all environmental, but I was amazed at how similar the kids were." The piles of twin data from this study have never been analyzed; a few book chapters and descriptions of one separated pair are all we have seen.[10]

A nagging question remains: Why did Viola Bernard decide that twins should be brought up apart? Her belief that twins should be separated was never accepted by mainstream psychologists or social workers. When Viola Bernard died in 1998, she left her papers to the health sciences library at Columbia University, but the "Twin Study (Twins Reared Apart)" file is sealed until January 2021. Bernard is remembered as "an eminent psychiatrist, psychoanalyst and child welfare advocate."[11]

Viola Bernard was not the first person to give twin research a bad name. In the mid-1940s, Nazi doctors conducted twin experiments trying to show that Jews and others were biologically inferior to Aryans. Consequently, twin research fell out of favor for many years.[12] But twin studies of intelligence, personality, and mental illness continued, and they showed that genes mattered—experience alone couldn't explain similarities in identical twins reared apart or why schizophrenia ran in families. The studies also popularized the idea that differences are not deficits.[13] Twin research began to make a comeback in the late 1960s, though its renewed popularity was not without setbacks.[14]

In the mid-1970s, the British psychologist Cyril Burt was accused of making up IQ scores, reared-apart twin pairs, and even his assistants.[15] These accusations were particularly scandalous because Burt's work had been well respected. People who disagreed with his belief that genes influence intelligence used Burt's alleged fraud to support their own environmental theories of behavior. No one refers to Burt's studies anymore, although two independent investigations found that he was not guilty of any wrongdoing.[16] But whatever the real story behind Burt's IQ findings, other reared-apart twin studies have found exactly what he had—that genes affect general intelligence.[17]

Today, reared-apart twins are being studied in the United States, Sweden, Finland, and Japan.[18] Although most people support this re-

SEPARATED AT BIRTH

search, not everyone thinks it's a good idea. Some investigators complain that identical twins reared apart are alike because their adoptive families treated them alike—or because they copy each other's mannerisms when they meet. Although these charges have proved to be unfounded, the critics are unmoved.[19] Fortunately, today's studies are giving us much more data—and many more stories.

On my shelf is a videotaped recording of reunited thirty-four-year-old identical twins Lucky and Diane. The tape captures their first wonderful moment of meeting—that split second of self-other recognition and out-of-control glee. "You're me!" Diane yells as the twins embrace and then hide their faces, as if to lessen the scene's intensity. Viewers are deeply moved by this image, and I have seen some look away as if to relieve the emotional rush. I never look away—I stare at the twins' faces when I see this tape, trying to feel their exhilaration.

Until now, I have been unable to disclose the stories in these pages. But several sets of twins and their families have now spoken beyond the data, reflecting on their lives as individuals—and as twins.

1

Beer Cans and Key Rings

"Hi, Doc."

Every once in a while I answer the telephone to the sarcastic but re-spectful greeting, "Hi, Doc." I know immediately that it's one of the fireman twins, Mark or Gerry. These identical twin brothers, who did not meet until they were thirty-one years old, had lived parallel lives as children, teenagers, and ultimately firefighters, but in different New Jersey towns. Their lives collided occasionally, such as when Gerry snubbed Mark's cousin Debra as she drove past a traffic jam Gerry was directing. And when "Mark's" father was told that his son was seen playing hooky, he laughed: "Impossible—Mark's right here."

After several minutes of conversation, I can usually tell if it's Mark or Gerry on the other end, although they sound the same. I know the brothers well from having tested them at the University of Minnesota. Both twins were half-amused and half-unnerved at being under a fe-male thumb, coming as they did from the male world of firefighting—perhaps their slightly mocking "Hi, Doc" was their way of letting me know that.

The fireman twins are great entertainment. They once downed Budweiser beers, their favorite drink, on live TV.[1] And they showed us their signature quirk—placing their pinky finger under the beer can and keeping it there until they took another breath. These bald, mous-tached, six-foot four-inch twins also carried key rings on the right side of their belts, leaned their heads back when they laughed, enjoyed a good party, and despised incompetent chefs. But it was their passion for firefighting that truly defined them. Both twins became captain of their respective firehouses in nearly the same year. And as Gerry insisted, "Firemen are not made, firemen are born. It's in the blood. We have the same blood so it's only natural that we should both be firemen."

I have two mental pictures of Mark and Gerry, one scientific and one intimate. The scientific side comes from their role as research participants, helping us decide the extent to which genes and environments affect behavior. The intimate side comes from their reactions to going from singletons to twins, from individuals to mirror-images, and from strangers to brothers. Almost immediately, Mark and Gerry were completely comfortable with each other, as if one twin allowed the other to be more like himself. There seemed to be no limit to situations that prompted comments like, "I need a beer," or "Time to party," behavior that could try other people's patience. But this was who they were and they both understood it without discussion. Mark and Gerry also enjoyed having fun at someone else's expense. I met them for dinner the night before we were to tape a talk show, and together they lifted me up and wouldn't put me down.[2] But balancing their light side was Mark and Gerry's dedication to the serious business of firefighting and saving lives. They wore their badges proudly.

About one year after Mark and Gerry came to Minnesota, I accompanied a film crew to the twins' homes and firehouses to re-enact events that had led to their reunion.[3] I had heard their story many times, but on that day there was a deeper drama to the tale. Perhaps this was because the main characters had been reassembled in the right places. I mostly watched the twin who was listening to his brother tell his side of the story—the quiet twin, whether Mark or Gerry, sat smiling as though he were tickled by this latest retelling.

It happened for Mark and Gerry in September 1985. About thirty thousand volunteer firefighters had gathered for the annual Firemen's Convention, in Wildwood, New Jersey. Captain Jimmy Tedesco had brought his wife, Renee, and fireman Bill Reckner had brought his wife, Marianne. The two wives were out on the boardwalk when they saw someone resembling Mark. When Renee mentioned this to Jimmy, he didn't pay attention because he knew that his friend Mark wasn't at the meeting. But the next day, several firefighters saw Gerry eating lunch. Thinking he was Mark, they called out to him, "Hi, Klunker!" but they got no answer. Up close, Gerry looked a lot like Mark, even though Gerry was one hundred pounds lighter. The sound of Gerry's voice was also familiar. Jimmy asked Gerry a series of questions:

Jimmy: Do you have a brother?
Gerry: How should I know? I'm adopted.
Jimmy: When were you born?
Gerry: 1954. [the same year as Mark]
Jimmy: What day were you born?
Gerry: [hesitating] Tax Day.

Jimmy left the convention determined to follow up on his conversation with Gerry. Jimmy knew that Mark had been adopted, but he had to check the firehouse records to confirm Mark's date of birth. It was April 15th—Tax Day. Then he called Gerry with the news. The skeptical firefighter said that he nearly dropped the phone at the chance that he was an identical twin. But Gerry's "let's see" attitude took over: "Twins or look-alikes, what the heck? Bring him down and we'll have a party whether or not it's true."

Jimmy put together a plan to bring the two brothers together: The meeting would take place five days later, on a Friday night. Jimmy would tell Mark that their company had been invited to the Wayside Fire Station in Tinton Falls (Gerry's firehouse) to inspect a foam unit. The only information Mark received other than the planned equipment inspection was that he would be meeting someone who, like himself, enjoyed "tipping his elbow."[4]

When Mark arrived he shook hands with Gerry, then walked past him, focusing on the new equipment. "It's nothing but an ordinary pump," Mark said. Then someone steered Mark toward the real purpose of the visit: "Look at Gerry, doesn't he look like you?" Mark took a closer look and said, "He's big like me. He's got the same nose as me. He's got the same moustache as me." But when Gerry took off his baseball cap, Mark was really amazed. "What's my bald head doing on his shoulders?" he asked. Gerry recalled, "It was like the twilight zone. I saw 'me' walk through the firehouse door one hundred pounds heavier." Then Gerry said what was on both brothers' minds: "I need a beer."

The brothers celebrated for the rest of the night and had a great time discovering how alike they were. Both twins loved Italian food and Chinese food. Both of them liked hunting and fishing. And both twins liked smoking, although Mark had quit by the time they met. They both wore big buckles on their belts and always carried knives. When the twins stripped to the waist in front of a mirror, they saw that their thick chest hair followed similar patterns and swirls. Even their weight difference was put in perspective—Gerry had lost one hundred pounds shortly before they met. Mark said that things got "spookier and spookier" when he heard Gerry's voice echo back as his own. The twins were learning what their shared genes could do.

Some people think of Mark and Gerry's meeting as a trick of fate that put one identical brother in a place where he was mistaken for the other one, but I don't agree. Our genetic background can be thought of as a "faithful squire," leading us toward people, places, and events that bring us pleasure and away from those that don't. Of course, our inherited tendencies give us lots of opportunities from which to choose, but the range isn't infinite. Mark and Gerry might have been satisfied being emergency rescue workers or paramedics, but they would probably have been miserable as computer programmers or bank tellers—those cerebral, sedentary jobs would have squelched their best talents. Being a firefighter requires physical strength, psychological stamina, problem-solving skills, and civic responsibility, and both Mark and Gerry had those qualities. Mark actually got into firefighting as a lark; his high school friends thought it would be fun to run red lights and see buildings burn. So Mark tried it. But when he rescued a girl from an accident and saw the gratitude on her face, he knew this was not a game. And he knew it was something he wanted to do.

Gerry said that he always wanted to be a fireman; he had chased fire trucks as a kid and had visited fire stations with his father. He applied for membership in his local firehouse twenty-five years ago. So I don't believe that chance explains why both twins were firefighters or why a firemen's convention brought them together. Of course, Gerry's decision to attend, Mark's decision not to, and Jimmy's running into Gerry come closer to the unpredictable events that can totally change our lives.

The reunion party's glee and excitement didn't last forever. Soon the twins started asking each other questions about their past. Both brothers had known since childhood that they had been adopted. Gerry had a younger sister, Marilyn, who was also adopted, and Mark had a younger brother, Alan, who was the surprise biological child of his adoptive parents. Neither Mark nor Gerry had had any inkling of being a twin. Mark's parents thought that he might have had a brother—but Gerry's parents knew more.

Gerry's parents, Shirley and Leonard Levey, lived outside New York City, on Long Island. When I met them, they leaned against their kitchen counter with their arms around each other. They looked down at the floor as they talked about a time and a decision that they thought would never come up again. Shirley Levey had dressed up for this occasion in a red blouse and a black skirt, and her hair was stylishly combed. She seemed nervous and teary, as though she expected someone to question the decision about which she too had doubts. Leonard Levey appeared more casual than his wife. His longish face and balding hair reminded me of Gerry, even though they were not biologically related. Both parents were nearly a foot shorter than their son.

Leonard Levey spoke softly: "When Gerry called to ask me if there was anything left out of the adoption story because, at that moment, he [Gerry] was staring right at his twin brother, I asked him some quiet, gentle questions." Levey said that he felt guilty because he and his wife had known that Gerry was a twin. Shirley Levey spoke next, trying not to cry: "We did everything we could to protect him. We told him he was a chosen baby and he took this in stride. We tried to do the right thing, but this was the one thing we did not do. This is the one straw that literally made me fall apart." Shirley said that she would have taken both twins, but she and her husband couldn't afford to raise two children at that time—they had already spent a fortune on unsuccessful infertility treatments. They kept Gerry's twinship quiet because they figured that his chance of meeting Mark was so improbable that it wasn't worth worrying him.

The Leveys' doctor had told them to pick the bigger baby, assuming that twin would be the healthier of the two. Gerry was the bigger baby when the twins were three days old, but identical twins' weights can change. Ironically, Mark became the heavier twin—and four years later the Leveys were more secure financially and adopted Gerry's younger sister, Marilyn. As Marilyn told her mother years later, "If you had taken both twins you wouldn't have taken me."

Mark's parents, Joe and Eleanor Newman, lived in a small house in a suburban New Jersey neighborhood. Mr. Newman was five feet five inches tall, about a foot shorter than Mark, but he was bald and heavyset like his son. Mrs. Newman was the same height as her husband and had brown hair and brown eyes. Joe and Eleanor Newman learned about their son's twinship via a "twin prank."

Gerry knocked on the Newmans' door two days after he and Mark had met. Joe Newman answered it and, assuming it was Mark, asked, "Where are your keys?" Gerry said, "I left them at home." Gerry sat down and turned on the TV set just as Mark would have done. Ten minutes later, Mark knocked on the door and again Joe Newman answered, asking, "Where are your keys?" Mark said, "I left them at home." Newman looked at Gerry, but he asked Mark, "Who is this clown?" "This is the twin brother I told you about," Mark said. (Mark had called his parents earlier to tell them that he had met his twin, but they thought he had been drinking.) According to Joe Newman, "They blasted my mind." Unlike the Leveys, Joe and Eleanor hadn't known that Mark was a twin. Mark said that his parents were in a "subdued state of shock."

If only the Leveys had been more financially secure, or if the Newmans had adopted two days earlier, Mark and Gerry would have been raised together. Sometimes one or both separated twins never learn that they are part of a pair, so they live life as accidental singletons. Mark and Gerry could have been such a pair.

Twins like Mark and Gerry are often asked, "Did you ever *feel* as if you had a twin?" Some people embrace the romantic notion that twinship can be known by virtue of sharing the womb, but there is no scientific evidence to support this claim. Mark's and Gerry's recollections confirm these findings, but they could be misconstrued.

Mark described the following dream: "When I was a teenager I dreamt that I was watching an operation in which an appendix was being removed. But the operation was performed on me. It was like watching myself. I never had my appendix taken out, but Gerry did when he was three months old." It is doubtful that Mark's "vision" would have suggested a lost twin if he hadn't met Gerry—dreams, after all, are open to hundreds of untestable interpretations. Like other reared-apart twins, Gerry sensed "a little empty feeling in the back of my mind." (He actually pointed to the back of his head when he said this.) "Maybe I had other brothers and sisters, but I didn't care to find them. I had my parents and they raised me. But always in the back of my mind I wondered if there wasn't something else in my life."

I have thought about how to explain such feelings. Most reared-apart twins were adopted, so they rarely resemble the members of their family. Mark didn't think he looked like either of his parents, although Gerry said that he resembled his father slightly. Mark also said, "Physically, my [nonbiological] brother, Alan, weighs as much as my left leg—I could tie him up like a sack in my pant leg. He's much more outgoing and a better money manager. I am single and free, he was married and is divorced. We have the same brains, but we are smart and stupid in opposite directions." Marilyn, Gerry's adoptive sister, said that she and Gerry shared nothing but their address: "We are very different people. But looking at Mark and Gerry—they are one."

Some adoptees wonder why they were adopted in the first place, but such thoughts generally do *not* reflect poorly on the quality of their adoptive homes. Instead, they may reflect curiosity over their biological origins and the universal importance of human relationships. Of course, Gerry's perceptions may have been tied to other things—many people, not just some adoptees, feel that there are empty spaces in their lives, possibly caused by failed relationships or unsatisfied goals. It is, therefore, unjustified to explain some separated twins' discontent by "intrauterine knowledge" of a missing twin. After all, Gerry did not share his brother's dream.

Mark and Gerry eventually learned that their biological parents had been married, but not to each other. The twins' adoption cases were handled separately, but their adoptive parents may have passed each other in court.

Would Mark and Gerry have turned out differently if the Newmans had raised them together, or if the Leveys had been smitten with the smaller twin? Both twins' families were lower middle class and Jewish, but not religious, although both twins had Bar Mitzvahs. Neither twin's father had gone to college—Leonard Levey had completed high school and was a printing production manager; Joe Newman had gone to high school and trade school and was a postal supervisor. Both twins' mothers had gone to college, although Shirley Levey hadn't finished her degree. Shirley had clerked at the state supreme court; Eleanor Newman had been a secretary. Gerry had a younger sister; Mark had a younger brother. Their homes seem similar, but the twins are alike in ways that are unrelated to their home environments.

The only firefighter in either family was Gerry's uncle, who lived in New York, but both twins nonetheless volunteered. Both sets of parents were "light social drinkers," but both twins drank large quantities of mostly Budweiser beer. Gerry wondered if he had inherited his biological father's drinking habits.[5] Shirley Levey was an opera, ballet, and

Gerry Levey (left) and Mark Newman both had Bar Mitzvahs in 1967, when they turned thirteen—but they celebrated thirty miles apart. (Photos courtesy of the Levey and Newman families.)

theater fan, but these interests never rubbed off on her son. "Hell, no, I'd be bored," Gerry said. Mark's mother played cards (and mahjong) regularly, but Mark plays cards only occasionally. Both twins like fishing, but only Mark's father took him on fishing trips.

When children are raised by warm, sensitive parents in healthy environments, they turn out pretty much as they would regardless of who their parents are.[6] We also know that reared-apart identical twins are as alike in personality as reared-together identical twins.[7] This doesn't mean that environments don't matter; it just means that the environments that matter most are the ones that people experience individually and do not share with family members.[8] Mark and Gerry didn't meet for thirty-one years, but their behaviors matched in ways that can only be explained by their identical genes. Unlike their other family members, they made loud, staccato-like laughing sounds, threw their heads back for effect, and answered questions with one-word answers. Their IQ scores were just two points apart. And there were those pinky fingers.

The twins' signature quirk—holding their pinky finger under a beer can—has drawn lots of attention. When I describe this shared trait to people, they are amazed or skeptical. Some people call it coincidence, but they are ignoring the scientific side of the equation. Gestures and movements are partly explained by how our bodies are put together, so it makes sense that Mark and Gerry would hold things the same way. The twins said that they use their pinky finger to support the can or glass as they drink. It is also likely that this position is comfortable for them because they have the "same" hands and fingers. Or maybe this habit partly reflects their worry over spilling the precious liquid—tendencies to feel worried or anxious are partly inherited.[9] Most people could be persuaded to try putting their finger under the glass when they drink, but they wouldn't do it naturally and might not like how it feels. Science is not far beyond speculation in explaining such behaviors, but greater identical than fraternal twin similarity suggests that genetic factors play a role.

Identical twins are a lot alike, but they are less alike than people think. Mark and Gerry, two volunteer firemen with no science background, grasped this concept easily. Gerry said, "I am me. Mark is me. We are one, but we are different. He has his life, I have my life, and nothing will change that." Mark listed their similarities: "likes, dislikes, prejudices, and mannerisms." Some of the twins' differences include music and sports; Gerry likes country western and the Washington Redskins, Mark likes rock 'n' roll and the Dallas Cowboys. But Mark said that they "like each other's styles." Some of the twins' interests match in other ways, even if the details differ. They both like forestry, but Gerry studied it at school, whereas Mark learned it in the field. When they met, Gerry installed chemical fire-suppression systems and Mark installed burglar alarms. Their only major nonshared experience was Gerry's Peace Corps service, which took him to Brazil for eight months.[10] But this experience didn't make a big difference between them.

Both twins have shown little patience with other people's failings. Gerry once created quite a scene during dinner: When a restaurant chef overcooked his steak, he uttered many loud, "unkind" words. My only option was to pay the bill and run out of there. In this situation, Mark took the "elder brother role," telling us that he had mastered his impatience and that Gerry would, too. In some ways, Mark was a small step ahead of Gerry, waiting for him to catch up. This is a common occurrence among twins. In fact, identical twins have unique opportunities to "see themselves" in different settings. This unusual learning process can protect them from mistakes and disappointments. Because one twin knows what the other twin is going through, it can also increase their mutual understanding.

To their families and friends, Mark and Gerry's similarities were overwhelming, but the twins took them in stride. Mark summarized it best when he said, "It was as if Gerry had just moved away for thirty-one years and came back for a visit—once we met, we only had to fill in the details." According to Gerry, "We were so alike that there was no need to get acquainted." It was gratifying to see how quickly the twins' relationship was developing. And it was fun to watch them pulling off pranks to divert the Minnesota research staff. I was upset when Mark and Gerry dunked their overnight activity monitors in beer at the end of the week, but their good-natured insults were hilarious. "Boy, are you ugly in the morning," Mark said to Gerry. (This seemed oddly self-deprecating.) The twins' playfulness and rapport were becoming their trademark. But meeting each other was "no big deal" to either of them—they refused to get worked up about it. That's how they were.

Mark and Gerry say that they have not changed much since meeting each other; according to Gerry, the only difference is that he has a brother. The twins' firehouse friends were very excited when they met, but once the initial shock had worn off, the twins were unfazed. Their reaction seemed partly driven by their "what the heck" outlook on life.

Moments after Gerry (left) and Mark met on September 20, 1985, at Gerry's firehouse in Tinton Falls, New Jersey, they ran to a mirror to compare their bodies. Here they are reliving that first incredible night when they discovered that their favorite beer was Budweiser and that they both held the can with their pinky finger underneath. (Photo by Nancy L. Segal, November 1986.)

Mark also said that after fighting fires both twins had seen a lot: "Nothing surprises us."

But other people saw things differently. After the twins met, Marilyn Levey, Gerry's sister, thought that her brother was happier and more contented: "He seems more fulfilled, as if finding a missing piece of the puzzle." Joe Newman, Mark's father, sensed that "Mark has found himself since meeting Gerry, and has become more outgoing." Maybe the "what the heck" twins couldn't see their softer sides—or didn't want to. Regardless, neither Mark nor Gerry changed his life in any significant way to accommodate his twin.

Curiously, Mark isn't bothered that he and Gerry were raised apart. He explained that twins growing up together try to differentiate from each other to develop separate identities. And he feels that this detracts from the fact that they are twins. But most twins enjoy being twins despite their occasional disagreements. I was convinced that Mark and

SEPARATED AT BIRTH

Gerry were happy to have found a new drinking buddy—the fact that this buddy was their twin was probably a plus.

Luigi's is the twins' favorite New Jersey bar and restaurant, so we stopped by with our film crew. Seated next to Mark and Gerry, Jimmy Tedesco (who first met Gerry at the Firemen's Convention) admitted that he had been uneasy about his initial reunion plan; he had worried about what might have happened if things had not turned out right. Would Mark have hated him for bringing up this part of his past? But Jimmy said that the chance was worth taking: "The best tribute I had in bringing them together was at Mark's mother's funeral, in 1986. Some of the relatives said that what I did was tremendous because Mrs. Newman would have wanted it to happen, and that she was going to the grave knowing that Mark knew he had a true brother. They said I should be proud and I am proud. I made it possible, I made it happen." I listened to Jimmy, but I watched Mark and Gerry. They removed their wire-rimmed glasses and wiped their eyes.

Mark and Gerry live about fifty-five miles apart. In the last few years, both twins have driven trucks in addition to fighting fires. They see each other occasionally, mostly at gatherings for firefighters, although they talk on the telephone every few months. Thinking over the twenty years since they met, Mark said that he and Gerry don't "get personal" with each other—they do not (and have not) exchanged much information about themselves over the years: "We never changed, we are living our lives as we want to. Gerry is just another relative—we are brothers, we are friendly, but we are not close [in the sense of sharing thoughts and feelings]. In some ways I am closer to my friends in the firehouse." The twins don't need to say much about themselves because they can intuitively grasp the other's mindset. The fact that they can do this is not a big deal to them.

Mark said that if Gerry were to come by for a visit, "it would feel like being with me. Even today, we are still walking the same paths, but doing it in different places." He added, "I would do anything for him without hesitation." Their closeness is unique and is defined on their own terms; it comes mostly from knowing that they are doing the same things. But something was about to happen that both twins would not be doing: Gerry was getting married.

Mark said, "My feelings are mixed. It's a weird situation. If we [Gerry and I] goof off on the phone, Susan [Gerry's fiancée] starts talking in the background. We're just breaking each other's chops, so she should leave us alone. Gerry is too much of a fun person to be made dull." Mark was not going to the ceremony: "It's Gerry's family's thing. And why should I pay $400 for a suit that I'll wear once? Besides, I might be having surgery." (Mark had injured his rotator cuff in a work-related accident.) I reminded Mark that he had gone to Gerry's sister Marilyn's wedding, also a family thing. According to Marilyn, Gerry had wanted him there, but Mark felt out of place. And recently, Gerry said that he doesn't have the family feelings for Mark that he has for his sister, Marilyn. Ultimately, and without hesitating, Mark did not go to Gerry's wedding.[11] His twin's new status may have hit his softer side; Gerry's wife, Susan, thinks that Mark is "scared and intimidated" by Gerry's marriage and "wonderful relationship" with his stepson. "We tried to get close to Mark, but he shut us out," she said, adding, "Gerry looked sad and said that he wished Mark could have been at the wedding. I think that deep down, Gerry loves his brother."

It's hard to know where the twins' feelings come from—too many good-natured insults, their "what the heck" attitude, or their escalating detachment. Maybe each twin wants more and thinks that the other twin wants less.

Mark joked that Gerry's getting married was basically the same as his going away on a "life sentence, not a vacation." We both knew the reference—Mark once said that meeting Gerry felt like his twin was just coming home after thirty-one years. Mark said, "Gerry is into being a dad to his wife's kid and I am being Mr. Bum. We were both Mr. Bum before that." Later Mark changed his mind. "Gerry is still a bum," he said, as if to downplay their differences.

But Mark was probably right the first time to think that Gerry was no longer "Mr. Bum." Gerry said, "I love being married—it's a steady thing." Gerry had been engaged to Susan twenty-five years earlier, but

SEPARATED AT BIRTH

they had broken up. Susan had since married and had a son, but she was recently widowed. Several years ago, she ran into Gerry at the 7-Eleven store where she was taking inventory; Gerry went to that store for coffee every morning. Susan heard his voice and said, "Gerald?" Gerry knew that the only people who called him Gerald were his mother, his sister—and Susan.

Mark didn't think that Gerry's marriage would change much between them, except for one thing: "Before we did things in parallel and knew about it—now we'll do things in parallel and not know about it." But they are not doing things in parallel, and they know about it.

Both twins are still involved with their firehouses, but their work situations have changed. Gerry is still driving trucks, but his work responsibilities have expanded. Mark is no longer driving trucks because his injury has kept him inactive. The twins' lifestyles have changed in other ways as well. Gerry drinks nonalcoholic beer and Mark drinks Coors Light. When the twins met each other fifteen years ago, they would have chewed up anyone who didn't drink the real stuff. But Gerry is raising a thirteen-year-old son and said that "there are some things you can't do around a kid." Mark's weight has gone up to four hundred pounds as a result of his inactivity, so he is counting calories. But more significant than the twins' changes in drinking are their changes in outlook. Gerry is happily married; Mark has been seeing someone on and off, but at age fifty, he is down on marrying. Mark is also tired of New Jersey's traffic, politics, and prices, so he is moving to Bullhead City, Arizona. Mark said that being away from Gerry will be "no big deal—we'll still see each other about once or twice a year." Gerry has accepted Mark's decision to move as he had accepted Mark's absence at his wedding: "Mark has to do what he has to do." But Gerry didn't sound happy.

If Gerry's mother ever regretted her decision to take just one twin, she doesn't regret it now: "We did the right thing, at the right time, for the right reasons." But if the twins had been conventionally closer she might have felt otherwise.

The attachment between Mark and Gerry seems undeniable, born of their acute sense of sameness. Marilyn Levey said, paradoxically, that Mark and Gerry are so identical that they have nothing in common: "The twins don't share their feelings, and once the media's interest in them died down, they couldn't connect." Mark and Gerry joke about their relationship because it's their way—but they may want more from each other. As Mark said, they have the same bald head on their shoulders.

2

Switched at Birth

George and Marcus Holmes were raised as fraternal twins in Ottawa, Ontario, in Canada. Records show that they were born on June 19, 1971. Their parents, Laura and Randy, both twenty-one and unmarried, put the twins in temporary foster care arranged by the Children's Aid Society. The couple married two months after the twins' birth and returned to reclaim their sons. Hospital staff had told Laura that the twins were fraternal, so she wasn't fazed by the fact that they didn't look alike. Once she had her boys back, Laura felt that her family was "complete," though she did have a daughter, Jessica, four years later.

Like many fraternal twins, George and Marcus do not look alike. George is five feet seven inches tall and weighs 168 pounds. A photograph taken in his early twenties shows his brown wavy hair parted on the left, falling several inches below his shoulders. His sharp blue eyes and penetrating stare suggest he is either highly observant or totally self-absorbed. Marcus is an inch shorter but weighs 226 pounds. His short dark hair is slicked off his forehead. His brown eyes and relaxed expression contrast sharply with his brother's concentrated stare. With his round face and full cheeks, Marcus resembles his father more than he does his twin; George's flared nose and thin lips make him look more like his mother, although he has his father's brilliant blue eyes.

Laura and Randy have always made their twins feel loved and

wanted. George and Marcus have celebrated every birthday together with two cakes, baked by their mother. They have always been fairly close to each other, but when they got older they had separate friends, partly because they went to different schools. Then, in September 1991, a chance event substantially transformed George and Marcus's relationship to each other and to their family. They were twenty-one.

In September 1991 Brent Tremblay, the adopted son of Carroll and Jim Tremblay, entered Ottawa's Carleton University, an institution with more than 15,000 students. Brent studied journalism and joined the Strategy Club, a group whose members play board games, cards, and chess. Many young people who are not enrolled at Carleton go to the campus to "hang out." Brent was twenty-one.

While Brent Tremblay was taking classes, George Holmes was working as an usher at Ottawa's Elgin Theater. But George liked games and had friends in the Strategy Club whom he'd visit in Carleton's lounges. One day, George's friend Sasha thought she spotted George and walked over. "Hi, George," she said, but the person she spoke to didn't recognize her. "My name is Brent, not George," the young man replied. Sasha was shocked and explained that her friend George looked just like Brent. She said George would come by in a few days and that they should meet.

Brent recalled that when George entered the lounge several days later, everyone stared: "I was surprised to see someone who looked so much like me, although his hair was a bit different. It was eerie—for both of us."

George and Brent liked each other instantly. According to Brent, their friendship was "natural and effortless." They liked Paul Newman and Richard Burton, but not Tom Hanks or Ben Affleck. They liked old films like M*A*S*H, Jaws, and Star Wars but were cynical of mass marketing, so they watched mostly low-budget films with clever plots and characters. They also liked the same kind of music. George followed grunge, a musical style popularized in Seattle; Brent didn't listen to it then, but he liked it a lot once he heard it. Brent says that they were very open to each other's thoughts and opinions, "giving weight

SEPARATED AT BIRTH

and respect" to what the other said. Neither one was athletic, but both were obsessed with football statistics and figures. And both were enthusiasts of an obscure board game called *Awful Green Things from Outer Space.* According to George, it was easy to talk to Brent because "we had the same ideas, thought patterns, and sense of humor."

George and Brent spent hours together, socializing and drinking beer with their friends. Besides their common looks and interests, people noticed that they held a glass the same way and had the same "odd way of pushing things aside." Some of their friends suggested that they could be twins—Brent's birthday was June 14, 1971, so they were born only five days apart.[1] George and Brent thought that their similarities were just coincidence, but mostly they were amused. They were friends for a year and a half before meeting each other's families; even Marcus, George's same-age brother, didn't know much about George's new friend. "I don't remember bringing it up," George said. During that time, George "hung out" more with Brent and his other friends than he did with Marcus, though he did spend time with Marcus and his two other roommates at the house they rented together.

But new facts were starting to surface. Most significant was Brent and George's realization that, as infants, both had been in the same temporary foster-care facility—at the same time. And their physical and behavioral similarities were overwhelming to them and everyone they knew. The possibility that they were related was now too real to ignore, but several scenarios were possible: (1) George and Brent could be identical twins, born to Laura and Randy. (2) George and Brent could be identical twins, but born to another couple. (3) George and Brent could be unusual look-alikes. George admitted that when he first met Brent it never occurred to him that they could be related. But after a year and a half, he admitted, "I would have been surprised if we had not been related—we had too much in common."

George and Brent took their time before sharing their suspicions with their families. According to Brent, "One reason we moved slowly was that we knew how many people's lives would be screwed up if we were related." Their chance meeting raised difficult questions for

Marcus, George's fraternal twin: Who was Marcus, and was he Laura and Randy's biological child? Was Marcus George's brother, or was he an unrelated child given to Laura and Randy by mistake?

When I heard about the Holmeses and Tremblays in April 1994, I was unprepared for the scientific chiller that would unfold.[2] Apparently, a succession of oversights by social workers and foster parents caused the accidental switching of two-month-old Marcus and Brent, and resulted in Brent's adoption by the Tremblays. These mistakes shattered the families' faith in medical professionals and public institutions.

Because Marcus and Brent were switched, Brent and George grew up separately as identical reared-apart twins. But *virtual twins (VTs)* were created when Marcus was paired with George.[3] VTs are same-age, biologically unrelated children raised in the same home, so they are "twinlike" without being twins. Most VTs know about their unusual relationship, but George and Marcus didn't—for more than twenty years they believed that they were fraternal twins. George and Marcus participated in my virtual twin study, but I was most curious about George and Brent's evolving relationship and how their meeting affected their families.

The true twins, George and Brent, now in their early thirties, were reluctant to talk to me at first, but they eventually spoke at great length over the telephone. Listening to them heightened my sensitivity to their similar voice quality and speech patterns. Both twins were artists at reconstructing their reunion and its aftermath, and they each spoke freely about the different life choices they had made. I also met Brent's parents: Jim, a semi-retired statistician, and Carroll, a retired registered nurse, when I visited Ottawa in August 2002.[4]

Jim and Wade (Brent's younger brother, whom the Tremblays adopted seven years after Brent) met me at the bus station. Jim is tall and slim with a friendly but businesslike manner. Wade is six feet three inches tall and weighs 255 pounds. He is a polite young man in his mid-twenties who was excited about his new teaching job. On the way to their home we talked about George and Brent's reunion, a subject that raised different emotions in each of us. Jim was angry and upset that his peaceful family life had been disrupted. Wade was excited and interested to finally tell his part of the story—he was fourteen when the twins met, and his understanding of events was largely overlooked. And I couldn't wait to learn new facts about this case.

Carroll greeted me warmly outside their neat suburban home. She had short brown hair and wore medium-size gold hoop earrings. Her house was immaculate; the yellow and white walls and furniture sparkled and everything was perfectly placed. I learned that the Holmeses' home atmosphere was more "relaxed"—the dining room had been turned into a family room packed with books, games, magazines, and videotapes. The Holmeses also owned a German short-haired pointer named Nikki whom Brent adored. But the Tremblays, especially Carroll, had objected to having a dog. "I am not an animal lover," she admitted.

Carroll was as eager as Jim and Wade to tell her side of the story. Revisiting some events was painful, and her voice broke occasionally. But there was an intensity to her talk, driven, I believe, by her desire to get the story told and told right. I asked Carroll and Jim to take me back to their experience with the Children's Aid Society of Ottawa, more than thirty years ago.

The Tremblays' and Holmeses' paths might have crossed in the fall of 1970, before the twins were born. Carroll and Laura had been seeing the same gynecologist, Carroll because she was trying to become pregnant and Laura because she was pregnant with twins. "We could have been in the same waiting room at the same time," Carroll remarked. After some unsuccessful attempts to have a baby, Carroll, age thirty-one, and Jim, age thirty-six, decided to adopt four-month-old Brent. He was one of three baby boys who had been placed with elderly foster parents. The foster couple, now living in Florida, couldn't cope with caring for three newborns, so two of them (George and Marcus) were moved to a different home. But before the move the babies' ankle identification bracelets were removed temporarily, and two of the tags (Brent's and Marcus's) were incorrectly replaced; here, apparently, is where the switching of the twins occurred.[5] George and Marcus stayed in their new home for only a few weeks before Laura and Randy came to claim them.

Had social workers or foster families examined the medical records, the error would have been obvious, because the "right" charts went with the "wrong" children. George's and Brent's folders stayed together during the second move, but entries in Brent's file did not match baby Marcus. For example, Brent's eyes were large and widely spaced, but Marcus's eyes were close together. A potentially serious situation was that Marcus had anemia. Carroll was told to administer iron supplements to Brent, but it was actually Marcus who had the problem. "What if I had been asked to give him insulin or something potentially toxic?" Carroll wondered.

Carroll recalls that Brent was a beautiful blond baby with blue eyes.

Identical twins Brent Tremblay (left) and George Holmes (center) were separated at birth. George and Marcus (right) were raised as fraternal twins—until Brent and George met by chance in their twenties. Brent and George felt an immediate rapport when they first met. (Photo by Wayne Cuddington, reprinted with permission from *The Ottawa Citizen*, April 5, 2000.)

SEPARATED AT BIRTH

She received him after a year of meetings with adoption agency staff, during which time she learned the baby's family history. The baby's father was an architect, his mother was a nurse (also artistically talented), and his maternal grandmother played the piano. So, over the years, Carroll was puzzled by the fact that "Brent had terrible handwriting and couldn't draw at all—nothing seemed to match. But Brent read a lot so I thought that maybe his father, being an architect, read a lot, too." Now she knows that she was looking at Marcus's family history all along. Marcus eventually became a carpenter, using skills he probably inherited from his biological father.

Carroll named her baby after George Brent, the actor who played Jane Powell's father in the 1948 musical comedy *Luxury Liner.* "I thought his last name would make a nice first name"; ironically, her son's identical twin was named George. But this was not the only strange incident involving names. In 1992—just three months before the twins met—Carroll and her sister, Cherie, went to Toronto's Woodbine Center to buy something "special and different" for Brent's twenty-first birthday. Riding the escalator to the second floor, Carroll saw a stand selling newspapers with mock headlines, and one caught her eye. It read, "Brent Cleans Room Finds Lost Brother." According to Carroll, Brent's room was a mess and Wade could conceivably get "lost" in it. Carroll bought the newspaper and the family signed it— "With all our love and best wishes. Mom, Dad and Wade." When she came across the paper a year later, she shuddered.

I asked Carroll and Jim to describe their first meeting with George. In fact, both families knew little about their son's new friend, although Brent had mentioned hanging out with someone who looked like him. Finally, after eighteen months of close friendship and fooling people, Brent asked his mother if he could bring someone home to dinner. She said fine, she'd have a roast ready by 6:00 P.M. The doorbell rang and Carroll answered it: "In walked a young man wearing Brent's jacket and hat. I knew it wasn't Brent, but I was shocked." Brent was standing behind George, wearing George's shirt and baggy pants. Carroll called for Jim and Wade to come in. They stared in amazement.

George and Brent moved to the couch, unintentionally allowing the others to see the similarity of their eyes, hands, and gait. Carroll said, "They both walked like they were on strings—they had the same shuffle." She and Jim asked George question after question about his birth and family. When he said that he lived with his biological parents and fraternal twin brother, the impossible notion that he and Brent were separated identical twins started to form in everyone's mind. Suddenly, Jim was afraid to ask any more questions. "It was like opening Pandora's box. You know, you live life in a little house, you protect the people in it and you don't want anyone to come in and spoil it."

Carroll, forgetting about the six o'clock roast, called her neighbors Debbie and Peter to come right over. They were eating dinner, but she insisted. Hiding Brent in the laundry room, she was eager to see their reaction to George. Debbie chatted with "Brent," asking him if he was getting his hair cut soon. (At the time George's hair was longer than Brent's.) When Carroll returned, she asked Debbie if she had seen Brent. "Yes," she said, "his hair is getting long." Carroll said that Peter had the same reaction, but he was "not one to mess around"; he put into words what Carroll feared most. "They are identical twins," he insisted. Eventually she served the roast (which by then was like a "brick"). Everyone watched as Brent and George carved up their servings in the same deliberate way.

After dinner, Jim drove Brent and George to Grand Central Station, a bar where they were meeting friends. They sat in the back seat of his car. "Oh, God!" Jim thought, listening to them chatter. Brent and George were oblivious to him, totally absorbed in their discussion of football facts and statistics: "I couldn't help but think how similar they were. When we got to the bar they just got out of the car. I think they said 'thank you.' We needed to talk about this when I got home."

Not surprisingly, a similar scene had taken place at George's house several weeks earlier. With Brent left alone in the living room, George's grandmother entered and gave "George" a hug and a kiss. But she wondered why he didn't hug her back. Brent recalls that Laura didn't take her eyes off him the entire evening and that Randy was "shocked."

George told Carroll that his mother, Laura, "was as upset as you are; she didn't sleep that night." In fact, Laura was so shaken that she took a leave of absence from work.

The events of twenty-two years earlier were slowly becoming clear. When Laura and Randy returned to the Children's Aid Society, they were given one of their identical twin sons (George) and an unrelated child (Marcus). That left George's identical twin (Brent) to be adopted by the Tremblays. Clearly, Laura was incorrectly told that her twins were fraternal.[6] Brent complained, "It was a monstrous failure of the system. A child could have seen through this. The foster parents photographed George, Marcus, and me holding three different stuffed animals and they used them to tell us apart. That was the foster mother's brain child—how would that tell us apart?"[7] George insisted, "I want a camera in the delivery room when I have kids."

Everyone's life was in disarray. Laura and Randy discovered a son they had never relinquished (Brent) and a son that was not supposed to be theirs (Marcus). Brent (who had been given up for adoption) learned that his biological parents had wanted him all along; he had always assumed they had rejected him. He also discovered his real date of birth, and an identical twin brother and younger sister. Carroll and Jim agonized over possibly losing the love of their adoptive son, whose temperament fit better with his biological family's than with theirs. George learned that his fraternal twin was not his twin, and that he had an identical twin all along. Jessica discovered that an older brother with whom she had been raised was not her brother—and that she had a different brother instead. Most difficult of all, Marcus struggled with the realization that his parents were not his parents and his twin brother and sister were not his siblings—in short, he was not at all who he thought he was.

The day I spent with Jim and Carroll Tremblay gave me a sense of what it was like for an ordinary family to feel its firm foundation crumble in a moment. As they recalled the various events and their emotions, their voices softened and they moved together as though seeking support from the one person who understood.

After that first evening with George, Carroll sought professional help to determine if Brent and George were twins. She called her pediatrician, Dr. William James, who suggested that the two boys drop by his office so he could look at them.[8] He was so amazed by Carroll's story that he continually scratched his head as he listened, actually drawing blood: "When I saw the boys a few days later I saw the obvious—they were very similar. In my own mind I was trying to say it wasn't true. I wanted to be cautious." After they left, he called Carroll and asked, "Do you want to open a can of worms?" He gave her the name of a developmental pediatrician, Dr. Susan Martin, but Carroll said it was up to the boys to decide. Meanwhile, George and Brent visited George's doctor, who arranged for blood work. It was late August 1993.

Early in September 1993, Jim, Carroll, and Brent pulled into the parking lot at Riverside Hospital, in Ottawa. They were there to learn the results of the blood tests that would tell if Brent and George were twin brothers. At this point, only Brent's and George's blood had been analyzed.[9] Exiting the car, Carroll caught sight of someone who looked like her son (George) walking next to someone unfamiliar—it was Marcus, George's supposed fraternal twin. She saw Marcus moments later, seated in the waiting room next to Laura, their mother. Jessica, their younger sister, was also present. But it was Randy, George's father, who made Carroll gasp: "I looked at him and saw those big piercing blue eyes. I thought to myself, 'He is Brent's father, we don't need blood.' But I said nothing."

The two families sat together in the tiny waiting area. Other patients were there, and several children were running around, screaming. This scene only intensified the anxiety they were all feeling. Carroll recalls, "Jim and I were thinking, 'How did we get your son?' and I'm sure Laura and Randy were thinking 'How did you get our son?'" Dr. Martin finally came in and read from the pediatrician's chart: "The results cannot tell us for sure if Brent and George are related or if they are twins. We need to do DNA testing, using samples from Laura, Randy, Brent, George, and Marcus."[10] But in reality, Dr. Martin was "struck by how similar the putative twins looked and behaved"; she was just being careful.

Brent and George were highly critical of the doctors who "blew us off," telling us we might not be related. "Before the DNA results, they gave us 'professional opinions'—how could they not see what everyone else could?" George wondered. According to Carroll, everyone was "deflated" because virtually nothing had been resolved.

The families returned to the hospital two days later for the second round of tests. The samples would be sent to Toronto for analysis, and results were promised within six weeks. Once their samples were drawn, Marcus, Brent, and George went to meet friends, leaving the two sets of parents alone. Immediately, the four began a fascinating and heartbreaking retrospective of Brent's and George's developmental timelines.

As babies and toddlers, both boys had been unusually easy to handle—they slept and played anywhere, on sofas, on carpets, and in cribs. And they never needed to be entertained; Carroll recalled that watching a bug or a butterfly afforded Brent hours of entertainment. Both boys read by age three and devoured books by age six. They would read as they walked, becoming so absorbed in the material that they would bang into walls. Both George and Brent were identified as gifted pupils when they entered kindergarten, and they were placed in the same kind of enhanced program. By then, both were wearing eyeglasses.

George's and Brent's intense early focus on subjects that interested them persisted. Randy told Carroll that once, while waiting for an elevator, George was so absorbed in his thoughts that he didn't get in once it arrived. (This story fits well with George's expression in the picture taken in his early twenties—observant but preoccupied.) Carroll recalled dressing Brent in his snowsuit to go out and play, but he just stood and watched the snowflakes fall: "He was mesmerized by what he saw." As young boys, both were shy and played with just a few close friends. At thirteen, both were playing chess and at fourteen both had trouble with the same school subjects. (The problem was not their inability to master the material but their lack of motivation.) George and Brent also collected comic books and board games—and consumed bunches of cherries. And unlike most sixteen-year-olds, neither had gotten a driver's license; each had taken lessons and progressed to the same point, but they were uninterested in driving.

⁂ There were some differences. Brent, the firstborn twin, was a half-inch shorter than George and had worn braces on his teeth to prevent him from developing an overbite. George, who hadn't had his teeth fixed, lisped slightly as a result. Brent had finished high school, whereas George was one credit shy of graduation. Brent had enrolled in college, first at Carleton University in journalism, before attending a string of local colleges, but he never finished a course of study. George never attended college but tried a number of temporary jobs. Nonetheless, their similarities outweighed their differences.

Both sets of parents worried that, growing up, neither George nor Brent conversed like other people. "You would be having a conversation with them and they would suddenly say something totally unrelated to the topic. It was like Brent was on another planet," Jim remarked. And both spoke in short phrases which may have helped them finish each other's sentences. Both boys were also very interested in science, especially astronomy. They didn't seem to have interests typical of other children their age, such as football or skating—although both were captivated by sports statistics, as Jim had discovered in the car.

Beyond George's and Brent's unusual behaviors, several odd occurrences now made sense to both families. A few years before they met, Brent's brother Wade was puzzled when his friends ran into George (thinking it was Brent) and wondered why he didn't speak to them. Brent's Aunt Norah once spotted "Brent" at a place he couldn't possibly have been; moreover, she mentioned to Carroll that he wore a different hairstyle. And a few years before Brent and George met, George's sister, Jessica, was riding a bus in downtown Ottawa when Brent got on and sat down without speaking to her. Jessica thought it was her older brother George and that he was snubbing her. One night in the late 1980s Randy and Laura attended a concert given by the Canadian band "Pursuit of Happiness." There were several thousand people in the auditorium. They were surprised to see "George" in the crowd, although he seemed to ignore them. They figured he was just ashamed to be seen with his parents on a Saturday night.

Given that the twins lived only about ten miles apart, instances of mistaken identity were not unlikely. But there were also some earlier near misses, chances when the boys might have met as infants or as young children. These events were potentially more serious from Carroll's point of view because associating Brent and George in infancy or childhood might have brought custody battles. Carroll learned that Marcus's biological mother had considered contacting the Children's Aid Society to find his adoptive family, to be certain he was faring well; she didn't intend to claim him. Marcus's mother never followed through—but if she had, the trail would have taken her to the Tremblays, where she would have found Brent instead of Marcus. "If this had happened it would have been a story upon a story." (Both families assume that, had the switch not occurred, Marcus would have been placed with Jim and Carroll.)

But that wasn't all. One of Wade's teachers, who knew Brent, had children who played with George and Marcus. Had this teacher looked more closely at George, she might have made a connection. Carroll's voice lowered to a whisper when she told me this: "We would have lost Brent." The fact that George and Brent met as adults was fortunate because custody was no longer in question. But Carroll's fears of losing her son's love and loyalty were real—and vividly expressed in a dream she had soon after the twins met: Unable to find her son, she drove to the Holmeses'. There was Brent, hiding in a deep hole. He was holding up a sign showing a dark "X" drawn across a picture of his mother's face. He didn't want to get out. Still, nothing could be certain until the DNA tests were completed.

On September 13, 1993, DNA test reports were faxed to Laura Holmes's office. The results were unsettling, but predictable: the probability that George and Brent were identical twins was greater than 99.9 percent. The probability that George and Brent were Laura and

Randy's biological sons was greater than 99.9 percent. The probability that Marcus was their biological son was 00.0 percent. As Jim put it, "This was the first step toward changing our family."

The DNA results were what everyone expected, but digesting the proof was difficult, because there was no more room for doubt. Everyone now had to deal with the hard reality. Laura phoned Randy, and they and their children met at home to talk quietly. One of the first and most important things Randy did was to take Marcus out alone for a drive. He assured him that he was, and always would be, their son.

While Randy was consoling Marcus, George called Brent to tell him the news. Carroll said that once Brent knew, he hung up the phone and asked her to come see him: "All he said was, 'George and I are identical twins.' I knew that already." Then they both cried. When I spoke to Brent, he told me he was more worried about his mother's reaction than his own. I heard his voice crack as he spoke: "It was an emotional moment. I felt the rug yanked out from under me, it was a complete upheaval. I thought, 'So, what do we do now?' My mother thought I would go off and live with George, but I knew I wouldn't."

Carroll said, "I realized he was an identical twin, but he was our son. But maybe he was not our son anymore—maybe we would lose him to another family. An identical twin is a real drawing card. If Brent had only found his biological parents he could decide whether or not to develop a relationship with them. But finding an identical twin means there is no choice because twins are too close to ignore one another. And Brent and George were already close. I worried whether we would lose out." She added, "It was a lot to dump on a twenty-two-year-old." She cried as she recalled that day.

Jim called the DNA results the "worst news" he could have heard: "Our family unit was destroyed—how would we regain it?" Initially, both Jim and Carroll tried to put a positive spin on things—instead of losing Brent, maybe they would "gain" George as a kind of son. But that never happened because George never felt the affinity with the Tremblays that Brent felt with the Holmeses. (At first, the Tremblays sent birthday cakes and Christmas gifts to George, but he eventually asked them to "back off.") This makes perfect sense because George had no link to the Tremblays, biological or otherwise. So, strange but true, Carroll acknowledged that her son had a brother to whom she had no real connection. She was bitter: "We gave George his twin, but we had no relationship with George—and we would have liked one."

In fact, even before the blood was drawn, Brent's friendship with George had dramatically changed his life. He experienced a quick closeness with his identical twin and slipped easily into a different social world. The DNA results only intensified their bond. Like his twin, Brent began drinking regularly, even though alcohol had been consumed moderately in his rearing home. Randy, the twins' father, noticed that Brent reacted badly to large quantities of beer and expressed his concern to Carroll. But nothing changed. Brent's laid-back manner, disregard for punctuality, and taste for fun aligned perfectly with his twin's. Carroll summed it up well: "George had more influence on Brent than Brent had on him—George was leading the life that Brent should have been living." Wade, Brent's younger brother, saw this, too: "Brent was very possessive of George and would break plans with me just to be with him. When George was at our house he was more of a brother to me than Brent was."

Carroll could see that Brent thoroughly enjoyed the Holmeses' laid-back family atmosphere—chasing the dog, playing games, listening to music: "He loved the Holmes household, especially their dog. Whenever we were there he would sit and pet it." She recalled that when Brent was a child the family had spent three weeks each summer visiting her sister, Cherie, in Thunder Bay. "My sister had three dogs, a mastiff named Aquarius, a Maltese named Mitzy, and a dachshund named Snuggy, and Brent was crazy about them. Jim remembers how gentle Brent was with the pets—you could see in his face how much he loved them. He would complain that 'Aunt Cherie has three dogs and we don't even have one.'"

Brent was comfortable in the Holmes household, so he and George spent more time there than at the Tremblays'. But Carroll said that occasionally Brent and George would come to her home to swim in the pool. She was fascinated by their behavior—they would approach the water stiffly before creeping in: "They never bashed the water like most guys do." Exiting the pool, they would dry themselves off, still talking, then delicately take the cheese and crackers Carroll had prepared for them. And they would toss a ball back and forth while talking sports non-stop. "But they spent more time at George's. Brent once apologized to me—'Sorry, I like that house better,'" Carroll recalled.

I could feel Carroll's hurt and disappointment. In her journal she wrote, "It was very obvious that Brent preferred the characteristics of his genetic background to the one he was raised in. It's in his genes." She was a mother wearing two faces: She had fought the foster-care facility on behalf of her son, for compensation and acknowledgment of wrongdoing. And she mourned the loss of the boy she raised lovingly, knowing he felt a better fit with another family.

I wondered what the Holmes family felt for Brent—did they feel the same kinship with him that George did? Laura said, "Brent is my son, but I am not his mother." Randy said that Brent was "like a nephew, not a son."[11] The media sometimes revel in the "instant psychological connections" described by some reunited relatives. These connections can happen, but they are not the rule. Laura loved her three children and had no reason to doubt her relationship to Marcus; Brent's parents loved and supported him, so he never felt an emotional void. Many parents and children (both biological and adopted) say that time is requisite to building the close personal relationship we think of as love. I also believe that since George and Brent were young, still developing their identities when they found each other, they could work their newfound brother into their lives more easily than Laura and Randy could work a newfound son into theirs.

Laura also wondered how many other infants had not gone home with their real families: "If this can happen with identical twins who look so much alike, then it must happen with others." She was a mother who sought the best possible environment for her twin sons

SEPARATED AT BIRTH

when she couldn't care for them herself. But she was immeasurably and irrevocably hurt by a system she trusted.

George said that the news of his twinship was "real and unreal." It confirmed what he was starting to feel strongly: "I would have been surprised if we hadn't been related, we had too much in common." But it was strange to think of Marcus as not really his brother: "I still consider Marcus to be a brother—and my family considers him to be a son." George felt sad that he and Brent had not grown up together, but he is glad that they met early enough in life to "recoup" their bond. Yet despite their closeness, George considers Brent a "friend, someone to hang out with," rather than part of his family.

When I asked George how his brother Marcus had taken the news, he replied: "I cannot speak for him. But he was thrown for a loop. He wondered, 'Where do I fit in?' although [he] said it was not a big deal." But George admitted later that Marcus was sensitive about what the DNA tests meant. I have known some adopted individuals who were stunned to discover that they were not genetically related to their parents. But Marcus's case was unusual because he *and* his parents believed he was their biological child, and he looked a lot like his father. No doubt his situation made the news especially tough.

A week after the DNA test results were known, Laura, Randy, George, and Marcus joined Jim, Carroll, and Brent at the Tremblays' home. The families wanted the Children's Aid Society to admit to its mistake and pay damages. They hired Arthur Cogan, a high-profile attorney who was accustomed to handling the press. Carroll sensed that Marcus was reluctant to come: "It was a lot for him to accept. He might have been the son we should have gotten."

As expected, the Children's Aid Society "dragged their feet" during the first year of litigation, so Cogan contacted newspapers and radio stations. Carroll recalled, "Once the story broke, the media jumped all over us. Several articles appeared and a movie deal was offered, but it fell through." Soon the media attention lost its "glamour"—Carroll complained that all sides of the story were not given equal time, and

George was tired of feeling like a "cue card." The families preferred to handle their emotions privately and to focus on the lawsuit. It was nearly eight years until the case settled, but not to everyone's satisfaction.[12] In Cogan's view, the Tremblays' disrupted relationship with Brent was not as stressful as the Holmeses' disrupted relationship with their adopted-away son: "The reality is that Laura and Randy received the wrong child."

One of Carroll's diary entries read, "I was so sure that we would have had this matter solved long ago, based on my faith in the judicial system . . . Everyone focused more on Marcus, but which is more traumatic? To find out you were not adopted and should have been [Marcus]—or to find out you were adopted and weren't supposed to be [Brent]? I do not mean to minimize the damages Marcus has claimed, but being put up for adoption was his fate."

Carroll's comments sound cold, but she was not unkind. Her reasoning about Brent was shaped by love and emotion, whereas her thinking about Marcus was guided by objectivity and reason. Cogan sided with Marcus: "He was rudderless and rootless when the story broke. Marcus was a lovely guy—he took it well, but you knew he felt hurt and empty." But Cogan also acknowledged Brent's suffering: "Brent didn't know any other home environment until he met George. Brent still blames Jim and Carroll for how their restrictive rearing affected him. Brent clung to George, who was more stable than he was." Jim and Carroll did have strong beliefs about "eating right and dressing right," which Brent understood, but resisted.

It is impossible and unproductive to weigh the different charges and damages. Everyone in the Tremblay and Holmes families was hurt by the mistake that happened years ago. Their pain is permanent— nothing can compensate for the time lost between the identical twins, brothers and sisters, parents and children. The events of this case and their aftermath leave us a lot to think about. Identical twins, even if separated, can reconstitute their twinship after being reunited, but how? George and Brent were probably able to reconnect so easily because they had lots of common interests and abilities. They were able to ease into a relationship that felt familiar and natural.[13] They were also young and unattached at the time of their reunion.

On the flip side, most unrelated individuals raised together, like Brent and Wade, and George and Marcus, don't resemble each other as much as biological siblings, if at all. Wade is outgoing, has lots of friends, and plays different sports, whereas Brent is contemplative, has a few good friends, and studies sports statistics. Wade was diligent when it came to school and work, but Brent didn't complete college or pick a career. Carroll called them the "doer" and the "thinker," and the same might be said of Marcus and George. Marcus is very sociable; George said that "competition for the phone between he and my sister when we were teenagers was fierce." But like Brent, George is more reserved and has fewer friends. Marcus finished high school and became a carpenter, while George ushered, guarded, and clerked for ten years before becoming a federal correspondence officer.[14] Marcus was always "into sports," one reason that George was a little more athletic than Brent; Brent had a sports-minded brother, but not a same-age brother with whom he hung out. Strangely, everyone said that Wade and Marcus were alike.

This story reminds us that who we are in our families is central to our identity, and it shows us that changes to our identity can be damaging. Eight people—Laura, Randy, Carroll, Jim, Marcus, George, Brent, and Jessica—had to rethink who they were and how to cope with the radical revision in their family structures. New kinships for which we lack names—for example, an adopted mother's relationship to her adoptive son's twin; a father's relationship to a son he thought was biologically his—were seriously tested. Not everyone emerged a winner.

We can only speculate if the families would have been better off if Sasha hadn't walked into Carleton's student lounge on that particular day. There would have been no emotional upheaval, but Brent and George would have been denied their relationship as identical twins. Fortunately, Marcus retained the love of the parents who raised him. He eventually found his own biological parents and siblings, and has since married and had a son. Carroll and Jim never really lost Brent's love and devotion. But they are not in touch with their son's twin and would like to be. Laura and Randy see Brent from time to time, most recently on his thirty-third birthday. George wasn't there.

I spoke with George and Brent about their relationship, past and present. I listened for choppy sentences and drifting thoughts, but heard none. Maybe this was because they were both focused on a topic of huge personal significance. Both twins were intelligent, articulate, and courteous.

I was surprised to learn that George and Brent, now in their early thirties, are no longer close—the last time they arranged to see each other was the summer of 2002. The source of the difficulty is their different lifestyles, which have not won their brother's approval. George never finished high school but was selected to work for the government on the basis of competitive test scores. Brent calls George's current government employers "vicious," but he applauds the fact that his twin got his job through merit, rather than a diploma. "This is one of our quirky opinions," Brent said. George even got his driver's license, but mostly out of necessity rather than a desire to drive or own a car. "Most of my twenties consisted of mooching rides," George admitted. He dates several women, but none steadily. He values his time and independence.

Brent enrolled in two universities and one college, although he never earned a degree. He has never held a full-time job, but he works a full schedule of part-time jobs, including teaching chess to young children. He also works for his country's opposition political party, the Canadian Alliance. He has a steady girlfriend, Suzanne, whom he expects to marry some day. Brent knows that George is "more settled" in his work than he is in his, but Brent believes these differences can "switch between twins." George isn't so sure.

According to George, back in 1994 "you would not find two people more in sync than Brent and me. My brother Marcus was doing his thing and we couldn't wait to do ours. But Brent and I maxed out on our time together and we have evolved differently." Even their hairstyles reflect their different life choices; George's is short, whereas

Brent's, in his own words, is "three feet long—like Ian Asterbury's from the rock band Cult." But George's hair was long when they first met. George was careful to be kind, but he is not proud of his twin: "I have no sympathy for able-bodied and able-minded individuals who do not do things for themselves. I see so much wasted potential. I don't see how we can hang out anymore. This feeling is coming more from me than from him." He added, "It's easier if I don't see him, but it is not a decision I came to easily. Maybe I am being unfair."

Brent said that meeting George has caused him to consider questions of free will: To what extent do genes make us do what we do? "George and I have the same 'wetware,'" he explained. "It's easy for me to see where he's coming from. We don't write each other blank checks." Brent also talked about how he and George had drifted apart: "The difference now is that George puts his nose to the grindstone. I like to think that, even today, our relationship would be effortless, that we would be on the same page, but we have busier schedules." I wondered if he felt somewhat rejected by his twin, and used their "busier schedules" as an excuse for why their relationship has cooled. After all, George said that the negative feelings came mostly from him.

George and Brent ran into each other at a bar called the Lockmaster on two or three occasions in late summer and fall 2003. According to George, when Brent wandered over to him, "there was a little awkwardness, but it was not too bad. I am really not up for making specific plans. I do have a small amount of regret that we are not in touch—but I am doing my thing." Brent said that they both like the Lockmaster because you can drink beer and play pool; in fact, he and George played a few games together, sometimes alone and sometimes with other people. "What was it like running into George?" I asked. "Not too bad," he replied.

3

Oskar and Jack

The story of Oskar and Jack is perhaps one of the most unusual incidents of identical twin brothers reared apart. Oskar was raised as a Catholic in Hitler's Germany and was a member of the Hitler Youth. Jack, by contrast, was raised as a Jew in Trinidad and became an officer in the Israeli Navy. It sounds like the stuff of a mediocre thriller, but it is real.

Oskar and Jack were born in Port of Spain in January 1933 and were separated when they were six months old. Jack was raised by his Jewish father in Trinidad, which was then under British control. Oskar was raised by his Catholic mother and grandmother in the Sudetenland, the part of Czechoslovakia transferred to Germany by the British and French in the 1930s.[1] When the twins finally met, briefly, at age twenty-one, each realized that had their situations been reversed, he could have grown up as the other. This "other" was an identical twin who looked like him and talked like him, but whose political views and historical understandings he found incomprehensible and intolerable. They didn't meet again for twenty-five years.

I haven't written the story I expected to write. I hadn't met the twins when they were studied at the University of Minnesota in 1979; I had only seen the newspaper headlines: "Twins: Nazi and Jew," and "Identical Brothers . . . One Raised as a Nazi, One as a Jew."[2] The second story included a snapshot of the twins with a Jewish star printed above one and a swastika printed above the other. But that's too simple. That's not how it was.

The story of Oskar and Jack began in 1929, when nineteen-year-old Josef Yufe set sail for Venezuela and Trinidad from his hometown in Romania. He left to escape the prevailing anti-Semitism and the strict Orthodox Jewish life his father expected of him. En route to his new life, Josef met a young German woman named Liesel, and they stayed together in the Caribbean for three years. Josef's dark hair and eyes, strong cheekbones, and confident stare suggested a European Clark Gable. Liesel's brown hair and eyes were less distinctive, but her smile was warm and appealing. Liesel's reasons for leaving Germany are unclear, though she probably hoped for a better life elsewhere. It was the first time either of them had left home.

No one knows for sure if Josef and Liesel ever married, but they had three children, a daughter, Sonja, born in 1931, and identical twin sons, Oskar and Jack, born in 1933. When their relationship soured as a result of Josef's "roving eyes" and excessive drinking, they separated. In the summer of 1933, Liesel returned to Germany with two-year-old "Sonni" and six-month-old "Ossi."[3] Why Ossi? Oskar was the more difficult child, a "cry baby," and Josef, who had no patience or compassion for children, preferred the more even-tempered "Jackie." (Jack was named after his father's boxing favorite, Jack Sharkey; Oskar probably got his German name from his mother.)[4] Oskar's fussy moods and irritating whine thus sealed the twins' fates: Jack became a British subject in Trinidad and played with the black children on the island. And he was raised Jewish. Oskar became a subject of the German Reich and eventually joined the Hitler Youth—by default, like all young German boys.[5] And he was raised Catholic.

Leaving a twin baby behind would have been heart-wrenching for any new mother. But Liesel believed that her family would reunite in Europe. The letters she sent to Josef were never answered, however. A year and a half later, a note from friends arrived from the Caribbean— Josef had married a beauty queen, Miss Trinidad, and would not be going to Germany. Liesel became depressed and took a job as a nursemaid in Milan, leaving Oskar and Sonja with their grandmother in the Sudetenland.

The twins' childhood years had striking similarities and differences. Each felt abandoned and rejected—Jack by an indifferent father who sometimes beat him, an absent mother, and a detached stepmother (Miss Trinidad); and Oskar by an absent father, an unavailable mother, and a disapproving grandmother.[6] Oskar's grandmother, a stout blonde woman, knew nothing of her grandchildren until they came home and, according to Jack, were "dumped" on her. She disliked Oskar immediately because his crying forced her student tenants to leave, causing her to lose income. She was strict with her grandchildren and beat Oskar from time to time. She also worried about his Jewish background. When Oskar was eight, he heard something about "Jews" at school and asked his grandmother what it meant. She said never to say "Jew" again.

Oskar's Jewish background worried him, too. When he was in secondary school, he was called to the vice principal's office. Upon arriving, he was told, "Salute! You are Hitler Youth!" He complied with a "Heil, Hitler!" Then he was asked about his father's last name: "Yufe? Doesn't that mean Jew?" He thought quickly: "No, it's a French name, it's pronounced 'Yufé' [Yu-fay]."[7] Oskar suppressed this episode and became an enthusiastic member of the Hitler Youth, convinced that what the Nazis said about the Jews, war, and country was true. On another occasion, Oskar and Sonja were rounded up with Jewish children and placed on a wagon for deportation. Their grandmother immediately alerted Oskar's Uncle Max, an influential Nazi party member.[8] Uncle Max assured the officer that a mistake had been made, and the children were released. Oskar was traumatized by the knowledge that he and Sonja might have been killed because of the Jewish heritage they didn't acknowledge. Fearful of what might happen to the children in the future, Oskar's grandmother had them both baptized and changed their last name to match their mother's.

Meanwhile, Oskar's twin brother, Jack, was facing a different kind of discrimination and a different fear. He was the only Jewish boy in his peer group and one of the few white citizens in a black country. He was teased because he was skinny and because his father spoke with a thick European accent. His greatest fear was that someone would discover his German roots, so he just said that his mother was living in Europe. In 1946 Jack joined the Sea Scouts, the first step toward joining the British Navy; he even earned an award from the king of England in 1949: "I had to be very pro-British. In my mind, being a Sea Scout lessened the importance of having a German mother."

Jack's Sea Scout master, Arthur Johnson, now eighty-two years old, was his role model and father figure. And he knew about Jack's past: "Jack was hard-working, trustworthy, and respectful. He was also a bit more patriotic than the other boys—being in Trinidad meant that he avoided the dangers in Germany, so he felt on safe ground."

When Oskar was five or six years old he noticed twin girls at school and asked his grandmother why they looked alike. She explained the reason and told him that he had a twin. When Jack was eight, Josef told him he had a twin brother living in Germany. But this news left no impression on Jack at first, because he didn't understand what it meant to be born at the same time as someone who looked just like him.

During World War II, the twins thought—even dreamed—about each other. Jack saw *Commandos Strike at Dawn,* a 1942 film about a Norwegian fisherman who takes action against Nazi troops occupying his village, then escapes to England.[9] Later, he dreamed about being a soldier and saw Oskar on the opposing (German) side. He awoke terrified because, in the dream, he was stabbing his twin. Oskar heard American planes flying overhead and wondered if one of them carried his brother. He thought about what would happen if he (Oskar) were a fighter pilot and shot down his twin.

Jack and Oskar turned twelve in 1945, when the war ended. At about that time, Jack received a letter from his mother, Liesel. She said that she was happy to have found him, and that she, Sonja, and Oskar were alive. She also asked for financial help. Josef was uninterested in helping her, but Jack sent them goods—sugar and other island prod-

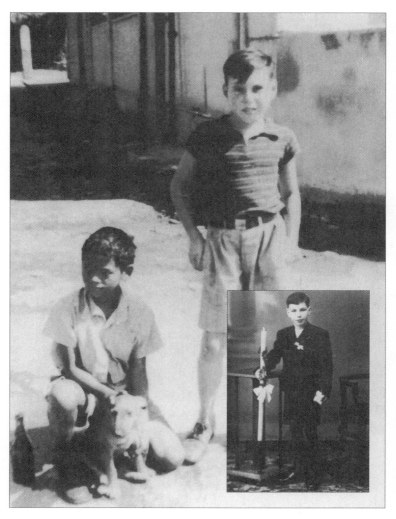

Oskar (inset) at his First Communion in the Catholic Church, at age ten. At that time he and his family were living in Freiwaldau, a district in the Sudetenland. Jack (upper right), also age ten, has returned from "exploring" Trinidad's mangrove swamps with a friend—the bottle to the left contains guppies that the boys caught that afternoon. Even though Jack's father made him attend synagogue regularly, he never had a Bar Mitzvah. (Photos courtesy of Jack and Ona Yufe and Oskar's family.)

ucts—with money he had earned working in his uncle's store. A few years later, Jack received a letter from Oskar suggesting that they meet. But Oskar was shocked by the photograph Jack returned with his reply: It showed Jack standing next to black and mulatto children in Trinidad. The twins' meeting was postponed, however, because when Jack was sixteen his father sent him to Israel to join the navy. Josef thought that military service would help overcome his son's apparent lack of ambition. While Jack was in the service he lost touch with his German family. And he met his first wife, Ona.

Jack and Ona met in 1953 at Kibbutz Ma'ale Ha'Chamisha, in Israel, when both of them were living and working there. Ona, an American Jew by birth, was attracted to Jack because of his "air of mystery— he had an accent, he was good looking, and he was not American." Ona was also intrigued by Jack's unique family history, though she didn't learn about it until after they were married.[10] Ona encouraged Jack to find his family, and he did so with the help of the British Red Cross. Jack was eager to meet his twin, but his first priority was meeting his mother.[11]

In 1954, when Jack was twenty-one, he and Ona traveled to Germany from Israel. Jack's Israeli Navy service had ended and he and Ona planned to go to the United States, where Jack's father had relocated. Time and maturity led Jack to rekindle connections begun through his earlier correspondence with his mother and his twin. He was curious about his German family.

Each twin wanted to be the first to see the other. When they arrived at the train station, Jack caught sight of Oskar and thought, "What a nerve, someone is wearing my face. It was also slightly embarrassing." Even though Jack had seen pictures of his brother, he now faced the reality of seeing someone who looked exactly like him. For Ona the meeting "had a Hollywood feel—finding a twin after so many years apart. They didn't look like clones. Jack was slender and Oskar was 'zoftig'—fleshy and robust. But meeting Oskar, who had been just a piece of paper and a photograph, was incredible."[12]

Jack (left) went to Israel at age sixteen to become a sailor. This photograph was taken after he completed boot camp and entered the Israeli Navy, when he turned eighteen. Oskar (right), at age fifteen, was a student at the Commercial School in the German state of Hessen, a secondary school that prepared students for various industrial jobs. He finished his studies at age seventeen, then worked full-time in the coal mines. Oskar sent this picture to his twin in April 1948: "To Dear Jackie, from Oskar," he wrote across the back. Six months later, Oskar sent this same picture to his father and twin: "Dear Father and Jackie, from Oskar," it said. It's likely that the first photo reached Jack after the second one—the twins complained in their letters that the mail deliveries were unreliable. (Photos courtesy of Jack and Ona Yufe and Oskar's family.)

The twins stared hard and often at each other, as most twins do when meeting for the first time, searching for similarities and differences. But in Jack and Oskar's case the fascination was mixed. Jack explained, "We saw each other as enemies, neither one of us would change. We looked at each other with suspicion." The bad feelings intensified when Oskar removed the luggage tags identifying Jack's country of origin as Israel.[13] Oskar warned Jack to say that he was visiting

Jack (left) and Oskar at their first, unfriendly meeting in Germany in 1954, when they were twenty-one. The family had gone for a walk and stopped in a park along the way, where this picture was taken. (Photo courtesy of Jack Yufe.)

from the United States. In 1943 the twins' mother, Liesel, had married a man who still held anti-Jewish views, so having Jewish relatives, especially in their home, would have been risky.[14] Jack and Ona stayed in a separate apartment to minimize the chance of Liesel's husband discovering his wife's Jewish connection. But the masquerade was easy to maintain—Jack said that Oskar's stepfather was "easy to bamboozle" because Ona was American, and both she and Jack spoke English. Like Jack, Oskar hadn't told his then girlfriend, Christel, that he had a twin until Jack came to Germany. And Christel learned from Liesel, not from Oskar, that Jack was Jewish—but it didn't faze her. "I was young and didn't understand the problem," she said.

Ironically, Jack was used to hiding his German roots in Trinidad. Now he was hiding his Jewish background in Germany, even though the war was over.

Not all members of Oskar's family were emotionally distant toward Jack. Ona remembers Liesel being "so warm and friendly" toward him. When they went to Liesel's home Jack delighted her—she didn't hug him, but she looked at him adoringly, reaching out to touch him as if to be sure he was still there. Several years earlier (with the help of a translator) she had written to her son: "My dearest Jücki! Up to now, I have not been able to forget, why I must be separated from all that meant love and happyness for me. We can only hope to see each other once more. My sonny child it is my greatest desire before I will have to close my eyes . . ."

"I was King of the Hill," Jack said. But Ona remembers that Jack was "standoffish—it was hard for him to reach out to her." Meanwhile, Oskar sat in a corner and "pouted." Oskar admitted, "She [my mother] saw the bad guy in me and the good guy in him [Jack]. I looked more like my father." Oskar had also angered his family by attending Communist and other political meetings in East Berlin after the war, though he says he merely went "to get answers . . . to know what happened."

The young people did "fun things" during the twins' six days together, visiting the Krupp Castle at Rheineck, riding on scooters, and eating at cafés. Jack recalled taking a boat trip on the Rhine River with his older sister, Sonja (who was raised with Oskar in Germany), Walter (Sonja's boyfriend), Oskar, Christel (the small, dark-haired woman Oskar later married), and Ona. Jack had hoped for private time with Oskar on the boat, "but he [Oskar] was so unfriendly, and he was not trying to hide it. He kept covering his eyes with his hand." But what Jack saw as rejection by his twin was more complicated than that, although Jack didn't hear the whole story until years later. It didn't help that the twins had to speak through an interpreter since neither was fluent in his brother's tongue.

The six days passed and Jack's curiosity about his German family was satisfied. He was delighted to have met the mother he never knew, but parting from his twin was a cool affair: "We could not renew a love that was never there to begin with. My twin was a stranger to me." The cold tone of their parting is understandable. To say that their lives from birth to age twenty-one were at familial, political, religious, and cultural odds hardly captures the breadth of their divide. These differences explain the "icy handshake" and "emotional distance" both twins recall during their first meeting in Germany.

After Jack and Ona left Germany, they settled near San Diego, where Josef, Jack's father, had started a business. Jack established himself as owner of El Progresso, a retail store in nearby San Ysidro.[15] Josef started referring to Jack as his brother rather than his son, something that Jack found hurtful, as though Josef was denying who Jack was. Jack and Ona raised two daughters, Rehova (Hobi) and Devra. But they separated in 1978 and divorced in 1985, after their two children were grown. In 1991 Jack married Ruth Vega, a younger woman of Mexican descent. They have two children, Anita and Kenny.[16]

Oskar stayed in Germany and married his longtime girlfriend, Christel. He worked as a miner and then as an electrical welder in the German Ruhr. "I have been into every pit in the Ruhr," he said. Oskar and Christel had two sons, Ingo and Rolf. Later, they became the grandparents of Julian, Christopher (nicknamed "Little Ossi" by his mother, Anke, because he was demanding and temperamental), and identical twins, Anna and Kathi. Oskar was very involved with his grandchildren—Anna and Kathi said that he pressured them to "eat healthy, avoid smoking and do what he told them." But "he idolized us. He was very happy we were on earth because we are twins," said Kathi. Time passed with little indication that Jack and Oskar would meet again.

In fact, the twins had little contact after their meeting in Germany. Oskar stopped writing because Jack didn't answer his requests to sponsor his emigration to the United States. Jack explained that bringing Oskar over would have increased the burden that Jack himself presented to his father. Josef refused to support Oskar because he was a "German." Furthermore, Jack was not a United States citizen and was being sponsored by Ona's father. Above all, "fears and worries" urged Jack to keep Oskar at bay: "He might have started depending on me if things didn't go right." Jack refused to feel guilty about his decision to withhold support from his brother.

While Jack and Oskar were out of touch, Ona said that contact between the families was "intermittent, but steady, maybe three times a year." Ona wrote letters and Christel sent Christmas cards, something that Jack said was "stupid" given that his family was Jewish.[17] Twenty-five years passed. Then, in 1979, Ona saw a *People* magazine article describing University of Minnesota research on twins reared apart. Jack wrote to the project director, Professor Thomas J. Bouchard, Jr., to see if he and Oskar qualified for the study. They did. Then Jack wrote to Oskar in Germany to see if he was interested. Oskar was "delighted" by the invitation: "It was really the last chance to get to know him properly." Jack was also extremely happy: "Maybe enough time has gone by that we can meet and be friends." Jack added, "That was some day. I thought he didn't like me." But he admitted that "a catalyst was required to bring us together." If not for the Minnesota study, both twins would probably have been left wondering how far they might have taken their twinship.

As the trip to Minnesota approached, Jack became more enthusiastic about what he sensed was his unusual life story. But Oskar was con-

SEPARATED AT BIRTH

cerned about public disclosure of his Jewish roots. Oskar's son Rolf later explained that Oskar worried about recent attacks on Jewish people in Germany; Rolf, however, wasn't concerned about his Jewish roots. "We don't see this as a dark side to our family," he said. "And it didn't bother Oskar that Jack was Jewish."

Jack and Oskar approached their second meeting differently from their first—hopeful, but uncertain that they could really feel like twin brothers. Memories don't fade, but maturity brings new perspective to old sentiment. Both twins knew that this was their last opportunity to try to reconnect. Jack also said that being identical twins was a driving force in their effort. So, despite their strong differences and lingering suspicions, both men were fascinated by their similarities and by the potential for a meaningful relationship.

Oskar arrived first at the Twin Cities International Airport on November 2, 1979. Once Jack landed, several minutes passed before the twins caught sight of each other because each wanted to see the other one first—just as they had at their first meeting twenty-five years before. Pillars surrounding the airport arrival gates gave both twins protective cover, but they couldn't stay hidden forever. Jack claims that he saw Oskar first, and his immediate reaction was that someone was dressed exactly like he was—in a light blue epauletted shirt with military-style pockets and square, wire-rimmed eyeglasses. "The glasses surprised me, but not as much as the shirt. I have ten or fifteen of them," Jack said.

Later that night Oskar saw a Jewish star hanging from Jack's neck and wondered, "What would Jack see me as?" But the twins had little time to talk about the past or present while they were in Minnesota. Study participants are kept busy during testing and are separated as much as possible to prevent them from discussing questions and answers.

Soon, reporters began following their story. Oskar later blamed Jack for the media attention that eventually reached his hometown in Germany. But according to Jack, Oskar took part in the interviews willingly.

Jack (left) and Oskar at the University of Minnesota, where they participated in the Minnesota Study of Twins Reared Apart, in 1979. The twins, age forty-six, hadn't seen each other for twenty-five years. If not for this study, they might never have seen each other again. (Photo by Thomas J. Bouchard, Jr.)

The twins discovered a lot about themselves during their week in Minnesota. They were very competitive with each other; each twin obsessively tracked the other's test scores, trying to beat him. They also learned that they both read books from back to front, sneezed loudly in elevators, wrapped rubber bands around their wrists, flushed toilets before and after using them, and wore tight bathing suits.[18] It's easy to call these habits coincidences, but they're probably not—more likely, they come from the twins' shared biology and ways of approaching the world. For example, both Jack and Oskar were sensitive to germs, so their penchant for flushing public toilets is understandable. The twins also liked controlling situations and watching people's reactions, so it makes sense that playing practical jokes (such as sneezing loudly in crowded elevators) would appeal to them.

The twins' matched behaviors, as well as their separate lives in Trinidad and Germany, have been described often. It's hard to imagine a greater contrast in upbringing between identical twins, and yet Oskar and Jack were very similar despite their childhood differences. But once the study ended, researchers and reporters paid little attention to what drove Jack and Oskar's meetings, which they looked forward to despite their conflicts. That it has taken this long for the personal elements of the twins' story to surface is understandable; the brothers needed time to test their fraternal ties. And some of their family members, especially their older sister, Sonja, didn't want their Jewish roots exposed. So when Jack invited me to his home, I couldn't resist a behind-the-scenes look at the relationship between two people with identical genes but opposing minds.

I first met Jack Yufe in September 2001. He wanted to talk to me because "so many things [about our relationship and our divisiveness] came out later." "Later" meant the years since the twins' 1979 participation in the Minnesota Study of Twins Reared Apart. During that time, Jack and Oskar took six or seven vacations together, sometimes just the two of them and sometimes with their wives and children.

When I arrived at the San Diego train station, Jack was leaning against a wall by the exit, an older version of the red-haired, freckled, and bespectacled image I had expected. At sixty-six years old, Jack was five feet seven inches tall, slightly overweight, and quite casual in appearance. This last fact surprised me because both twins had been fashionably dressed in most photographs. He smiled when he saw me—he knew that I knew a lot about him, and besides, we had a Minnesota connection.

But I saw more than Jack's age and attire; I saw a powerful physical divide between the two twins. Jack would have blended in with the Jewish crowds I have seen at synagogues, while Oskar would have been noticeable, almost out of place. And yet Jack and Oskar were genetically identical. Our religions and backgrounds aren't inscribed in our faces, but they can be reflected in the habits, attitudes, and customs of our culture. The Jewish star around Jack's neck aside, his casual appearance and relaxed pose contrasted with Oskar's thick moustache and reserved expression. Maybe the warm California sun and cold European winters had left lasting marks. Or perhaps I saw each twin embedded in his unique circumstances.

We drove to Jack's home, a modern, two-story structure with a large driveway and pool. The walls were covered with black-and-white photographs of Jack in Trinidad and Israel, as well as certificates he had earned as a swimmer and sailor. And there were boxes of pictures of his father, Josef, his step-siblings (from his father's multiple marriages), Jack's two wives and children, Oskar's family, Oskar and Jack's mother, Liesel, and their sister, Sonja. There were also pictures of the twins, news clippings, and videotaped interviews he and Oskar had done with the media.

Jack wanted to tell me about the additional similarities he and Oskar had discovered over the years. He had a list: wrapping tape around pens and pencils to get a better grip; underlining heavily when reading books and magazines; picking up articles left on desks and tables; demanding a special chair in the living room; and insisting that food be brought to the table promptly. The twins also had an "extreme" taste for butter; Jack joked that he ate more butter than bread. When eating in restaurants, both twins moved vases and other objects to the side of the table to maintain eye contact with others—and were frustrated when the wait staff moved them back. Both twins were short-tempered, absent-minded, and demanding of their children. And both carried pepper spray and dealt similarly with "raspy people."

On a trip to Paris, the twins' wives, Ruth and Christel, commented that Jack and Oskar walked, moved, and nearly tripped in exactly the same way. Both wives also carried large purses to accommodate the paraphernalia their husbands always brought along. And they noticed that both twins scratched their dry scalps with their fourth finger. On one vacation the twins agreed to meet for breakfast. In the morning they emerged from their adjacent hotel rooms at exactly the same moment—Jack said that it was like "looking in a mirror." And both twins had been in car accidents at nearly the same time. Jack also remarked that when he flew out of Portugal after one of their trips together, he was bothered by the closeness of the lines for passengers going to Germany and England.[19] "They have been enemies for years," Jack said. Oskar had left the day before, so Jack didn't know if his twin had also been disturbed by the lines—but he was sure that Oskar had.

Jack's penchant for spicy food (which he was used to eating in Trinidad) was shared by Oskar when Jack introduced him to it. Oskar didn't grimace or reach for water when he ate a hot pepper for the first time. Jack recalled asking Oskar how he liked the food, and Oskar answered, "Good. More." Both twins enjoyed music—Jack liked Trinidad's "soca" music (a blend of calypso and soul), while Oskar liked Germany's "Volksmusik" (a counterpart to country western). But Oskar liked the music from Trinidad when he heard it. Jack didn't dislike German music, but "I wouldn't put it on," he said. In fact, Jack visited Germany just twice since the twins met—in 1982 for a film project that fell through, and in 1994, "when Oskar first got sick and I wanted to be with him." However, Oskar had been to San Diego several times and would have gone again if his health hadn't worsened.

But more important than dwelling on their similarities, Jack wanted to reflect on how far he and Oskar had come as twins, and on

Jack (left) and Oskar, age sixty-one, with Oskar's twin granddaughters, Kathi (left) and Anna, age eight. Jack visited Oskar in Germany in 1994 when Oskar first got sick. On this day they stopped by a children's playground near Oskar's home. (Photo courtesy of Ingo, Oskar's son.)

how much was left unsettled between them when Oskar died in 1997. Sometimes other people's observations are insightful.

Jack said that his daughter Devra told him that meeting Oskar gave Jack the advantage of seeing himself in another person. Devra's insight resonated with Jack, maybe because he knew that he and Oskar watched each other closely when they were together. There was a competitive tension between the twins, possibly linked to their first meeting in Germany, when Jack got all the attention. And when they were together, each twin could see "himself" as he might have turned out. According to Jack, Oskar told him, "If we had been switched, I would have been the Jew and you would have been the Nazi." But Jack didn't need to be told. He also knew that, under different circumstances, both might have been raised in Trinidad—or in the Sudetenland.

Jack's former wife, Ona, was intrigued by Jack's life story when she first learned about it. But when I met her in February 2003, she hadn't thought about the "twin thing" for some time. She and I watched the 1995 documentary *Oskar and Jack,* which she had seen eight years earlier.[20] The film, by Frauke Sandig of Germany, shows Jack and Oskar describing their separate life stories, in Trinidad and the Sudetenland. It ends with the twins' visit to Trinidad and their discussion of how each became the person he is. Both times she felt emotionally disconnected from the film—it had been a long time since the twins had met, and she had not been a major player in their reunion. Ona said, "Seeing the film is like watching other people. Now I am mostly moved by each twin's growing-up experience." In retrospect, she felt sorrier for Oskar than for Jack because, aside from parental rejection, Oskar lived in terror—he had a Jewish background and lived in the Third Reich. Her feelings surprised her.

I never met Oskar. The twins had been studied at Minnesota before I arrived, then Oskar died in 1997 from lung cancer linked to his job in the mines. But I learned a lot about him from his German family when I visited them in July 2004. The twin's half-brother, Peter, and his wife, Adelheid, both English teachers, were my hosts, translators, and interview subjects. I was delighted but surprised that Oskar's family agreed to speak with me because they were worried about their privacy. But over two family meetings and a magnum of wine, they decided to proceed with the story.[21] "Oskar would have wanted us to get the job done," said Oskar's older son, Ingo.

Peter met me at the Recklinghausen train station in the western part of Germany. He looked nothing like Jack. Peter was nearly sixty, with dark gray hair and a gray moustache, and he was neatly dressed in a striped shirt and tan shorts. He was business-like in a charming way, and very warm and accommodating. I had dinner with him and his wife, Adelheid, at their home later that night—Adelheid had visited Oskar often during the last year of his life. Then Oskar's son Ingo arrived. At age forty-six, Ingo was a familiar version of Oskar (and Jack); he had the twins' characteristic sharp eyes and high cheekbones. I would see these features repeated in Oskar's younger son, Rolf, and in Ingo's twin daughters, Anna and Kathi. Oskar's sons didn't find out about their father's past until he and Jack went to Minnesota, when Ingo was twenty-three and Rolf was eighteen.

I talked with Ingo alone after dinner. It was the first time he had discussed his feelings about Oskar with anyone. His face turned very red at times, and he left the room twice to grab a smoke outside. The emotions that his wife, Barbara, said he never expressed were starting to show, and eventually we had to stop. But Ingo agreed to talk more the next day, and the day after that.

Ingo drove me back to my hotel that night. On the way he said that his family and his brother's family planned to visit Jack in California the next year. "Why do you want to visit Jack?" I asked. "To see him," he answered.

Over the next five days I spoke with many members of Oskar's family.[22] Before leaving for Germany, I had taken another look at *Oskar and Jack,* the film I watched with Ona. I really wanted to see the film with Oskar's family—what did they think about it? Were they surprised by something Oskar had said? But Peter warned me in advance that this might not be possible: "You shouldn't forget that it might be painful for them to watch that all again after Oskar's death."[23] Still, Peter spoke with Ingo, and without my asking, Ingo announced that we would see the film at his home. He added, "No one in the family has been able to see this film. We cannot hear his [Oskar's] voice, we break down." But seven years had passed and Ingo thought it was time to watch it.

Two days later, I was sitting at Ingo's dining room table with Ingo, his wife, Barbara, their twins, Anna and Kathi, Rolf and Anke, their sons, Julian and Chris, Oskar's wife, Christel, her friend Horst, and Peter and Adelheid. Coffee and cake were followed by wine and conversation about school, work, and travel. When it was time to watch *Oskar and Jack,* Rolf left with his young son, Chris. Rolf later explained that he could anticipate his family's reaction and couldn't bear to see it. He did say that Oskar was delighted with the film when it premiered in Germany, but was critical as usual: "My father said that it could have been better."[24]

Ingo was very serious. He waited until everyone had gathered quietly around the television before starting the tape. But when he hit the play button, we saw a different tape—scenes from Rolf and Anke's *polterabend,* a party that takes place the night before a wedding. I watched the family watching it. It mostly showed Oskar and Christel and other couples dancing and celebrating. Christel, who was seated across the room from me, was smiling and laughing with the others, but it also looked as if she might be blinking back tears. Everyone else in the family seemed upbeat to be reliving this celebration. But after a few minutes Ingo stopped the tape, lit a cigarette, and started the documentary. Oskar and Jack appeared, as adults and as young children in pictures. There were close-up shots of both twins telling their life stories, first Jack, then Oskar. Ingo stared hard—and when Oskar started talking, Ingo looked down at the floor, trembling. Christel and Kathi cried, and Ingo and Anke left the room. I stopped the tape. This documentary was more than just a story for this family.

I found Ingo alone in the kitchen. "The voice is terrible," he said.

Ingo and I talked for a long time about Oskar and about Oskar and Jack. I asked him again why he wanted to visit Jack in California;

he hadn't really answered that question when I first brought it up. "Maybe seeing Jack is a way to revisit Oskar, to keep him alive at some level," he said, adding, "I can't watch the tape and I don't know why." Next I spoke with Christel, while Ingo translated. I asked them both the question I really wanted to ask Oskar: Did Oskar ever talk about how his life would have turned out if he had been raised by his Jewish father in Trinidad? Ingo and Christel believed that Oskar had thought about this possibility, but never spoken about it. "My father was a realist," said Ingo. "He didn't think about theoretical things." But Oskar had raised this point with Jack—"If we had been switched, I would have been the Jew and you would have been the Nazi." But what was Oskar really thinking?

Oskar's family was very gracious, especially after I had caused them pain. Perhaps they were doing it for Oskar—after all, he would have wanted to get the job done. Nonetheless, questions remained.

After seeing each other in Minnesota, Jack and Oskar continued meeting as adults, trying to restore their lost twinship. They make us wonder: How can we hope to embrace someone whose thinking is so opposed to our own? For Jack, the anticipation of seeing his twin drove the relationship: "I would run enthusiastically to the airport. This is my best memory of Oskar. We liked meeting each other—but then we would get into the routine of difficulties and competition." The twins couldn't reasonably discuss events and outcomes from World War II because they disagreed too strongly over responsibility and justification for bombings and other acts of war. Oskar's repeated reference to German soldiers as "we" infuriated Jack. And Jack heard Oskar refer to Franklin Delano Roosevelt as Jewish. "How do you deal with that?" Jack wondered. He did so mostly by avoiding such topics: "I just dropped it—what can you do?" But for Jack, the "worst thing" about Oskar was his inability to make a decision quickly. According to Jack, "Oskar always waited to get the best deal, on hotel rooms, on lunch tables, whatever. I'm not this way—but I used to be."

The irritation was mutual. Once in Trinidad when the twins were getting into a taxi, Jack replied, "Yeah, man" to something the driver had said. Thinking he had said "German," Oskar asked Jack, "Why did you say you were German?" According to Jack it took two years to put that incident to rest. And Oskar was livid when Jack "dared to speak up to him in his own country [Germany]"—but the next day they acted as though nothing had happened. "That's the way it is with twins," Jack explained.

The twins also tried to steal the limelight from each other. When Oskar cursed a Russian train conductor who didn't allow the twins to sit in first class with second-class tickets, did he do so to impress Jack? When Jack demanded a bag from a shopkeeper and didn't get one, was his violent reaction intended to gain Oskar's respect? Or was it their short tempers taking control?

In addition, the twins were at odds over Jewish-Palestinian issues. Oskar sided with the Palestinians, which Jack attributed more to Oskar's old enmity toward the Jews than to his sympathy for the Palestinians. The twins' half-brother, Peter, thinks that Oskar sometimes opposed Jack on purpose, just to sound right: "Maybe Oskar felt blamed by others [for Germany's war activities] so he took the German side just to counterbalance Jack."

Oskar also seemed curious about his Jewish past. Jack recalls Oskar's fascination with a Jewish wedding in San Diego's Balboa Park. Oskar, Jack, and Jack's son, Kenny, were in the park one afternoon when Oskar got separated from the group. Retracing their steps, Jack and Kenny found Oskar absorbed in the marriage ceremony. Now that Oskar's Jewish roots weren't threatening as before, perhaps he could show interest in the past he had denied. In fact, Oskar once reflected that being separated from his twin was probably a good thing. He alleged that Dr. Josef Mengele, the Auschwitz physician who performed horrific medical experiments on twins and dwarfs, would have found them.[25] "It would have been harder to hide two of us," he reasoned.[26] Fortunately, Oskar was never circumcised as is customary for Jewish males on their eighth day of life, and so he lacked a visible sign of his Jewish heritage.[27]

Years after the war, Oskar and other miners were sent to Poland for a work project. Oskar visited Auschwitz during a free weekend, though he told his colleagues he went to Krakow. His family knew nothing about this trip because he never told them. But he told Jack that he went—although he said nothing more. "Oskar went because he cared, because he wanted to see for himself," said Jack.

So Jack and Oskar kept in touch, knowing that their relations would deteriorate each time they met. Jack said that they kept meeting because they were twins: "Being a twin isn't special, special implies that you are above others—but it's unique and Oskar also felt this way. We both knew we were from the same egg and same birth, and there were many similarities."

Most abilities, values, and attitudes are equally shaped by genetic factors and idiosyncratic events.[28] But depending on the circumstances, genes or environment can have a greater effect on an individual. Jack said, "Of course, our political thinking was all environmental." Their separate cultures clearly influenced their thinking, but they used the same coping strategies. As children, both twins embraced the culture of their homeland, in part because both twins felt different from their peers. Besides Oskar's concern over his Jewish roots, he was teased for not living with a mother and father like his playmates. Jack's German background disturbed him because of British warnings of a German invasion of Trinidad. Nevertheless, Jack said that both twins handled their childhood situations in the same way—Oskar by becoming "very German" and Jack by becoming "very British." Their forceful personalities were starting to show.

Jack and Oskar illustrate the divide between content (the habits and beliefs of their culture) and commitment (their level of involvement in their respective cultures, deriving partly from their genetically based personality traits). One day Oskar asked his family, "Am I like Jack?" They replied, "You are like him [aggressive, critical, demanding], but you are less extreme." And when Jack used these words to describe Oskar, his wife, Ruth, said, "Sounds like someone I know." According to Rolf, both twins disliked these particular traits, which they saw in themselves and in each other.

Neither Jack nor Oskar was open with his feelings, so my time with their families was revealing. Clearly, both twins had enormous influence on the people around them. They could both get people to do things—to a point—even if they didn't want to. For example, on one of Peter's visits to California, Jack insisted that Peter go with him to a Trinidadian dance in Los Angeles, even though Peter was reluctant. But Peter refused to fly to Trinidad with Jack and leave his wife, Adelheid, behind. Ingo and Rolf said that when they first visited Jack in San Diego they felt as if they had "two fathers." Jack insisted that they eat fish rather than marmalade with their rolls because it's healthier, and Oskar agreed. They ate the fish even though they didn't want to. Another time, Jack told them they had to ride bicycles for thirty minutes before they could have breakfast. After three days of this the two brothers moved to a hotel. They were "glassy-eyed."

Peter said that Jack "lives in the past and waits for the future"; and though Oskar also lived in the past, he was more attuned to the present. Perhaps because of his grandchildren, his illness, or his age, Oskar had mellowed in recent years, becoming a real family man. He saw his children nearly every day and was part of every one of their decisions, from child-rearing to house-building. Knowing this, I wasn't surprised by what happened at Ingo's house when we watched the documentary film.

Thinking back over their first meeting, Jack wondered if both twins might have expected a hug, which neither was willing to initiate. Jack was used to physical affection among Trinidadian men, but Oskar was accustomed to German men's physical restraint—in Germany, physical affection between men implied sexual interest.[29] But Peter said that "reserved embraces" were appropriate between relatives. No doubt, Jack and Oskar's inability to show their emotions increased the gap between them at that time. Oskar's son Ingo recalled that when he first saw Jack in San Diego he had expected a hug, but Jack had backed away.

Jack said that his relationship with Oskar was "like having a wife younger than you are and always hoping it will get better." There was clearly an attraction between the twins and the potential for a close relationship, but as with some couples, their differences in opinion would invariably take over. Still, their connection was undeniable because of what they could see of themselves in each other—and each time they met they hoped for a fresh start. They made some progress; what Jack thought was Oskar's indifference during their first meeting was partly explained by his sleep deprivation and the glare of the sun: "These reasons for Oskar's behavior never came out in Minneapolis during the study, they only came out much later."[30] But Oskar was also angry with his father for having deserted him, a childhood feeling that Jack's visit to Germany probably aggravated. Years later, Oskar still referred to his father with dislike and disappointment for abandoning him. Paradoxically, Jack felt the same way, even though Josef had raised him.

Oskar's son Ingo recalled that when Oskar was sick in 1996 and 1997, he looked forward to Jack's calls, which "brightened his mood." During that time, Jack read several medical books, hoping to learn about a breakthrough to help his twin.

Jack was not at his store when the phone call from Peter came, so his wife, Ruth, later told him that Oskar had died. Oskar's death stirred a mix of emotions in Jack, albeit unexpressed. According to Ruth, Jack felt angry and upset that Oskar had died, yet his reaction seemed cold. She said that he stayed away from the funeral because he didn't want to feel the emotion or face the reality of his loss. But Jack agonized over whether or not to go, even after his therapist advised him not to. His final decision was based on "logic and reasoning"—he didn't want to disturb Oskar's family, whom he called "lovely people"; had he been there his presence would have reminded them of their deceased father, grandfather, brother, half-brother, and spouse. And he would have been uncomfortable being in a church—even in death, Oskar managed to anger Jack by requesting a Catholic service.

Soon after Oskar's death Jack reconnected with southern California's Trinidadian community. "He came out of seclusion," one of his new friends said.[31] Jack also phoned his German half-brother, Peter, even though they had never been close.[32] "I need you," he said, according to Peter. Peter and his wife, Adelheid, visited Jack in California within a few weeks of that call, but they spoke on the phone nearly every day before that. Jack insists that he called Peter for information about Oskar's death—the funeral plans and Oskar's last wishes. (Oskar had no last wishes for Jack, at least none that he expressed to anyone.) He said that he called Peter because Peter spoke better English than the rest of Oskar's family and would be less upset by his questions. But Peter wondered if Jack was looking for a substitute twin—or at least a continued family connection. Peter and Adelheid have visited Jack four times since then, most recently in August 2004. When they left, Peter said that Jack turned away so they wouldn't see his tears.

Jack admitted that during the last few years there was little closeness between him and Oskar and few opportunities for them to meet. He also acknowledged feeling guilty for not having encouraged Oskar to move to the United States after they met in Minnesota: "If he had been living and working here, he would have been out of the mines that killed him."

Jack and Oskar may pose one of the most extreme cases of identical twins reared apart, but the reality is not as extreme as what the headlines proclaimed. Oskar wasn't proud of Germany; he was critical. Both his sons said that their father watched many documentary films on the Holocaust. Ingo explained: "He [Oskar] would make us sit and watch them when they were on television. He would say, 'Ingo, you must look at this and be understanding. The poor Jewish people.' Now I do this with my twin children." And while Oskar was raised Catholic, he rejected religion and didn't raise his sons to be religious. He always seemed to be searching for the right theory or the best way to live. "My father was looking for direction," said Ingo.

In contrast, Jack is confident of his political and historical understandings. He is a self-described agnostic, but he is a strongly identified Jew. So I wondered if Oskar was less a product of his cultural and political background than Jack was of his, and Oskar's family agreed. Oskar enjoyed being in the Hitler Youth because he could skip church and play sports, both of which appeal to most young boys. Growing up, Oskar endorsed the views of the Third Reich, but he didn't hold on to them, and he spent his adult years searching and questioning. He considered himself a complete German, despite his differences with his country's past. Jack once tried telling Oskar that Trinidad was his country (after all, Oskar was born there), but Oskar insisted that it was Germany—the land of trees, woods, and hills. But he was never a Nazi.

Had Oskar remained as committed to the ideology he embraced when the twins first met in their twenties, their story might have ended there. But maybe not.

Both Jack and Oskar took great interest in their personal histories and what they revealed about how biology and culture affect human behavior. Oskar's wife, Christel, said, "It is unfortunate that they no longer have the chance to continue their lives together. There was a unity and harmony about them." She remembered a day when Jack and Oskar were so deep in conversation that they walked past the house: "They loved to analyze things." That they persevered in their difficult relationship is testimony to the power of twinship.

When Oskar died, Jack said that he wanted to remember his twin as he was—"feisty." They shared this quality and it was familiar to both of them: "I enjoyed Oskar's company and looked forward to being with him." When I asked Jack if they loved each other, ultimately, he replied, "Love each other? We don't even know if we liked each other."

This was not a story of Nazi and Jew—this was a story of identical twins who, despite their extremely different backgrounds and cultures, eventually accepted each other as part of their lives. And they cared about each other. Their relationship was undeniably tense and con-flicted, but that may have had less to do with their different life histo-ries than with their same overbearing personalities. They argued about history and war, disagreements driven by where they were raised. But if Jack and Oskar had been reared together, they would have been the same tough enemies and the same tough allies—they would have just found different things to argue about.

The thought of how easily each twin might have grown up as the other seems like a disturbing truth, but both brothers knew that such choices were not theirs to make. "Children have no say in what they are taught," Jack said. "If we had been switched, I would have taken Oskar's place for sure. It doesn't bother me. But I'm glad I was not on the other side." Jack said that though Oskar maintained "absolute silence" about his feelings on this topic, Jack was sure that Oskar found it disturbing.

In a rare photograph hanging on Jack's wall, the twins are wearing British and German helmets, only they have "switched" positions. This role reversal was surely done for fun—or maybe each wanted to see how it would feel to be on his twin brother's side.

POSTSCRIPT. In October 2004, I was about to send this manuscript to my editor when I received a package from Jack. It contained no note or cover letter—just piles of photographs, letters, and other items from the twins' past, wrapped carefully in plastic bags. The photos, mostly black and white and in odd, out-of-date sizes, showed scenes from the twins' lives in Trinidad and Germany. I had seen some of them when I visited Jack in 2001. But stuck between the pictures was something I hadn't seen—the luggage tags Oskar had pulled from his twin's suitcase when Jack and Ona came to Germany from Israel in 1954. Oskar had kept them at some risk to himself, given his stepfather's anti-Jewish views. He handed them to Jack during one of his last visits to San Diego. There was also a stack of letters in Jack's package; most of them were fresh photocopies, but a few were ragged originals.

Letters exchanged between Jack and Oskar in the early 1950s show sides of the twins that I hadn't expected to see. Each twin was supposed to be undemonstrative and unemotional—both families said so. But these young men's letters were full of excitement, longing, and curiosity over an identical twin brother they had never seen:

Jack to Oskar (September 4, 1950): "Write soon when you receive my letter because I am awaiting eagerly to hear from you. Your loving brother, Jack."

Oskar to Jack (September 13, 1950): "I received your letter from the 4th Sept . . . We should be very much enjoyed if you could make it possible to come see us . . . Hoping from you an answer as soon as possible. I am greeting you affectionately as your brother Oskar."

Jack to Mother, Brother, and Sister (June 4, 1954): "Needless to say we [Ona and Jack] are both excited about the trip [to Germany] . . . Pardon my childish scrawl. I am just excited so I am shaking a bit. Love Jackie."

But the warmth that came so easily in their letters turned into tension when they finally met. It lasted the entire six days of Jack's visit, and for the next twenty-five years. And it got in the way of the relationship the twins tried to develop later on. The space between them was more than their political differences; as the letters show, Jack and Oskar could be as emotional as anyone. But they couldn't be emotional in person. Reading their letters was like discovering a part of them that others couldn't see. After all, most people haven't seen their correspondence. Maybe Oskar and Jack would have been closer as brothers if they had just written or phoned each other after leaving Minnesota rather than meeting. But what they couldn't say to each other in words they said with their actions—Jack by saving the letters and Oskar by saving the tags.

Some people might object that Oskar and Jack weren't emotional at all, that they just liked to save things, a trait that could be tied to their shared genes. That may be partly true, but what they decided to save reveals a lot about the bond they shared.

"My dear brother!" Oskar began . . .

II

VARIATIONS ON
COMMON THEMES

My high school friends Barbara and Judy are identical twins who were convinced that they were fraternal. But what they couldn't see and hear in those days, others could—they had the same dark hair, the same large eyes and wide smile, the same uncertain laugh. As adults, they decided to find out for sure what kind of twins they were, perhaps because they noticed that their children shared some unusual behaviors. Eventually, DNA testing proved that they were identical. "It's a nice, profound feeling," Barbara said.

Whenever I meet identical twins or people who know them, they start listing the twins' behavioral differences: "She's the loud twin and I'm the quiet twin!" or "Those two are total opposites!" But eventually, everyone gets around to talking about what identical twins have in common and how much they enjoy being with each other. Despite the fact that identical twins look and act so much alike, people look for their differences, even exaggerate them, because it's unnerving not to be able to tell two individuals apart.

People want to know how alike identical twins really are, but there isn't a simple answer to that question. And a convenient similarity index isn't available. The best we can say is that identical twins are more alike than anyone else; some pairs are more alike than others; and no pair is exactly alike. Identical twins are closely matched in body size and structure, but twins in a particular pair might differ in running speed if, for example, one had been in an accident.[1] These same twins could have identical IQ scores, but one might weigh more than the other if the accident made him or her less active. Such differences between twins are not unusual.

The identical twins and triplets described in the following three chapters show striking similarities and differences. Twin girls Melanie and Mira were diagnosed with selective mutism (SM) when they were four. SM is a rare condition in which extreme shyness compels some children to stop speaking. The twins, who now talk in whispers to certain people in certain places, both have the disorder, but one twin is more severely affected than the other. The fact that both twins show this behavior suggests that genetic influence is important—but the difference in their condition means that something environmental is also at work.

Identical triplets Owen, Tom, and Frank are nearly perfect copies of one another—their shaved heads, outgoing personalities, and clever speech make them hard to tell apart. But Tom is a homosexual, whereas his two identical brothers are not. These triplets provide great material for debates over what causes some people to be gay. Why Tom and not Owen? And why not Frank? These are questions that still puzzle the three brothers and their family.

The third twin pair, Andru and Audrey, used to be Agnes and Audrey. One of these identical sisters had hormonal therapy and surgical reassignment to become a male. As a child, Agnes identified with boys and acted like a boy, choosing trucks and guns while Audrey asked for dresses and dolls. Agnes's feelings of being male grew stronger in her late twenties, when life as a female became intolerable. Andru and Audrey say that they have always been each other's strongest support system—they still are, but things are not the same. Andru changed sex, leaving Audrey without her twin sister.

These twin and triplet sets are miniature laboratories. But there is more to these stories than hard data; tracking their lives illuminates the conscious decisions, emotional upsets, and chance events that help shape who we become.

VARIATIONS ON COMMON THEMES

4

Selectively Mute

I watched them as they arrived for the morning kindergarten session. Five-and-a-half-year-old identical twins Melanie and Mira were blonde and beautiful. Their thick straight hair fell softly to their shoulders, their bangs edging the tops of their bright blue eyes. They wore the same white and yellow shorts and T-shirts with white and yellow daisy trim. Anyone would envy their lovely looks. But Melanie and Mira lived in fear and worry, their palms turning cold and clammy when strangers passed. When they entered the classroom they clung to their mother, Donna, a grown-up version of her pretty twins. The girls looked exactly the same, but the greater severity of Melanie's symptoms would soon be apparent.

If you have gone to school you remember it: the great adult "quiet conspiracy": "Shh, no talking!"[1] Teachers look around, fingers pressed to their lips to still the chatter and laughter of their pupils. Quiet reigns for a time, but it is quickly broken by a giggle, a cry, or a shout that children can't suppress. Noise levels escalate as if on cue and the ritual repeats itself. Silence feels unnatural to most boys and girls, but some of them, like Melanie and Mira, welcome it, seeking calm within their quiet storms. Fearful of new adults, places, and peers, these children rarely speak outside the comfort and security of their family and home. They cannot be coaxed from their hard verbal retreat. Watching them is fascinating and heartbreaking. Who, or what, in their social worlds could arouse such anxiety?

Looking at Mira and Melanie in their classroom, I wondered, "What are they afraid of?" Donna and I had reviewed the twins' short life histories and drawn a blank. The lack of a precipitating factor was puzzling. Only one possibility was raised: Donna and her husband, Mark, had divorced, a traumatic event for some children. But that possibility was quickly dropped. The twins were only one when their parents split up, and Donna insisted that the girls' verbal development had proceeded on schedule. Their infant babbling had progressed to short phrases and sentences by the time they were two. And they were speaking and arguing with each other and with their older brother, Jim, when they were three. So Donna was shocked when Melanie and Mira's preschool teachers told her that neither twin spoke to them or to their classmates. The problem persisted.

A perceptive teacher recognized their puzzling condition a year later. The twins are among the .001 percent of school children suffering from selective mutism (SM), a social anxiety disorder characterized by lack of speech in some situations despite normal speech in others.[2] Their behavior reflects exquisite sensitivity to interactions with new people in new places. Such sensitivity may have a partial genetic basis—family members of children with SM are often shy or withdrawn. The twins' mother, Donna, a college student, felt "high, but manageable levels of anxiety" when she prepared oral assignments. Her experience suggests a milder version of the social fears expressed by her daughters. Perhaps she passed this predisposition on to the twins, whose elusive trigger was simply attending school. But SM has also been linked to delays and disorders in language and motor skills.[3] Melanie, but not Mira, scored "below level" in kindergarten reading readiness. Child behavior experts cannot explain how these vulnerabilities end up as silent behavior.

The twins' behavior baffles Donna. "At home they talk normally, they fight, they play and carry on a conversation with anyone with

VARIATIONS ON COMMON THEMES

whom they are familiar," she explained. "Familiar" is the key word. The twins and other SM children only speak to the small circle of people they have always known. For Melanie and Mira this means their mother, their father (whom they visit every two weeks), their mother's new husband, Danny (whom she began dating soon after her divorce), their brother, Jim (who is older by three years), their maternal grandparents (with whom they have lived since age one), their paternal grandparents, and a little girl who knew them as babies. When I met the twins at age five, they didn't speak to their step-grandparents, their father's new partners, the little girl's mother, unfamiliar children, or any new adult.

Adults cannot see the world through a child's eyes, at least not the eyes of these children. I wondered what life was like for Melanie and Mira. Maybe they misread social signals, mistaking smiles for threats or dialogue for dislike. Perhaps keeping quiet was the only way they felt safe—giving them social insurance against unwanted attention or intrusion. Donna, frustrated by her girls' verbal impasse and knowing that I studied twins, called me hoping for answers.

Back in the kindergarten room, I saw one twin tug on her mother's shirt sleeve, a sign that she had something to say. Donna bent down and offered her ear to the child, who cupped her hand around her mouth before producing a barely audible whisper. No one was allowed to see her speak![4] Donna also worried that Melanie ("the problem twin") was "bringing Mira down" (the "faithful twin"). "Why can't Mira just be herself? I am more frustrated by Mira's 'twin loyalty' than with Melanie's social anxiety," she said.[5] Why Melanie was the silent leader and Mira the willing follower is unknown. Nothing in the twins' birth histories or subsequent development could explain their current behavior. But the girls' different behavioral patterns had emerged early. Holding Melanie's hand at a parade when she was five, Donna noticed that her daughter's palms were sweaty. Donna also recalls having to calm Melanie down after she grew alarmed during a family visit to a local restaurant. Both twins scored high on the problem behavior les of a questionnaire I gave Donna to fill out; however, Donna indicated that Melanie, but not Mira, exhibited crying, worrying, poor eating habits, specific fears, nightmares, and bed-wetting.[6]

Donna agreed to let me watch Melanie and Mira at school. I wondered how they would manage their classmates' chatter, stares, and physical contact. Would they participate in scheduled activities or cling to each other? Would they seek help from their teacher or struggle on their own?

The first event of the morning was taking attendance. The children moved to their assigned spots, brightly colored squares on a giant carpet. Melanie and Mira sat about eight feet apart from each other with some children in between. When pupils' numbers were called, each child screamed, "Here!" with enthusiasm and gusto, as though competing for a loudness prize. When the twins' numbers were read there were short pauses, followed by "Here!" coming from an adjacent spot; the task of identifying them had been given to other pupils. During these few seconds, faint signs of discomfort showed in the twins' faces and gestures—a shy smile, a finger in the mouth, a downward turn of the head.

With attendance completed, the teacher, Mrs. Green, gathered the children around her for story time. The twins listened intently, their facial expressions changing appropriately as events unfolded. Both girls reacted to their teacher's questions by nodding or shaking their heads. They sometimes sought their teacher's assistance by tugging on her arm or sleeve, then pointing to the problem. Later, I would see Mira silently mouth the words to a song the children sang during their music lesson—but she stopped suddenly as though fearful of what might happen if she were noticed. I sensed that at times, Mira tried to step out of her quiet world, but something was holding her back.

As the morning wore on I became more and more captivated by the twins. Their faces were so expressive—their eyes were wide and bright, their cheeks were flushed, and their mouths changed from a slight frown to a half smile, reflecting the human urge to communicate. Both twins were attentive during activities, conveying their thoughts

Melanie (left) and Mira, age five, smile brightly but silently at the camera. They are in their grandmother's home, where they lived with their mother and brother. (Photo courtesy of the twins' mother, Donna Gordon.)

through expression and movement. It seemed like an incredible feat. Like masters of mime, the twins had perfected the art of unspoken conversation. SM children often communicate via movement and gesture, their silence signaling withdrawal from normal interactions. But Melanie and Mira's quiet vitality in social groups was strikingly at odds with typical SM behavior—I wondered if their lack of speech was their way to attract and control others' attention.

Activities change quickly in kindergarten classes. During a drawing session, each child returned to his or her "spot" on the carpet, and paper and crayons were distributed. The other little girls made frequent overtures to the twins; these children apparently loved to assist Melanie and Mira, and though their help was never solicited, it was accepted without resistance. The "little mothers" were quick to lend a crayon, erase a stray mark, or offer advice, accompanying their acts with slow, melodic words and phrases usually reserved for infants, toddlers, dolls, and pets. Perhaps their "talking down" to the twins had a soothing, reinforcing quality. Verbal gratitude for their deeds seemed unnecessary—an approving look or an encouraging gesture was payment enough. This remarkable dynamic, once established, appeared unstoppable. Male classmates showed little interest in the twins, but they were just as oblivious to the other girls.

Watching Melanie and Mira was like staring into a bright light. I was not the only one affected this way; several teachers were also struck by the twins' unusual expressiveness. It was curious to see how well they were accepted by their classmates. Silent children might invite cruel names that could be repeated often with the knowledge that they would never answer. The twins had not been happy in their previous classroom, but Mrs. Green had prepared her pupils for the twins in advance: "Melanie and Mira are just quiet. You should treat them like everyone else."

Mrs. Green also shared an important insight with me: "They have an elusive quality. This, coupled with their identical twinship, makes them irresistible." The twins were a novel attraction and sought after as friends.[7] But Melanie and Mira aroused frustration, especially on the part of their mother, teachers, doctors, and probably some classmates. Donna had to administer ability tests to the twins, taking the place of their teacher. She has also had to deal with adults who, unaware of the twins' condition, reprimanded her when the girls did not say "thank you." And Mira's computer teacher, "intimidated" by her silence, seemed unsympathetic. But the twins' defenselessness and fragility had considerable appeal, and they were conventional beauties. Most people wanted to help them.

I acquired a new understanding of the girls' behavior as the day wore on. Many parts of their story did not read like those of other children with SM: SM children are generally withdrawn, but Melanie and Mira were the most popular children in the class. They captured center stage easily and stayed there effortlessly—it was the other children who worked to keep them there. The twins' silence, presumably rooted in

VARIATIONS ON COMMON THEMES

their fear of a perceived threat, brought the social attention they enjoyed *because it was given on their terms*. Mrs. Green admitted that "they do like to be recognized by other kids." When it was Melanie and Mira's turn to be class "Star(s) of the Week," they stood before the other pupils and "told" their life stories by pointing to a picture chart that their mother had made. Such public performances are shunned by SM children, leading me to believe that a unique social order may have been maintaining the twins' silence.

There is growing recognition that oppositional, controlling behaviors occur alongside SM's signature social fears.[8] Children like Melanie and Mira may use manipulation to get desired social outcomes in their interactions with others. This fact, and the quiet spotlight that the twins enjoyed, may have reinforced their behaviors, making them hard to change because they brought pleasant payoffs.

As noon approached, the children took their lunches to the long tables outside. They could sit wherever they liked along the low benches. There was considerable scrambling among the girls for Mira as the favored lunch partner, and while Melanie also drew attention, she seemed slightly detached. But the extent of physical contact among the girls was extraordinary. Melanie and Mira, who sat apart, were constantly patted and touched by the other girls, whose maternal tendencies seemed to peak around the twins. The physical contact was returned but never initiated by the twins. Regardless, the other girls continued to talk to them, never discouraged by their silent responses.

During recess, Melanie and Mira each started out with a separate friend, but the pairs eventually became a group of four. Each twin's attention focused more closely on her friend than on her sister. Even when one girl dropped out, both twins seemed more concerned with the remaining child than with her twin. A teacher's aide was surprised to see the sisters playing together. I also learned that "when one twin is sick and stays home from school, the other does just fine." This observation is significant because it rules out the possibility that the girls' SM was caused by the intimate bond between twins that leads to tacit understandings, sometimes minimizing their need to speak. Most identical twins do share private thoughts and experiences, reveling in their close society, but they continue to talk. The *lack* of speech associated with SM and the *distorted* speech associated with identical twinship are not the same.

Distorted speech, or "twin language," refers to unusual words and phrases used by about 40 percent of young twins. Such speech is unintelligible to others, and may or may not be used exclusively between the pair. Identicals may be at greater risk for such behavior than fraternals because of their more similar mental and temperamental traits.[9] "Twin talk" is thought to arise from twins' close social relations, compounded by reduced language learning opportunities from reduced parental attention. Parents of twins try to divide their time equally between both children; paradoxically, they speak more to their children than do parents of non-twins—but each child has fewer chances to talk.[10] Separating affected twins improves speech quality and word knowledge by encouraging them to communicate with others, but SM does not work that way. Melanie and Mira's SM did not diminish despite their playing apart. I still suspect that their condition originated in social fears but is sustained by their social maneuvering and by the positive interest that identical twins attract.

Mrs. Green lent me a videotape of Melanie and Mira singing in their home. The twins were standing side by side, swaying to a rhythm that they created. Like most children being filmed, they smiled self-consciously, looked at the floor, and hid behind their hands. But they responded to musical requests from their mother and future stepfather. Without hesitation, the twins sang duets of "Five Little Pumpkins," "Baby Beluga," and "I Have a Little Turtle." In their "closing act" each twin told the same joke separately, one after the other. These images contrasted sharply with their in-school silence.

The next year brought new developments. Donna was surprised when DNA tests confirmed what everyone else believed—that Melanie and Mira were identical twins. Her reaction did not surprise me; because most mothers rarely confuse their identical twins, they think

VARIATIONS ON COMMON THEMES

they must be fraternal. These parents are highly attuned to subtle differences between their twins, perhaps as a way to distinguish between them. When most of us see twins for only a moment, we have no time to notice their slight differences. Identical twins look identical to us, so, paradoxically, strangers may judge twin type more accurately than parents or others who have known twins all their lives. I was right about twin type for 94 percent of the pairs in one of my studies, compared with only 74 percent of their parents.

Donna told me that the twins repeated kindergarten the following year, but as of January 2001, they were in separate classrooms. Mira had moved to a new room with a new teacher, while Melanie ("who was having a harder time" both socially and academically) had stayed with Mrs. Green in her familiar classroom. As a new pupil, Mira enjoyed celebrity status for a short time, but that phase passed. Since Mira had been the one to forge the friendships when the twins were together, Melanie struggled on her own. But she finally found friends.

Reasoning that they might talk to familiar children in familiar settings, teachers encouraged Donna to invite the twins' school friends to their home. The first attempts were unsuccessful because the friends simply copied the twins' gestures. But with the approach of fall 2002, there were some hopeful signs. Both Melanie and Mira started whispering to familiar school friends, *if* the friends were at their home. Once the twins started speaking to these friends, they continued to do so at school. The twins' whispering is familiar in form but foreign in function. They cover their mouths and the listener's ear, not to keep others from hearing, but to keep them from seeing the conversation; thus, the pattern the twins used with their mother was repeated with their friends.

Donna also told me that Melanie and Mira had joined a Girl Scout troop when they were seven. They still participate in bimonthly meetings, but they speak only to familiar children (girls with whom they regularly play), and never to adult troop leaders. The adults at the meeting direct questions to the twins through their friends, who "translate" their answers. This behavior set the scene for the next time I watched the twins—their eighth birthday celebration, held at a local bowling alley.

I have attended many children's birthday parties. I have blown out candles, opened presents, and distributed favors. I have done this with the zeal of a birthday girl, the impatience of an invited friend, and the forbearance of a supervising adult. Most children's parties are known for their noise and confusion, so I could scarcely imagine what to expect from a celebration where talking was clandestine and controlled by the small hosts. Eighteen female guests were due to arrive, and all but one, Ann, had been to the twins' home before.

I arrived early to get a seat by lane one—I wanted to see whether the twins' first sight of their friends triggered fear or delight. Remembering their school behavior, I expected them to enter cautiously and sit on the sidelines. I was wrong.

When I saw them they looked familiar, though their faces and bodies showed a slight maturity. Melanie's hair was a bit longer than her sister's, the only distinguishing physical feature I could find. Typical of eight-year-olds, each twin was missing some baby teeth. They wore jeans and matching white and navy T-shirts with "Angel" scribbled across the front. They took off their white sneakers in order to slide more easily down the lanes in their socks. There was a quiet radiance about them, and they seemed excited by the events of the day. Perhaps this might be just an ordinary children's party.

The guests arrived and put their presents on a table by the door. When they joined their hosts, it was a "love fest"—the twins and their friends wrapped their arms around each other and hugged, behavior that they repeated throughout the afternoon. There was lots of smiling and touching. According to the twins' stepfather, Danny, these exchanges were "standard procedure" when the girls arrived at school. I wondered if Melanie and Mira's silence was partly responsible; they may have rejected verbal advances, but they accepted embraces and, more important, returned them. Mrs. Green had observed that both twins have a "strange affectionate way about them." The only child not

VARIATIONS ON COMMON THEMES

caught up in the twins' greetings was Ann, though she was welcomed by the other girls.

Suddenly, it seemed as though the twins were conversing with their friends. Days earlier, Donna had made it clear that though Melanie and Mira were starting to talk, they did so only under highly restricted conditions—they spoke only to children who first visited them at home. They also "talked around" adults (that is, in their presence, but not to them). Donna observed that "Mira has formed a close bond with her teacher, amazing because she has never spoken to her." Despite some progress, Donna feels that her twins are still trapped in their quiet world. In fact, school administrators gave her permission to videotape their oral assignments at home.

The twins' party was quieter than any children's party I could remember. This was because the verbal exchanges between the twins and their friends were mostly whispers, muted and subtle, passing from covered mouths to covered ears. This kind of communication added to the twins' intrigue; after all, whispering is an exclusive activity, a signal that information will not be widely shared. The girls probably didn't murmur behind their hands to conceal their speech, but it may have unintentionally suggested privileged access. When Melanie instructed a child on how to roll the bowling ball, she put her arm around the girl's waist, then whispered in her ear. This could have been misread as a "confidential" communication.

Despite some social gains, Melanie spent a significant amount of party time with her grandmother, talking quietly and leaning against her. Retreating from friends and activities is unusual behavior for children celebrating birthdays. Mira didn't join them.

Both Melanie and Mira showed an assortment of nonverbal behaviors throughout the afternoon. They sometimes looked deeply into the eyes of other children while staying expressionless. Adults seemed to disturb them—Mira, poised to whisper, suddenly looked at me and stopped. Later, she seemed puzzled by the board above lane one that automatically displayed each girl's score. Rather than ask her stepdad outright, she gestured toward it, adding a circular sweep of her hand as though asking for an explanation. Unlike his wife, Danny refused to bend down to make his ear accessible. "I want to encourage them to speak normally," he said, causing Mira to stand on her tiptoes to try to reach him. Donna, unaware of her husband's behavior until I mentioned it, understood: "He is occasionally tough with them, but he usually lets them get away with things. Anyway, they'll just come to me if they can't get what they want from him."

I commented to Donna that her girls seemed lively compared with how they had behaved in kindergarten. "Yes," she said, "they are more outgoing when they are not in school. But they are quieter than they might have been because of Ann. She has never been to our house, and her being here changes everything." Danny agreed. It seemed extraordinary that the presence of one girl—a small child with a stringy ponytail—could have such influence. But SM children vigilantly track social contacts. The twins' occasional displays of non-whispered but softly spoken speech might have been more frequent had Ann not been there. I would later see Mira reply briefly to Ann, who sat opposite her when the children had cake and pizza, but she showed hesitancy and restraint. Melanie did not talk to Ann at all.

When it was time to sing "Happy Birthday," the children gathered around Melanie and Mira, who stood together beside their cake. Mira smiled more than Melanie, prompting someone's younger brother to announce, "Melanie never smiles!" It was a painful moment—public recognition of a problem everyone knew about but wouldn't mention—but it passed quickly. Melanie stayed expressionless. Was she fighting the sting of these words, or was she accustomed to them? Then, as the familiar birthday song began, I watched her join in on the first word ("happy"), then stop and look sad, almost alarmed, until the song ended. Was this attention discomforting because it was not given on her terms? Mira seemed undisturbed by the ritual, but she didn't sing. All of this worries Donna.

Recently, Donna has questioned the accuracy of her first thoughts on the twins' social role division: "Mira carried the selective mutism with her into her own classroom when they were separated, so she is not just following Melanie. She has her own issues. She just got eyeglasses, and when we got to school, she cried and cried because none of the other children have them. When her teacher asked her if her glasses were the problem, she shook her head yes." Still, Mira tolerates stress better than Melanie. According to their pediatrician, the twins' elevated stress levels have weakened their immune systems. Both twins recently suffered from dehydration serious enough to require overnight hospitalization for Melanie. But they seemed healthy enough at their party.

The best part of a childhood birthday celebration is opening the presents. I remember tearing into them, ignoring the cards and yelling at anyone who tried to open a gift for me. Maybe this explains why I found Melanie and Mira's opening of presents such a mysterious process.

The twins sat together on the floor surrounded by their friends. By then, several adults had arrived to pick up their children, and they stood outside the circle watching. Donna took presents from the table and handed them to the friends, who passed them to the twins. It was a subdued affair, lacking the fury and frenzy I was used to—rushing through each present in anticipation of the next. But this orderly routine was established quickly, and once individual presents were in each twin's hands, their friends helped unwrap them. As in the kindergarten drawing class, their assistance was not solicited; nor was it rejected. Another surprise was the amount of time the twins spent examining the cards, items that most children toss aside. At various times Melanie seemed uncomfortable, possibly overwhelmed. Occasionally, she gestured with her hand and body as though to silence her friends. She and Mira did not display their gifts immediately, but did so only when they were ready. Their friends waited eagerly, but the twins had the group's attention, so why rush things? Finally, all the presents were opened, and the party ended.

The girls' good-byes were accompanied by a final hug, somewhat hurried because parents pleaded, "We have to go now!" I rode home with Melanie and Mira's maternal grandparents, Dick and Carla, with whom the girls had lived for most of their lives. As we walked toward the car, I remarked again on the girls' progress. "Yes," Carla said. "We hope it continues." But Dick's comment gave me pause: "Mark [their biological father] really doted on his son, Jim. He was always more interested in Jim than in the girls." If this were true, it is still unlikely that their father's behavior caused Melanie and Mira to be silent—paths from parental treatment to verbal silence are impossible to trace. And the twins' symptoms did not appear until two years after their parents divorced. But maybe the twins' perceptions of their father increased their anxiety somewhat. I wondered what Donna might think.

Donna admitted that her former husband regarded his son and daughters differently: "Mark helped me take care of our son, Jim, when he was a baby, but he thought that the twins were a lot of work." According to Donna, during Mark's scheduled visits with the children, he spends more time with Jim than with Melanie and Mira. "Jim is his clone," said Donna. "Jim is just like Mark—some people say that they look alike, although I don't see it. And Jim is the only boy in the family." Donna also said that while the twins willingly visit their dad, Melanie in particular makes it a point to call her at home when she gets there. And the twins always take something of their mother's with them, such as a sweatshirt, "possibly for comfort."

Most physicians agree that single traumatic events rarely cause SM; they generally regard the child's temperament (for example, anxious or fearful) as a risk factor. But temperaments interact with environments and experiences—serious mismatches sometimes produce grave consequences, but good circumstances may offset them. Donna described the twins' brother Jim as a socially comfortable but excitable child who would get "sick to his stomach" when anticipating even fun activities. Maybe he would have been the more anxious child if the twins had been the favored ones.

If only we could know what Melanie and Mira think about when

VARIATIONS ON COMMON THEMES

they are alone together and when they are surrounded by their friends. Are they content with their world, or are they just coping as best they can? To what extent do they maintain their selective silence from a fear of intrusion or a desire for attention? How will they think about their childhood when they are teenagers and young adults? Will they feel embarrassed? Will they feel smug? Will they remember it? Will Mira blame Melanie for controlling her behavior at times? Or will they both remain socially anxious, staying silent when they feel threatened?

The twins' story saddens me because of the potential I see in them. Both girls are pretty and lively. They have families who love them. They have teachers and classmates who are willing to accommodate their needs and desires. But all that does not buffer their perceived threats from new people and places. If only I could see the world through their eyes to understand their condition.

There were times when I, and I'm sure others as well, wanted to confront the twins and shout, "Why not just say it? It's so much easier that way." But it would not have been easier for them. Until the source of SM is identified and a solution is found, it's hard to offer clear parental guidelines. Perhaps the best that families can do is organize social events at home, making SM children feel as comfortable as possible. Some psychiatrists are successfully treating SM children with tranquilizers. Psychotherapy has also been effective in some cases.[11]

I tell my students that we can learn a lot about human behavior by studying the wide array of developmental differences. I believe this is true of selective mutism, despite its obscure origins and underpinnings. Twins like Melanie and Mira highlight the great versatility of human communication—talking was unacceptable to them, but they found ways to make their feelings known. Mira's gestures may have been guided partly, but not completely, by internal speech. About 60 to 65 percent of the meaning in social situations comes from nonverbal cues, but something was keeping the twins from realizing the other (verbal) 35 to 40 percent.[12]

Donna once asked her girls why they don't speak more to other children. One of them answered softly for both twins: "Our friends like us the way we are."

5

Straight, Gay, and Straight

In June 1975, Michelle Marks learned that she was carrying triplets. She was thrilled but also anxious about the babies' health. Fortunately, all three identical boys were born healthy. Owen, the firstborn, came home when he was five days old. His twenty-month-old brother, Bob, seemed happy and excited to see him and even gave him a kiss. When Frank, the thirdborn, came home two days later, Bob looked at the baby and said, "Owen!" Tom, the secondborn, arrived two days after Frank. Bob, perhaps feeling confused and put out by then, made his intentions clear: "No more Owen!"

Michelle's husband, Dan, was delighted by the birth of his triplet sons. Dan, who managed his family's clothing business, gave Michelle three diamond bracelets for three future daughters-in-law. No one knew that one of the diamond bracelets would eventually stay locked in the safe—because one of the triplets, Tom, was gay.

Identical triplets are rare, occurring in only about 1 of every 50,000 births, but that isn't what drew me to this story.[1] Now in their late twenties, Owen, Tom, and Frank pose a curious and as yet unanswered question: How can people with identical genes end up with different sexual orientations?

Identical twins are more likely than fraternal twins to have the same sexual orientation, so we know that genes play a role in sexual preference.[2] Studies disagree, however, as to the extent of that role. Researchers studying male twins in gay bars have found greater genetic influence on sexuality than have researchers studying twins from population registries; this finding is attributed to the fact that twin brothers going to gay bars are more likely to both be gay. What exactly is inherited has also been debated. Some studies show that childhood gender nonconformity (wanting to be a member of the opposite sex, or preferring the games played by the opposite sex) represents the inherited part of sexual orientation. But the fact that some identical twins and triplets differ in their sexuality suggests that birth events (possibly in the form of different prenatal hormone exposure) or social experiences might influence sexual preference.

I learned about the triplets in 1997 at a psychology conference, where I saw a photograph of them at age twenty-one. They were indistinguishable except for slight weight differences. Their dark curly hair seemed to grow straight up from their heads, accentuating their pale faces and foreheads. Their full pink cheeks made them look very childlike. They seemed to want to laugh, and they looked like the kind of guys who would be fun to have around. When I learned that the triplet in the center was gay and his two brothers were not, I was amazed that such matched exteriors could hide such contrasting interiors. I felt this again when I met the triplets several years later—one triplet a day for three days—even though these identical brothers were far from carbon copies of one another.[3]

Owen looked pretty much as he had in the photo, except that his head was completely shaved. He had the same flushed cheeks that I remembered—his are redder than the others', prompting Frank and Tom to joke that he ate their fourth brother. He wore a loose T-shirt over baggy shorts and sandals. Owen was businesslike but had a quirky sense of humor; he insisted that Tom decided to attend the same college as his brothers because a local restaurant served the best nachos. Owen saw himself as the "elder statesman" of the three, whose job it was to look out for his brothers' best interests "whether they have wanted me to or not."

Owen worked as a customer service representative for a telecommunications company, but he would rather be inventing computer games with animation, great stories, and great characters. Owen was the only married triplet, having wed his college girlfriend in 1999. He is now a new father to a baby boy.

Tom was Owen's virtual duplicate, but slightly shorter and heavier. His head was also shaved; he was the first triplet to have done this, to fill a role in a Shakespearean play. He wore a bright red shirt and tan shorts, and a chain of cream-colored pukka beads around his neck. He has a taste for what his mother called "flamboyant clothes," a habit that began in high school, when he owned a sequined vest and multi-colored beach pants. Tom was open and friendly and, like Owen, met me with a huge smile—his high-pitched speech was embellished with head tosses and hand gestures.

Tom's last few years had been difficult. Financial misfortune forced him to live at home; he lacked a satisfying personal relationship; his parents struggled with his gay lifestyle; and he detested his job as a financial services representative. He is interested in doing "a thousand other things"—acting, singing, healing.

Frank had been in a car accident two weeks before I met him and showed signs of vertigo and other problems. Several years before the accident he had developed multiple sclerosis (MS), a disease of the nervous system, and the car accident had aggravated some symptoms.[4] (Owen also has the disorder, but his condition is less severe than Frank's. Tom has had hand tingling and stiffness but is generally symptom-free.) But despite his pain, Frank insisted on seeing me. He couldn't drive to my hotel, so he convinced his mother to bring him to a local restaurant where we would meet. Frank had the "same" shaved head as Owen and Tom, and he wore a loose white shirt over shorts. He also wore a watch bracelet on one wrist. Frank was slightly heavier than his brothers, a possible legacy of his former weight training or the inactivity resulting from his MS. He was also less effusive, probably because of his health concerns; meeting me took incredible effort on his part. Like Owen, he sees himself as the protector of his brothers.

MS forced Frank to leave a project management job that he liked to live at home and work in his family's business. When I asked him what he wanted out of life, he told me, "I could be a great millionaire. I would also want to be a philanthropist just to help someone out. I could also be a doctor to take care of sick people. Maybe I could open a line of fitness centers. If I could do anything I would also be an actor or an author."

Tom is like Owen and Frank in many ways. But homosexual twins often act and feel "different" from their identical siblings, even at a young age. Their mother, Michelle, insisted that she gave all three boys the same opportunities while they were growing up: "If there was a prize for equal treatment, I did my damnedest!" But from the start, Tom was different from the other two, and Michelle was highly attuned to their differences. She could always tell who was crying: "Owen had an ordinary cry like most babies; Tom would wail—he was needy and dramatic; Frank's cry was the most persistent."

The triplets' early cries developed into more apparent behavioral differences when they were two months old. According to Michelle, "Owen was easy-going; Tom was emotional and sensitive; Frank was happy and sweet." In childhood, Owen became "the stubborn one," Tom stayed "the sensitive one," and Frank grew into "the athletic one." Their first haircut at age three was written up in the local newspaper— the accompanying photograph showed Owen and Frank smiling and Tom sobbing.

The triplets' childhood was typical of middle-class Jewish children raised in the suburbs. They rode bikes and played baseball. They took trips to sports stadiums and to amusement parks. And they had Hebrew lessons and piano lessons. But each activity didn't bring the same pleasures or challenges to each triplet.

The "Big Bike Races" took place in their neighbor's driveway when the triplets were four and their brother, Bob, was six. These races were captured on home movies. Seeing them as an adult gave Owen a new perspective on Tom: "There would be me trying to beat Frank. Bob hated to lose and he'd throw the wheels and tell Frank that he sucked. But Tom disappeared from view—riding and competition were not big in his world." The boys also made a boxing film when the triplets were six. Frank and Bob were slugging it out while Tom, who was paired with Owen, was crying because he didn't want to do it. Tom says that the films are hard to watch because he sees his early sensitivity and toothy smile: "Our attitudes showed stirrings of difference."

The triplets played Little League baseball when they were seven. Tom was scared of being hit by the ball, so his father bought him a protective body shield. The first time Tom wore it the ball hit him in the back. Eventually, he stayed in the instructional league, while Owen and Frank moved up. But Owen admitted that he and Frank weren't great ball players, either.

Memories are reworked over time, so it is hard to know if Tom's early experiences are tied to his sexual orientation. But some may be meaningful. "When I was little I got a thrill at ball games," Tom explained. "I was fascinated by the urinals in the bathrooms because of all the varieties [of male organs]." Some kids peek, but Tom recalled these experiences vividly. And he says it hasn't changed for him—it has never changed. As a boy, he recalls relieving himself quickly to allow "time to look" without being away from his family long enough to arouse suspicion.

As a child Tom ran after girls because they were easier to chase than boys. "I was known as the 'kissing bandit' by age five," he said. But when Tom was eleven or twelve he grabbed a boy and held him down while he planted kisses on his face. And his taste for the theatrical was becoming more apparent. When the triplets appeared on a cable TV station at age thirteen, he announced that his father was rarely at home—then he burst into tears. Tom admitted that his father was usually around, though not always affectionate, and that he [Tom] was happy at home. "I just had a dramatic spurt that day," he said.

Michelle recalled another dramatic but maddening moment. The triplets were asked to do a singing audition for a McDonald's television commercial. Michelle said that they sang all the TV commercials on the way to the studio, but when they were asked to perform, they were silent and were sent home. Owen explained that they would only sing for their mother. Eventually, the triplets sang together at their friends' parties—and at their own Bar Mitzvah. After the service and the "triple treats" meal, they sang "Peanut Butter and Jelly" and "We Think We're a Clone Now." In high school they all starred in a Rice and Weber musical.

Owen was enthusiastic about the triplets' roles in the play. Frank called it "the best triplet moment besides the Bar Mitzvah," but added, "it was not the ultimate for me, the individual." Tom remembered it as "my family's proudest moment of me"—but he had a migraine headache after each performance: "I sang from *Children of Israel Are Never Alone*—'For I know I shall find my own piece of mind, for we have been promised a land of our own'—I felt it was a lie to sing something I didn't believe in. I was in love with the Pharaoh."

High school can be trying for students outside the mainstream. Tom didn't "come out" officially until college, but his clothing, speech, and mannerisms made him different from the other students. Some of them suspected that he might be gay. But Tom was never ostracized by his classmates because he had two ordinary (that is, heterosexual) brothers to shield him. "We were short, but we were three," he explained. "It was like armor. Being smart, a senior, getting leads in school plays, *and* being a triplet made me cool. If I had not been a triplet I might have had trouble." Frank agreed. "People didn't mess with us because we were triplets." Owen also recalls things being pretty peaceful: "We had 'Afros' so we fit in rather well in an ethnically diverse school. People thought we were Jamaican."

Tom never discussed his sexuality with Owen or Frank in high school, but classmates could see what his brothers may have suspected. Owen said, "I heard from mutual friends that Tom was pining for some guy. I don't think my reaction was that he must be gay—instead, I thought, 'Oh, that's just Tom.' Maybe from Frank's and my perspective it was not that he was different, but we thought his behavior was just normal for our brother." When Tom kissed a male student in a play, someone suggested to Frank that his brother was gay. But Frank told him, "It's just a scene."

Tom was at a theater festival away from home when he fully realized that he was gay, and the knowledge hit hard. He was sixteen. His parents, Michelle and Dan, knew that Tom was upset when he came home, but neither one suspected the reason. Later, Michelle overheard a conversation and found some letters that gave it away. The conversation (between Tom and a female classmate) was about something that had happened at the festival—the girl was interested in Tom, but he had turned her down. "He tried to explain to her why he had rebuffed her, that it had nothing to do with her," Michelle explained. "Maybe he was learning about himself, wondering why the girls wanted him, and he didn't want them." Michelle also read some letters that she said had fallen out of Tom's knapsack. One letter expressed Tom's romantic feelings for an actor in the school play, and another one (to Tom from a friend) congratulated him on coming out to his close friends. "I'm a nosy mother," Michelle admitted. "I asked him about the letters, but he felt that his life was being invaded."

At that point, Tom's sexual preference had not been discussed openly by his family. But Michelle said, "It was all out there." Tom says that his parents "should have known better, they both have gay friends." This was a tense time for many reasons—the triplets' high school graduation was approaching and they hadn't decided which college to go to.

Michelle and Dan had put down three deposits at three different schools. But Frank was involved with a young woman and wanted to stay close to home. Tom was struggling with his sexuality and wasn't sure about living away. Owen was the only one who wanted to go to college out of town. Ultimately, only one school offered the right blend of journalism (Owen), drama (Tom), and sports (Frank). The triplets weren't pressured to go to college together, but they did. During their freshman year and away from home, Tom opened up to his brothers.

The conversation took place as they were heading to their weekly "brothers night out." "I was a bit scared to tell Owen and Frank," Tom recalled, "but when I did they said, 'like duh!' I guess I was really gay or acting gay all along." But Frank remembers it differently: "At first I was shocked and I compensated by making jokes—'Hey, you are no gay guy!' But then I saw that he was having a tough time and I realized that whatever he chose—girl, boy, animal—my main consideration was that he be happy." He added, "Tom was always more emotional than the rest of us. But I always thought, 'that's just Tom.' But when he actually told us it was like touching hot and cold at the same time. There was an abruptness to it all."

Owen said, "It was his way of presenting it that was more of an issue. He and his boyfriend kissed in front of Frank and me at dinner. But I said 'okay.' This is the unique way we have, an acceptance that this is our brother and we will back him up. Even if we don't agree with him he has our unconditional love. I just didn't see much impact from this for us as brothers—so after he told us I said, 'Let's go to dinner.' But if Tom had been my child it might have been different."

Tom agreed that his brothers were accepting of his sexuality, but he had reservations: "They included my boyfriend in all our activities. They would say they supported me 1,000 percent, but I don't always feel this way. It was new and freaky for them. They were mostly interested in the technical aspects—'How is it done?' they wanted to know. And Frank has complained to our parents that if I [Tom] don't have to date Jewish partners, why [do they]?" Tom also complained, "My brothers are not able to set me up!"

Tom hosted a party during a semester break his freshman year to announce his coming out. According to Owen, their friends said, "Fine, we knew it all along" and were supportive. But how did their friends know for sure what the brothers didn't, or only suspected? Owen explained, "It's weird, but my expectation in high school was that Tom was straight. In my family, we didn't discuss it—we listened to our parents' dreams of a perfect life." Frank said, "Thinking back, why didn't we recognize it? If it walks like a duck, it must be a duck." The triplets' older brother, Bob, was "shocked" when Tom told him, though he was "getting back channel from Owen and Frank." "But what do I care? At the end of the day he's my brother."

Tom's struggles sent his family into counseling during his freshman

VARIATIONS ON COMMON THEMES

year in college. Michelle said, "We went because he was unhappy. We explained that we love him—but he couldn't expect us to change everything we believed in." Tom said that the family counseling was unsuccessful: "I was told I was going through a phase." And while he is still angry at his mother for reading his letters, as well as some journal entries, he knew that what she read had scared her. "It's tough to get over that even after eleven years," he admitted. "She didn't know what was wrong." Michelle hadn't mentioned reading Tom's journal.

Michelle doesn't blame herself for Tom's homosexuality. But she did say, "You go back and ask, 'What did I do?' Maybe I wasn't aware of his emotional traumas." Mostly she is puzzled at how one of her identical triplet sons could be gay "because their experiences were exactly the same." The experiences were the same, but the triplets were not.

Over the years, Michelle and Dan don't think that they have held Tom to higher standards than those they set for their other children. But Tom disagrees. Michelle and Dan have allowed him to bring his boyfriends home for dinner, but they can't spend the night. Of course, Owen and his wife, Lisa, couldn't stay together in her home until they were married, but Lisa could sleep in the guest room at the triplets' house. Tom believes that his parents' love for him is partly conditional on his living a lifestyle acceptable to them. His parents have denied him a diamond bracelet when he picks a partner—he wants it, not for its monetary value, but for its signal of acceptance.

Michelle was relieved whenever we left the topic of Tom's sexuality and began talking about what she loves most about her sons: "They have an animation about them. They walk into a room and there is electricity all over them." Telling me this made her feel like she was the mother of the family she had always envisioned, free from this one nagging problem. According to Owen, Michelle wanted to keep Tom's sexual orientation hidden from friends and neighbors. Understandably, when one child in a family is gay, everyone wonders about the others.

Several years ago the triplets were at a party when a gay man asked Owen if he was gay. "No, I'm married," he replied. Lisa, Owen's wife, showed the man her wedding ring. "So what?" he replied. "I wear a ring, too." I asked Lisa if she worried about Owen's sexuality. "No," she said, "he has a straight brother, too."

Owen began seeing Lisa during his freshman year of college, but Tom said that their relationship was "slow moving." "They dated for a year before they were boyfriend and girlfriend—it took Owen eight months to kiss her," he told me. When Owen was part of a college study he was asked if he "had ever been sexually attracted to a man or boy." He replied, "not sure."[5] When he was recently asked about this response he replied, "I would imagine that the question posed was a hypothetical question seeing how I haven't had sex with a male partner. I answered the question truthfully at the time that I wasn't opposed to it or turned off by it so I considered it 'desirable' or considered the possibility desirable. But maybe my comments should have been viewed as a 4 instead of a 5?"[6]

Owen said that marrying Lisa was the hardest decision he ever had to make. Like his father, he considers women the strength of his family, and the ultimate decision-makers: "I mirrored this [my father's feelings about women] with Lisa." He probably also knew that time spent with his brothers would be limited once he was married.

Owen's marriage was, according to Tom, "wonderful and hard—I wasn't convinced that he wanted to do it, even though Lisa had all the qualities he wanted." At the time, Tom saw his own life being "spelled out in a funhouse mirror, an alternative of what I am." He also asked, "What is good about being a triplet? My hands are always being held, I always have someone to walk with. When we are together, there is a core of confidence, and I take big steps—otherwise, I stumble." He recalled that, at Owen's wedding, the triplets sang songs from *The Lion King*, one of which included the line, "Our trio's down to two."

Tom and Frank admit that these days the triplets get together less often as just three, and Owen gets "digs" from the others about "asking Lisa's permission to see them." But Tom and Frank now think of Lisa as the "fourth triplet"—and she feels married to all three.

Like many researchers and their mother, the triplets wonder why one identical brother is gay. Tom has asked himself, "Could it be the way I was raised? Was it being Jewish? Could it be some higher power?" Owen thought that genes played a role in Tom's sexual orientation, but he couldn't say more. And Frank was no closer to solving this puzzle than most scientists, but scientists don't bring humor to the table the way he did: "Maybe Tom is gay, Owen is bisexual, and I am a lesbian." Then he grew thoughtful and asked, "Why Tom and not me? Maybe something just stimulates you and you go down a different path. Tom knew deep in his heart who he was and Owen and I knew who we were. Tom always tried to separate himself—I did it subconsciously with weights." He added, "We have the genetics of a munchkin. But I worked harder at sports than my brothers did—just grip it and rip it."

Frank occasionally twirled the watch bracelet dangling from his wrist. He hasn't had a steady relationship for some time, and he worries that he picks girls with "mental problems." Frank admitted that he gets "hit on by gay guys more than by women." He says it is "weird" that he is more low key than Tom, but then Tom says that Frank "dresses more gay" than he does. "I wear a bracelet," Frank explained, "but I ignore fashion, except that I like nice shirts." (Earlier, Frank had mentioned having "an eye for clothes.") According to Frank, "Tom thinks that gay men show themselves off to advantage, and I [Frank] have a better build than he does. But I don't question whether I am gay." Having MS, however, has made Frank question who he is and what he wants.

Frank was worried but also "outraged" when he heard that Owen had MS. Frank told Owen, "This is my private party—I don't want you to have it." Frank says he wants to help Owen get over his symptoms. The triplets are a close threesome, but each one is also searching for himself. I wondered, Would Tom have been outraged if Owen or Frank turned out to be gay?

Frank recalled a time several years ago when he and Tom were in a gay bar. Two guys came up to him but didn't show any interest in his brother. One asked for Frank's phone number and the other, who was deaf, wrote on a napkin, "I like your bald head." He told them, "Hey, I'm not gay, but if you like what you see, I've got a carbon copy right here."

For the most part, "Tom is just Tom," and the triplets continue sharing their favorite things. They are "voracious readers"; two of them stood in line and all three polished off *Harry Potter and the Order of the Phoenix* the weekend it became available. The fantasy part of the book appealed to them most. And they still play video games together for hours, just as they played *Dungeons and Dragons* as kids. They have also created their own food culture—they are junk food junkies who mostly crave pretzel rolls and gourmet popcorn. And they love orange juice, but, according to Owen's wife, Lisa, they smack their lips when they drink it. "It drives me up a wall," she said.

The triplets still share a love of acting. Not long ago, I forwarded each brother a copy of a casting call for identical triplets to appear in a major motion picture. Frank replied, "Always been a secret dream of mine." The triplets were filmed along with other twin and triplet sets, but this opportunity didn't lead to others. According to Owen, "The three of us are wandering aimlessly—what do we want to do?"

Owen, Tom, and Frank independently—and *absolutely*—agree that their sexual differences haven't hurt their close relationship. They boast that when they are together, "there is *nothing* we cannot do. When we are together, it's like looking at someone seven feet tall" (the triplets are each about 5'7"). They also know one another's strange habits and sometimes "prey upon them." But their teasing is never meant to hurt or insult, only to get a rise out of the others. When they hang out together, they freely call each other "jerks" and "assholes" because their comfort level allows them this kind of fun. Owen says that the brothers "exude a positive glow—we never get tired of answering questions about being triplets." And they prefer the company of three to any combination of two. Frank said that "this makes it easier to divide up the pie." According to Tom, "It's like firecrackers under our toes. Two are good; three are magic."

6

Agnes to Andru

I first saw them in a photograph. They were standing close to-gether, so it was hard to know where one set of arms and hands began and the other ended. They had on soft gray T-shirts and worn blue jeans, and they seemed comfortable and secure together. In most ways they looked like the countless other twins I have known, but not quite. The photograph told the conclusion to a story that probably began be-fore the twins were born—because, as alike as they looked, these iden-tical twins were fundamentally different. One twin's face was framed by long wavy curls, whereas her identical twin sister's face appeared under a short cropped haircut. The soft curves and contours of one twin's body contrasted with the hard lines and thickened muscles of the other's. Six months of hormonal priming and surgical reshaping had sculpted Andru from Agnes, fulfilling Agnes's desire to get rid of the female body that didn't match her male mind. Andru's identical twin sister, Audrey, was still a woman.[1]

My association with these twins began in spring 2002 with a call from a television producer who was doing a story on transsexualism.[2] The protagonist was Agnes (now Andru), who, at age thirty-three, was undergoing surgery to change her sex from female to male. Agnes's identical twin sister, Audrey, was married and expecting her first child. As Audrey observed when we spoke, "We are both going through a re-birth—I am becoming a mom and Agnes is becoming a man."

I looked at the twins' pictures, beginning with those taken in early childhood. Shot in backyards and playgrounds, these visual records are retrospective time lines. They showed differences in the twins' facial expressions and body postures, driven largely by their different experiences and viewpoints. I saw nothing remarkable about the two small girls standing side by side in yellow dresses and yellow bows. A set of identical faces peered at the camera, showing the strained look of children uninterested in posing and eager to play. In middle childhood their faces and bodies were maturing in sync, but by late adolescence there was a visible difference between them. This change was most apparent in a family photo showing the twins, their parents, William and Anna, and their sister, Cindy, who is four years younger than the twins. Both parents were smiling and seemed happy to show off their children. Audrey was grinning self-consciously, almost flirtatiously, showing off her long hair and developing figure. Cindy, who had Audrey's dark-brown curls and feminine physique, was also grinning. She could have been mistaken for Audrey's twin; indeed, that's who I thought she was at first. But there was another, somewhat familiar person in the picture who looked expressionless and unyielding in an army jacket. I knew this was a family of three sisters—was this person Agnes?

The twins' pictures capture important transitions in their lives, but they also leave empty spaces. The photos imply an abruptness to Agnes's gender awareness that is misleading. Her identification as a boy didn't emerge suddenly in adolescence; in fact, Agnes never doubted that she was a male. Her problem was that her male sensibility didn't match her female body. And yet her twin sister, Audrey, had always felt fully female.

Andru and Audrey welcomed me into their world and did their best to help me understand it. Their space is like that shared by many twins—close, private, and sheltered. They shared a room with their younger sister, Cindy, until high school (when Cindy moved to the living room) and slept in the same bed until junior high. Their relationship has been close since childhood and has stayed close even after Agnes became Andru. "I am his biggest fan and he knows it," said Au-

VARIATIONS ON COMMON THEMES

Agnes (left) and Audrey at age two. This is their mother's favorite photo of her twins. (Photo courtesy of Andru Perez.)

drey. I first spoke with the twins about one month after Andru's first transition from female to male was complete—his breasts were gone and he had started testosterone treatment. Both twins are smart, people oriented, and down to earth. But their shared traits have taken them in different directions; for example, both twins are extremely helpful, but Andru is a practical caretaker whereas Audrey is a maternal advice-giver.

"I always felt that she was my brother," said Audrey, "although as a child I didn't fully understand that. Kids were less gender-typed than they are now. Agnes did 'boy things' like wrestling. And she was my protector. When I was five or six I woke up in the middle of the night with a bloody nose and Agnes showed me what to do. And when I was ten I had a boyfriend. I remember looking out the window and feeling horrified to see Agnes beating him up."

For most identical twins protection runs two ways, giving them a twenty-four-hour safe house. Now Audrey is the protector—she has been the buffer between Agnes and their parents, who were shocked and saddened when their daughter decided to change sex. Agnes, usually the tougher twin, was very emotional over her decision to become a man. According to Audrey, Agnes pleaded with her, "Come visit me. I need you." "So I went," Audrey stated. "I don't read her mind, but I know her so well that I anticipate what she is feeling. When I got there Agnes told me. She wanted my approval. She didn't have to ask for it, she knows I'll always stand by her. I said, 'Okay, now you'll be a boy.' She asked me to help her tell our parents."

Andru focused on their earlier years: "Growing up I didn't feel like other girls. I would get so angry and frustrated, even violent. Audrey picked up on this, and I would go to her for strength. I protected her in a brotherly way, in a physical sense." He continued, "Audrey and I don't compete, but Audrey and Cindy do—they are girls."

The twins' perspectives reflected their unique life experiences, but they were very attuned to each other. This wasn't surprising—they had already pulled off several successful substitutions, such as the time Audrey skipped cheerleading to meet her boyfriend and Agnes became

VARIATIONS ON COMMON THEMES

Audrey (left), the twins' younger sister, Cindy (seated), and Agnes pose for a family photo. The twins were twenty and Cindy was sixteen. (Photo by Olan Mills Studio; courtesy of Andru Perez.)

a cheerleader for a day: "I was thinking that I was a Frankenstein in this little outfit." But such switches were no longer possible, even on the telephone. "May I speak with you about Andru?" I asked Audrey the first time I phoned her. There was silence, and I imagined her mentally racing through her list of friends and acquaintances. "I guess I'm not used to it yet," she confessed.

Andru and Audrey were the first and second children of eighteen-year-old parents, William and Anna Perez, who lived in a small Southwestern town. Anna's pregnancy was uneventful, though twins weren't diagnosed until two months before their delivery at eight months. Agnes, the firstborn twin, was smaller at birth and weighed less than her sister while growing up.[3] Audrey described the family as "lower class"—William worked in construction and Anna stayed home to raise her three daughters. Agnes, Audrey, and Cindy inherited their father's dark hair and eyes, a legacy of his Mexican heritage, which clashed with their mother's pale "Pennsylvania Dutch" features. William was the "oldest member" of his family and Anna was the "most responsible" member of hers. Their large extended family looked up to them to set the standard for how to raise children.

Audrey and Agnes were "androgynous-looking" kids. Anna kept their curly "unmanageable" hair short, which probably explains why people admired her "cute little boys." But when the little girls grew up and chose their own hairdos, Audrey picked a "pretty one," while Agnes was uninterested. "Hair just covers your head," she used to say. Their childhood was a series of gender-typed contrasts: pink-blue, skirts-slacks, dolls-guns, nightgowns-pj's. Both girls played with Barbie dolls, but Agnes cut Barbie's long hair and added a moustache. When their younger sister, Cindy, was born, Agnes thought that the baby was for Audrey, and she wondered, "Where is my little boy?" She thought that babies came in pairs, and it never occurred to her that she might get a girl.

Both twins played football as children, but according to Andru, "Audrey sucked at it." Andru, but not Audrey, joined the local wrestling club and was city champion in fifth grade and runner-up in sixth.

Agnes's boyish behavior charmed her parents, so they gave her all the boy-type toys she wanted—such as a rifle set and a GI Joe doll. "They were fascinated by me," Andru said. "My dad always wanted a son, and he thought it was 'cool' that I was so strong and independent. I was a little buddy to my uncles. They called me the 'jungle boy' and they called Audrey 'the sniveler'—she was always crying." But Audrey objected: "Maybe I wasn't more sensitive, maybe I was just a girl."

When the twins were five or six they played "doctor" with their neighborhood friends. While comparing their private parts, Agnes failed to find a penis between her legs like the little boys. "Things must have gotten weird for her after that," said Audrey. Regardless, Agnes's belief in her boyhood continued, but reality hit her at age ten. She lined up with her male playmates to see who could "pee the farthest," but she couldn't urinate standing up. "Why can they [the boys] make straight lines and I can only make a mess?" she asked herself. Her male friends had no trouble running, catching, and wrestling with her, but this time she had crossed a crucial line. "Whoa!" they said. "You're not a boy!" But Agnes *knew* that she wasn't a girl. "I felt genderless," she said. She thought that being female was a joke played on her by her family and friends.

Puberty's mental and physical changes can overwhelm adolescents even when their minds and bodies agree. But when their minds and bodies conflict, children's selfhood comes under attack. For Agnes, menstruation and breast development were betrayal by a body that didn't fit. "Oh, God, I'm gonna die!" she remembers thinking. But these physical changes were a "neat experience" for her twin sister, Audrey: "I got my period first, at thirteen. I thought, 'I'm a woman now!'"[4] Audrey's first kiss was memorable, but Agnes's first kiss was repulsive. Something must have happened during the twins' birth, rearing, or both to influence Agnes's thoughts and feelings.

Researchers have looked at various theories of why some people feel that they belong to the opposite sex.[5] But after years of study, the origins of transsexualism are unclear because transsexual individuals vary in their family background and physical characteristics.[6] Agnes and

Audrey (left) and Andru, at age thirty-two, a few days before Audrey got married. The twins were having fun just before the bachelorette party. They hadn't seen each other for about a year. (Photo by Audrey's husband, Steve; courtesy of Andru Perez.)

Audrey's early divergence in gender identity suggests a hormonal difference in their shared womb strong enough to redirect the mental plan of one twin. The twins' family treated Agnes differently than they treated Audrey, but this was probably a consequence of the twins' behavior, not a cause. As Andru said, "Young children have an innocence that can't be messed with—you are who you are." When the twins were fifteen, Audrey found books on homosexuality that Agnes had hidden under their bed. "I had a gut feeling that nothing would ever be the same again," she said. But what young children can get away with, older children cannot.

High school is a time of self-definition. Older adolescents are less restricted by family rules than younger children, so individual differences among them deepen and like-minded teens form clusters and cliques. Agnes wavered between two worlds, one that was conventional and open and one that was anomalous and hidden. She was popular, "criss-crossing many social corners"—the brains, the jocks, the geeks—but never getting close to one. Still, her classmates elected her as junior class vice president and senior class president. Perhaps these honors helped her to keep her male sensibility concealed: "I was very much out there. I was great at sports, I was funny, I participated in pep rallies." The twins' friend Carol had known Agnes and Audrey since junior high school and had double-dated with Agnes their sophomore year. "We thought she was just a tomboy," she said.

According to Anna, "the twins ruled Woodrow Wilson High School." Both were in the student council and Senior Hall of Fame. Agnes ran for the cross-country team and Audrey managed the wrestling team. Agnes was voted "Class Clown," while Audrey was voted "Class Best Friend." In yearbook photos, Audrey looks feminine whereas Agnes looks neither masculine nor feminine. When it came to dating, Agnes went through the motions, going out with male friends but avoiding sexual contact; she actually had more "boyfriends" than her sister. But in retrospect, Agnes looks unhappy in her prom pictures—taken the night that Audrey was happily crowned Homecoming Queen.[7]

When the twins were eighteen, they enrolled in separate colleges in their home state. Agnes studied psychology, then joined the Army Medical Corps; Audrey studied business. Then both twins took classes at the same school. "We didn't get along too well at that time, so we lived apart," Andru said. "She was neat and I was messy."

The twins' academic interests partly overlapped, but their sexual preferences didn't. One day during her freshman year Agnes called her mother, crying hysterically—she was being forced to change dorm rooms. When Anna arrived, she saw that Agnes was afraid to leave her mother and her roommate alone together. Agnes had confided in the girl, never expecting that she would threaten to tell Anna about her sexuality. When Agnes finally said, "Mom, I think I'm gay," Anna felt relieved. "Oh, is that all?" she asked. "I thought it was something serious."

Audrey's college experience was the opposite of her sister's. She had many boyfriends "but dated just one boy at a time." Some of them asked about her sister's sexuality, but none of them worried that Audrey secretly wanted to be a man. "I have a knack of picking good guys," she said. "Some were curious, but I was open and honest. Some of them teased me—'Are you sure you're not a boy?'—but they were just joking." Audrey also remembers running into one of Agnes's former classmates. "I used to date your twin sister," she said. But that didn't bother Audrey—in fact, the twin sisters celebrated their twenty-fifth birthday together on a double dinner date. "We each kissed our boyfriend and girlfriend at the same time," Audrey said.

Audrey knew that her happy years were miserable ones for her twin sister. Audrey said, "I get so emotional about it. It's hard for me to look back. The unhappiness Agnes must have felt because her inside and outside didn't match. She was in therapy for years." Agnes even attempted suicide when things seemed overwhelming. She also tried to find ways to live comfortably—one way was to come out gay.

Coming out gay at the twins' tenth high school reunion, at age twenty-eight, was Agnes's penultimate bid at defining herself; she saw it as a lifestyle that approached social acceptability. But if she had to be gay she was going to do it her way. "I'll be a pretty lesbian," she said. Audrey recalled how attractive her twin sister looked at the reunion: "Our male classmates said, 'Wow!' Agnes had a cute figure—she was built like a boy, but she was petite with slim shoulders. She wore a black dress and lots of red lipstick. But several years later, it was a different story." The "lipstick lesbian" was a masquerade—Agnes wasn't a gay woman, she was a woman with the mind of a man. It was time for her to realign her body and her brain.

A few years later, Agnes started corrective surgeries and hormone treatments. In doing so, she joined the sparse ranks of females seeking

VARIATIONS ON COMMON THEMES

treatment for gender identity disorders: Transsexualism is estimated to occur in 1 in every 100,000 females and 1 in every 30,000 males.[8] It has been a gradual process. Agnes was first diagnosed with gender identity disorder according to standard medical criteria, then counseled to help her handle post-surgical realities.[9] Dr. Michael Brownstein, a San Francisco plastic surgeon, managed her case. Some insurance plans cover some costs, but Agnes financed her operation on her own.[10]

Agnes had breast removal, or "top surgery," in December 2001.[11] She entered the San Francisco Medical Center confidently, accompanied by her friend Tina. Her physician drew dark lines across her chest, indicating where he would cut and what he would remove. He explained that the last part of the procedure involved grafting on the nipples and areola, spacing them widely to create a male look. The double mastectomy cost $7,000 and took two hours. When the operation was over Andru felt liberated—a blue balloon announcing, "It's a Boy!" was tied to her bed. "For the first time I looked the way I had always envisioned when I shut my eyes," she explained. "Opening my eyes before had been a betrayal—I had breasts." She would no longer have to tape her chest to conceal it.

The night before the surgery Agnes called her sisters and her mother to tell them that she loved them. She asked her mother to call her father at work to say that she loved him, too. She cried.

Andru began testosterone injections in January 2002 and has since been self-administering them every two to three weeks. He responded quickly to the treatment; his voice deepened, his muscles enlarged, and his beard grew. Having a mastectomy before hormones was a good decision on his part: "I could be a flat-chested woman, but I couldn't pull off being a male with breasts."

True to his distinctive style, Andru spelled his new name "Andru" (it means manly) instead of the conventional way, "Andrew." And he chose Francis for his middle name. He wanted his two names to be like his twin sister's (Audrey Fran) and different from his old ones (Agnes Fay). "That person no longer exists," he said, sounding a little weepy.

But it was true—his birth certificate, passport, and other documents were legally changed to reflect his new sex. By becoming male, Andru made history by giving science one of the rare pairs of identical opposite-sex twins.[12]

I saw the continuous transformation of Agnes to Andru in photographs he posted on his website. In one picture Andru proudly displayed his chest, newly flattened, with dark scars surrounding the areas where Agnes's breasts used to be. I hugged my arms reflexively around my upper torso when I saw it. And I thought about Mandy, my high school friend who had undergone chemotherapy for breast cancer. Mandy lost her diseased breasts, while Agnes discarded her healthy tissue. It didn't seem just. But I don't know what it's like to be Andru—or Agnes. I could only listen to him and try to understand.

"I have lived as a one hundred percent male since February 2002," Andru announced. "Are you really a man?" I asked. Andru's website had described him as being somewhere between male and female. Andru explained his "in-between state" by talking about his "girlish character." He elaborated: "I articulate a lot with my hands and guys just don't do that. I am very tender and touchy, traits that are more feminine." Andru admitted that he could be a man only to a point because "real men" are born with penises. "But what makes a man?" he wondered. "Some men lose their penis in accidents or in war, so are they not men?"

I knew how Andru struggled with questions of what makes a man, but I wanted to hear from Audrey and Cindy.

Audrey never questioned her own femininity. "I think women are beautiful and erotic, but I'm not sexually attracted by them. So in some ways I have the same feelings as my sister, but without the sexual side. I never questioned who I was. You go through a phase—am I pretty? You know, all the girl things. I am a girl through and through. I am also open-minded; lesbians don't bother me. I am 'homo-emotional' because of what Agnes went through." Cindy has the same outlook as Audrey: "Most women would say that a female's body is more attractive than a male's body—of course, it depends on the bodies."

VARIATIONS ON COMMON THEMES

Cindy is "a split between Andru and Audrey," a former cheerleader, a tomboy, a flirt, an athlete. She is engaged to be married, and she says that it wouldn't bother her if she had a gay child. Meanwhile, Audrey is preparing for her twin's future as a man.

When Audrey was pregnant, she addressed notes from her unborn son to "Uncle Andru." She plans to tell John, now nearly two, about her sister when he is old enough to understand. But she expects that there will be hard questions along the way. When John sees his mother's childhood photos, he will want to know the name of the identical-looking girl standing next to her. And John will wonder why Uncle Andru isn't in the family pictures.[13]

In fact, Audrey refused to see her twin until the transformation from Agnes to Andru was complete. "Seeing the middle stages would cloud the memories," she explained. But Audrey made an exception by inviting Agnes to her wedding in September 2001, though Agnes mostly kept out of sight. "It wouldn't have bothered me if she had been more out there," Audrey said. "I think she stayed in the background mostly for my husband Steve's family." Lots of pictures were taken that day—one showed Agnes standing outside the men's room, putting on makeup.

But Memorial Day weekend 2002 was Andru's real coming out.

Andru returned to his childhood home to see his family for the "first time." He and his friends spent an afternoon with the twins' younger sister, Cindy. Cindy has been a great supporter of her brother. "There's a lot of crap in this world, so why not live as happily as you can?" Cindy reasoned. She said that Andru was acting pretty manly until a moth landed on him—he jumped up suddenly, shouted, and waved his arms around. "He acted like a girly girl," she said, "and we said that you just can't do that."

According to the twins' father, William, "At first, it was like a death in the family. But then I realized that this is my same child. There were some tough days—I hashed it over and now I don't care what sex he is." Anna felt the same way: "After the dorm incident I had migraine headaches and went on short-term disability leave. I hurt for Agnes, for what she was going through, and I hurt for myself. But I was thinking that I'd rather she become a man than go on drugs or commit suicide." Mostly, William and Anna were saddened because they missed their daughter.

Most people never see sexually altered versions of themselves. And only a few twins know what Audrey has known and is in the process of knowing.[14] Maybe because Audrey understood her twin's suffering or because she was broad-minded, she seemed satisfied with her twin's change, even upbeat: "When I saw Andru this past May I was unbelievably happy because she looked like a man, not like that actor from *Saturday Night Live* [Julia Sweeney, who played the androgynous character "Pat" in the early 1990s], but truly masculine." Audrey was also relieved that the person she saw in May 2002 was not a stranger: "Andru looked like every man on our dad's side of the family—he was familiar, not like someone I didn't know." Andru recalled that Audrey hugged him and cried—he said that she cried because he looked good. But Andru also thought that Audrey seemed "kind of sad." Maybe Audrey was happy for Andru but sad for herself.

In most of our conversations, Audrey said "Agnes" more often than "Andru," "she" more often than "he," and "her" more often than "him," though with time the "he:she" balance evened out somewhat. We hardly see the faces and features of our family and friends because we like them for who they are. And our feelings about them stay the same even when illnesses, accidents, or aging cause physical changes. But few people change their sex. Agnes's habits and values probably didn't change much; his friends told him, "You are still you." But her body changed and her old identity went with it. Agnes as Agnes was gone, and for Audrey it would take time before her twin's new name and body caught up with her old mind. So for a while, Audrey and Agnes-Andru lived as awkward triplets. Even now Audrey likes using their old nicknames, "Ag" and "Aud." "I can hold onto a little bit of the past," she said.

Reflecting on his new life in July 2002, Andru seemed generally content, highly energized, and somewhat anxious: "I have always tried

VARIATIONS ON COMMON THEMES

to be the best I could be, so why should anyone expect less? I am proud to be going against the norm and not staying inside a box. I should be proud to live life fully—and I am coming to terms with it." Andru noted that the visibility of transsexual people has increased over the last few years. So if he felt regret, it was not for choosing to be a man but for having had to make that choice—though he added, "I chose to live my life happy, but at some level I had no choice." Life may be easier for him as Andru than as Agnes, and for other female to male transsexuals, but life is not easy.

Andru admitted that, like everyone else, he had bad days and good days—on bad days he felt like a "freak" and on good days he didn't. "If I could be normal I would be," he confessed. He felt he could lean on Audrey when times got rough—"Audrey's love for me is greater than her discomfort with this"—but Audrey lived nearly two thousand miles away and was busy with her baby. Andru ended our conversation by admitting, "I am skinny for a guy."

By July 2002, Andru's voice was deeper than it had been several months earlier, and he had a goatee. Remembering his worry over his slim build, I wondered if he was "bulking up." "Yes," he said. He also said that life had been great; he had been seeing a woman for five months and had accepted a new job. He had worked for his new employers for several years before that—as Agnes—but when they hired him as Andru "no one skipped a beat."

Andru and Audrey spent a weekend together in August 2002, when Andru met his new nephew, John Michael, for the first time. He felt like John's "male guardian." But according to Audrey, Andru talked to him just like she would—"he used kissy kissy baby talk." When Andru asked Audrey if she would donate her eggs so that he could have a child some day, she agreed without hesitation: "I would do that for her and her mate. But I wouldn't carry the baby, my own pregnancy was too difficult—otherwise I would."[15] Thinking about her own son, John, Audrey hoped that he would not be feminine. "I hope that my open-mindedness doesn't backfire," she said.

That weekend was also a time for conversation between the twins.

Andru had come a long way in his physical transformation from female to male. But Audrey thought that her twin looked like a thug and told him so: "Andru's head was shaved and he wore big jeans. I said, 'Are you going for the ghetto look?' Andru has been teased at times—his feminine mannerisms make some people think that he's a gay man. He's been called a 'jotón'—Spanish fag—in his local neighborhood." Audrey thought Andru was too nice, and that he should think more of himself and stop worrying about ending relationships. "He should just blow the girls off," Audrey said.

Audrey's words were harsh but understandable. Maybe they were provoked by her feelings of rejection (being male was more important to Andru than being her twin), affection (she wanted Andru to be happy), frustration ("you did it, now live with it"), and grief (she mourned the loss of her sister). That weekend, Audrey vacillated between forgetting that her twin was male and remembering that he was. Andru's physical change overwhelmed her "for their first ten minutes together," then she began calling him Agnes. She thought that her twin was genderless when they were children, and she still thought so.

Agnes has been Andru for several years, and they have been proud, sad, and trying times for William and Anna. The Perezes have lived their lives largely through their children, who were the first in each of their families to go to college and to live and work outside their small town. Both sides of the family have viewed William and Anna with respect and admiration because they seemed to get it right—they had a home, a job, and kids. Agnes's decision didn't change that; nor did it change how the extended family felt. In a 2002 holiday letter to his "wonderful uncles and aunts," Andru wrote, "I am asking to come home. To be loved and hang out with my family like I used to." When he saw his relatives the following May, his grandmother put her hands on his cheeks and said, "You are the handsomest boy."

Audrey has seen Andru once since that weekend, but she hasn't had a "real" conversation with him. I have—in April 2004.

It's amazing what hormones, surgery, and a male psyche can do for a female body. When Andru answered the door to his home, I thought, "This is a guy—a pumped-up, filled-out Bruce Springsteen." His dark hair was cut short and a beard, moustache, and assorted stubble covered his face. The sleeves of his dark T-shirt were tight against his well-developed muscles, and tattoos ran down both his arms. He stood slouching with his hands in his pockets. Andru admitted that everyone calls him "Mr." or "Sir" and that he likes it. But he is sometimes recognized from his TV interview, so he worries about his privacy—strangers have approached him to talk about his sex change in front of people who don't know his past. For this reason and because e-mail stalkers became too curious or obsessed, Andru dismantled his website. When I told him I would be in town, he agreed to meet me, but he warned, "I am guarded and private in regard to my personal life."

But Andru did talk about a lot of things, some very private. Maybe because he sensed my real interest in his twinship or because I am a twin, he opened up to me. He was articulate, insightful, and very funny.

Andru's family is coming to terms with his new life. His parents have started calling him "Andru," but his father sometimes forgets and calls him "mihija"—my little girl. "I wish we could just sit down and talk," Andru admitted. He also talked more about his life as a man: "I am a man at the internal psychological level, but I won't be complete until I get bottom surgery. A hundred legal documents can't do that for me." Andru initially opted for metoidioplasty, release of the clitoris from its "hood," giving the appearance of a male organ. But now, for the same money, he can get the "full cadillac"—phalloplasty to create a penis. "Why settle for a Hyundai or a Saturn?" he asked.

Andru is also a married man and happier than he has ever been. He and his wife, Laurie, were wed at the "Hearts of Reno" chapel on November 29, 2003, exactly one year after they met. Some members of Laurie's family went to the wedding, but only her brother and sister-in-law know about Andru's past. None of Andru's relatives were there—William and Anna couldn't leave a sick grandmother, Audrey couldn't leave her son, and Cindy had just returned from a relaxing vacation to a demanding job. Moreover, the wedding plans had changed several times. But William and Anna tell Andru to kiss and hug Laurie when they call him.

Laurie, a twenty-three-year-old receptionist at a cat clinic, came home from work while I was visiting with Andru. She is a tall, slim, and strikingly attractive redhead. She didn't know about Andru's sex change until two months into their relationship. They met at a party, then communicated for a while by telephone and e-mail. Laurie had seen recent photos of Andru and Audrey, but she had assumed that Audrey was "his ex." One day Andru said to her, "I have a twin—and I have a videotape to show you." "That's how I learned about him," Laurie told me. And when she found out that Andru had an identical twin, she wanted to meet Audrey, though when she did it was "not a big deal." Laurie met Audrey briefly at the airport in May 2003. "Audrey was a pretty version of Andru—gorgeous, in fact," Laurie told me. "They don't look alike to me. However, they're both hyper, they talk quickly, and they use their hands a lot. And they get so excited to see each other."

Andru no longer says that he has an identical twin, just a twin sister. He still feels like a twin, though he knows that the novelty of looking alike is gone. When he meets other twins, though, "there is an instant connection." And he has happy childhood memories: "When I look at our old photos, I think, 'wow, how cute.' I remember when we were little girls, tossing flowers at a wedding. We were holding hands." Now Andru says that his conversations with Audrey have become superficial: "I want to know what's going on—like, how does she really feel about it? But we never have a chance to talk." He added, "I have known Audrey all my life, but Audrey and Laurie have more in common with each other than they do with me—and I have more in common with Audrey's husband, Steve, even though he is sort of distant." When I looked puzzled, Andru explained, "Audrey and Laurie do acrylic nails—so what would I talk about?"

Laurie snuggled up to Andru on the couch as I was getting ready to leave. That night they were driving north to celebrate Laurie's brother's birthday. They plan to have two children, one using Laurie's eggs and one using Audrey's. They are legally married as man and wife. Meanwhile, San Francisco's same-sex weddings and Massachusetts's constitutional support for gay marriage have been controversial.[16]

William and Anna last saw Andru in August 2004. They take occasional trips to a place of prayer in Nebraska, part of the Lakota Sioux Native American Indian tradition.[17] There, they ask for insights for themselves and for their family. Andru sometimes joins them, but he seems less certain than his parents of the rewards: "I also go there for clarity—whatever that means." In 2004 he took Laurie, giving his parents a chance to get to know her better. The four of them shared a hotel room one night. Anna said, "Andru put on his shirt real quick when he got up in the morning—probably to hide the scars from the breast surgery. When I see the scars I think, 'That was my daughter.' But we're comfortable undressing around each other because Andru has a mother-daughter connection." William admitted that he wasn't comfortable seeing his son undressed. And he worried when Andru wanted to join him at the gym—where would he shower?

Audrey said that she would feel completely at ease undressing in front of Andru—they used to compare their bodies in front of the mirror—though she isn't sure how he would feel undressing in front of her. But the twins haven't seen each other since May 2003, and their meeting was brief. I met Audrey in September 2004, just a few months after I met Andru.

I recognized Audrey right away when she picked me up at the airport—she had flown in with her son, John, to visit her parents. Audrey was the pretty twin, a female Andru; it was the same DNA, only filtered through a woman's mind and body.

We drove to "The Island," an area where her family was picnicking for the day. William and Anna were all hugs and kisses when I met them. They were just like the twins had described them—friendly, proud, and fiercely protective of their children. They answered my questions without hesitation, that day and over the next several days. Mostly, they were relieved to tell their story after feeling wrongly portrayed by the media; they had supported Andru completely, but that hadn't come across on the Discovery Channel. William explained, "The narrator said we refused to be interviewed, but it was all too sudden. Just two months before, we thought Andru was gay—then we learned about the sex change when the film was about to be made. We needed time to think as a family and we couldn't do that in front of the camera."

Audrey sat with her arms around John: "Everyone expects me to be miserable about my twin, but I'm not. Of course, getting married, having a baby, and getting a new job have been great distractions. And I have to be strong for everyone. I love my twin, but I don't live near him." I could tell that I knew more about each twin's recent past than they knew about each other's. I told Audrey how Andru and Laurie had met, and I described Andru's apartment, his neighborhood, and his appearance. Today the twins e-mail each other about their work (both are in computer technology), but they never really talk. "If he asks me for my honest opinion he will get it," Audrey said. But both twins say the opportunities to talk aren't there. Audrey admits that she would "love" to sit down with Laurie: "At first, I wondered what kind of person would marry him, but I didn't think about it with an open mind. I want to live vicariously through her—how did they meet, when did they fall in love, etc., etc. Laurie loves Andru enough to take him as he is so it must be unconditional love."

The next day, I showed Audrey recent photos of her brother. "There is Agnes," she said. "I see my twin—it's who it's always been." She cried a little. Then she said, "The pictures are surreal. I look at Agnes-Andru as my twin, as being truly genderless." The twins' parents also saw the photos. Anna said, "I don't see pretty Agnes, I see my child being happy. What can I do?" William said, "I continue to love her. I say this to all my friends." That afternoon, a women's clothing catalog arrived advertising shorts, tops, and sports bras—the kind some women use to conceal their breasts. It was addressed to Agnes. I wondered if it reminded Anna that Agnes no longer existed, but she said that seeing the catalog didn't bother her.

Both twins say that their parents blame themselves for how Agnes turned out, but William and Anna say they have no regrets. "If Agnes wanted to wear pants, we let her wear pants—who cared, as long as she was happy?" said Anna. Audrey agreed: "Agnes was who she was, and for whatever reason, my parents did the right thing. They saved Agnes by letting her be a bit like herself, at least for a time."

The Perezes have been watching programs about families with gay and transsexual sons and daughters, and they can't understand how parents can reject their children. They also talked more about the 2003 television program featuring Andru's story—Anna remembered that it had aired on Mother's Day. William and Anna learned about the project just days before the camera crew arrived. And they didn't know much about Andru's breast surgery. "If she told me it didn't sink in. Was I hearing what I wanted to hear or was I not listening?" Anna wondered. William had thought that Agnes was having breast reduction.

We watched the film together. When Andru appeared on the screen, Audrey's son, John, who was seated on her lap, yelled out, "Mommy!" and everyone laughed. We continued to watch, but we stopped the tape when someone wanted to talk. William said, "In my heart I will always have three daughters—but I have a son, too. If you love your kid, you'll accept it." He recalled the time that he and Andru had gone out for breakfast: "'What'll it be, guys?' the waitress asked. That had pleased Andru." William added, "When we have a chance to talk man to man I could understand it—until then I am in the dark, I just don't know. I had thirty years with Agnes, I know her better."

Anna remembered Andru's call from the hospital the day before the breast surgery and admitted, "I didn't know it was so deep. I didn't want to lose my daughter. I asked her, 'Are you sure you want to remove your breasts?' Maybe I didn't take it seriously enough. I wish she had changed her mind. I wish I had been there for her. But we accept all of it."

For William and Anna, loving Andru, supporting him, and accepting him were never in doubt. And they are all for gay marriage—maybe because they believed in letting their own children do what made them happy. "She opened our eyes," William said proudly, thinking about the gay bars, dances, and poetry readings he and Anna went to when Andru was still Agnes. And Andru feels good about his family: "I am who I am in a positive sense because of my parents, not in spite of them."

Anna drove me to the airport the next day to catch my flight home. For some reason she started thinking ahead. "The girls' birthday will be in December," she said. Then she chuckled.

Andru and Audrey's matching genes didn't predict their contrasting gender identities; Andru felt like a man even though he had been born a woman. Still, even after his transformation he had feminine traits—emotionality, tenderness, and a motherly approach to newborns. Thus whatever happened to Andru (inside or outside the womb) affected his sexual feelings, but not all aspects of his personality and temperament.

Andru and Audrey are a rare work of nature. They show us that who we are can transcend what we seem to be—and that a twin sister's love can embrace a twin brother, even if he's always been a twin sister. Maybe Audrey knew this all along; in June 1974, when the twins were five, Agnes prayed to God to make her a boy for Christmas that year. Audrey kneeled down next to her and said, "I hope you get what you want."

POSTSCRIPT. Andru and Audrey spent ten days together, with their parents, over Christmas 2004. Five days after flying home, they were called back for their grandmother's funeral. They hadn't seen each other for a year and a half.

According to Andru, "There was no extra excitement—it felt like only a day since we'd met." For Audrey, seeing Andru "wasn't a surprise. He was the same old person, only he looked more normal because his appearance and his behavior fit." "Honestly," she continued, "I looked at him, and wow, I couldn't picture him as a female."

Andru's wife, Laurie, came with him, but Audrey's husband, Steve, stayed home. Laurie got along very well with Andru's relatives, and John Michael, her nephew by marriage, called her "pretty lady." Andru and Laurie plan to have children—maybe even twins. Laurie and Audrey might each donate an egg for in vitro fertilization by sperm from the same male. The embryos would then be implanted into Laurie's uterus. If successful, the result would be an unusual version of superfecundated twins—twins related through the father but not the mother. Superfecundated twins occur naturally when women release two eggs that are fertilized by the same male, or by different males, on separate occasions close in time. But twins sharing fraternal but not maternal genes do not happen naturally. In Andru and Laurie's case, the twins would be genetic half-siblings—and the twin deriving from Audrey's egg would be Andru's biological child because he and Audrey have identical genes.

Audrey admitted, "I am envious of Andru and Laurie; they are amazing together. I wish that my husband was so nice and affectionate." I mentioned this to Andru when he passed through Fullerton in January 2005, and he flushed with happiness. "Are you so solicitous of your wife because you've seen things from the other side?" I asked. Andru said no. He explained that he had been self-absorbed five years ago during his transition to becoming male. Now that he is more settled in his personal life he can focus attention on someone else. And though he knows it sounds strange, he doesn't want Laurie to work: "I wouldn't feel successful if I couldn't put a roof over our heads." He admitted, "I am a better man than I was a woman."

III

EXTRAORDINARY
CIRCUMSTANCES

People sometimes find themselves at the center of extraordinary cultural, historical, or political events. These experiences can substantially change their lives, either positively, negatively, or both. When twins are involved, we have a unique opportunity to see the effects of these life-altering experiences from two related, but different, perspectives.

The three pairs described in this section show what can happen when person, time, and place come together to create exceptional circumstances. Their experiences are variously joyful and tragic.

January 25, 1985, was the fortieth anniversary of the liberation of Auschwitz. That day the surviving Mengele twins, the victims of cruel medical experiments conducted at the Birkenau camp near Auschwitz, reunited as a group for the first time since the war. Shortly thereafter, I met identical twins Stephanie (Stepha) and Annetta at a public hearing in Jerusalem. The twins were separated from their family during the Nazi occupation of Czechoslovakia in the late 1930s and early 1940s. They were eventually sent to Auschwitz. There, twinship acquired shocking new meanings that left lasting impressions on the victims' bodies and minds.

Stepha and Annetta managed to stay together and survive; they now live in Melbourne with their families. The twins welcomed me into their homes for several days and shared their life stories with me.

Their experiences will resonate with Holocaust survivors and their families, as well as with students and scholars of that terrible time.

The Mengele twins are not the only twin victims of hatred and discrimination. The World Trade Center attacks on September 11, 2001, caused the deaths of nearly forty twins, robbing their surviving twin siblings of their unique connection.

Nearly everyone knows where they were and what they were doing when the two planes hit the twin towers on September 11. In the days that followed, I heard about several twins who had lost twin brothers and sisters in the attacks. The first twin survivor I met was Linda McGee, a forty-year-old third-grade teacher from the Bronx. Linda lost her twin sister, Brenda, that day. At first, Linda was shy when it came to speaking publicly about Brenda, but that has changed. She is determined to let the world know what it means to lose a twin sister. Linda has a lot to teach us not only about the grief of a single twin but also about the human spirit and our need to maintain a connection to those we have loved.

The extent to which China's One-Child Policy decided the fates of infant identical twins Lily and Gillian is unknown. The policy, in place since 1980, limits city families to one child and rural families to two.[1] It has encouraged many infertile couples outside China to adopt the unwanted (mostly female) babies; in fact, approximately 4,500 Chinese children received United States visas in 2001.[2] Twins, however, have been exempt from the fines imposed for additional births. The Chinese see twins as signs of good luck—the first Twins Cultural Festival, held in Beijing in October 2004, drew 500 sets of twins and triplets, both male and female.[3] We don't know exactly how Lily and Gillian were separated, but perhaps China's preference for male children and the uneven implementation of the One-Child Policy were factors.

Two Canadian couples—one childless, the other mourning the death of their infant son—knew that Chinese girls were available for adoption in the West and decided to complete their families. The couples received identical-looking babies; then DNA testing confirmed what everyone knew anyway: The two girls were identical twins. Since

EXTRAORDINARY CIRCUMSTANCES

the day their daughters came home, these two families have met often. They are letting the girls' twinship flourish and are thereby witnessing a unique human study: the behavioral and emotional development of identical twin girls raised as twins but in separate families. The ordinary intentions and actions of these two couples, wanting children and going about getting them, yielded extraordinary results that the four parents still can't believe.

What happened to these three twin pairs and their families doesn't happen to most people. But just by being themselves and responding to the circumstances in which they found themselves, they show us what twinship means and where our loyalties lie.

7

Two Bodies and One Soul

My plane from Los Angeles landed at Melbourne's Tullamarine Airport on January 15, 2004. After claiming my bags, I hailed a taxi to take me to North Balwyn, a suburb of Australia's second largest city. The driver, a forty-something woman named Paula, heavy-set with blonde hair and a thick accent, was from Poland but had lived in Australia for twenty years. When I told her where I was headed, she remarked, "North Balwyn is a fancy area—lots of rich Jews live there."

Paula didn't know that I would be spending the next five days with seventy-nine-year-old identical Jewish twins—and concentration camp survivors—Stephanie (Stepha) Heller and Annetta Able. When they were eighteen years old, the twins spent a year at Theresienstadt, a ghetto work camp in Terezin, Czechoslovakia, thirty-seven miles from their home in Prague.[1] In December 1943 they were transported to the Auschwitz concentration camp, one hundred and sixty miles southwest of Warsaw. There, they were subjects in the bizarre experiments conducted by Dr. Josef Mengele, the infamous "Angel of Death." Paula's words made me even more determined to tell the twins' story.

Mengele was born on March 16, 1911, in Günzburg, Germany.[2] He received a doctoral degree in anthropology from the University of Munich in 1935 and a medical degree from Frankfurt University in 1938. After holding several medical positions and serving in the medical corps, Mengele transferred to Auschwitz as a physician in 1943. There he conducted unmonitored and unrestricted experiments on twins, dwarfs, and people with unusual physical traits (for example, poly-dactyly—having more than five fingers). The purpose of these experiments has been controversial. Some historians believe that Mengele conducted them to find the causes of twinning, ultimately to increase the German population. But this seems unlikely because the best candidates for such studies would have been the twins' parents, whom he ignored. Other people think that he intended to show genetically based group differences and thereby prove Aryan superiority and Jewish inferiority. But physical or behavioral variation among ethnic or population groups does not allow value judgments of these differences. Perhaps Mengele simply sought a lasting place in science and believed that his research at Auschwitz would help him reach this goal.[3]

The Mengele twins, mostly children, were an exclusive minority among inmates at Auschwitz. Housed in an adjacent camp called Birkenau, the twins received better rations than non-twins. The extra food kept them alive a little longer, but only so that doctors could experiment on them at will; most of the twins eventually perished. The twins were sketched, photographed, weighed, and measured. Some were injected with typhus, exposed to X-rays, and transfused with incompatible blood. Impregnation of identical female twins by identical males (to see if they conceived twins) was Mengele's plan, but the camp's January 1945 liberation interfered. By then Mengele had escaped, taking his twin data with him. He eluded capture in South America for about forty years and was presumed to be hiding in Paraguay. He is believed to have drowned in Brazil in 1979.

The health and adjustment of the Mengele twin survivors were largely ignored in Holocaust literature until 1985.[4] In January of that year, eight of the twins visited Auschwitz-Birkenau to commemorate the fortieth anniversary of the camp's liberation. And in February about eighty of the approximately one hundred and ten surviving twins—then adults in their fifties and sixties—gathered at Yad

Vashem, Jerusalem's Holocaust Martyrs' and Heroes' Remembrance Authority, for a three-day public hearing on Mengele's crimes.[5]

I traveled to Auschwitz-Birkenau and to Yad Vashem with the twins. I wanted to represent researchers who worked legitimately and ethically. I also knew that some Mengele twins hoped to find their missing brothers and sisters in Jerusalem, and I thought these twins might benefit from what I knew about the psychological effects of twins being separated and reunited.

At the Jerusalem hearing, people listened silently to the twins' testimony on their camp experiences. A pair of brothers (thought to be twins by Mengele's officers) had received throat injections; Mengele wanted to know why one "twin" had a lovely singing voice whereas the other "twin" couldn't carry a tune. Another witness testified that young male-female twins had been sewn together, back-to-back, like a conjoined pair. Some twins who had received X-rays and surgeries were left unable to have children. And one identical female twin from Australia described a plan to have her and her sister made pregnant by identical male twins. This was Stephanie Heller.

Stephanie (Stepha) and her sister Annetta had been invited to Jerusalem by Australia's *60 Minutes* television program. The show's producers demanded exclusivity to their story, so they shielded the twins from reporters. I met them after the testimonial sessions at the hotel. They looked exactly alike—both women were about five feet tall and had large brown eyes and stylish haircuts. They wore similar tailored suits and white blouses. Their only apparent difference was that Annetta had dyed her graying hair red.

In February 1985 the Holocaust twins were bound by their desire to find Mengele and bring him to trial, not knowing that he was already dead. The 1985 hearing was a turning point for many of the twins because for the first time they openly expressed their feelings about their past. Stepha and Annetta were such a pair.

Over the years I lost contact with the Australian twins. Then, in October 1994, a letter arrived from Stepha, saying that she and Annetta had read about my work in a twin research newsletter. I replied immediately. Stepha's next letter included an invitation for me to visit her and her twin sister in Australia. Her letter ended, "Yours, Stephanie and Annetta." She had signed for both twins.

The Hellers' home was modern and spacious. I rang the bell and Robert (Robby), Stepha's husband (and also first cousin), answered the door. Robby was eighty-three years old and five feet eight inches tall with a slim, compact build. With white hair, dark eyes, and tailored clothes he was a distinguished figure. He smiled and patted me on the shoulder, though we had only met through e-mail.

The twins, Stepha and Annetta, were standing behind Robby when I arrived, and they greeted me with hugs and smiles. Stepha was thinner than I remembered, having had three back surgeries, the last one in 2003. Her hair was gray. She told me that she had been slightly gloomy the week before, owing to her medications, but that now she felt upbeat and enthusiastic—though she worried that this visit would fall short of my expectations. Annetta's hair was shorter than her sister's and dyed blonde. Her voice, expressions, and gestures mirrored those of her twin sister, though she did less of the talking. Annetta lived just blocks away from Stepha and came to her home nearly every day, just as she had even before her husband, Jiri, passed away over twenty years ago.

It was nearly one o'clock when I arrived, so we sat down to lunch in a big kitchen with a wonderful view of the garden. "We spend most of our time here," Robby explained. Although I had come to interview them, the twins and Robby peppered me with questions about my background, my work, and my love life. Family ties and social networks are enormously important to Stepha and Annetta, as they are to other Holocaust survivors whose parents and siblings were exterminated in Hitler's gas chambers. Stepha's twenty-one-year-old granddaughter, Julie, wrote, "Granny will spend five minutes with a person and be able to tell you their life story, names, jobs, and problems of all their family members." After that lunch, I believed it was true.

The next five days in North Balwyn began the same way for me—a

EXTRAORDINARY CIRCUMSTANCES

solitary morning run, then breakfast with Robby. But the rest of each day was unpredictable. We talked, shopped, looked at photographs, and watched videotapes. The twins were charming and vivacious—and candid. On the third day of my visit, Stepha, Robby, and I drove to Philips Island, where the Hellers have a summer home.[6] There, I watched the nighttime parade of small penguins emerge from the ocean and waddle to the land. And I asked questions and listened.

It became clear almost immediately that Stepha and Annetta are extremely close sisters with interlocking lives. Both said that being twins was their defining characteristic, followed by being Jewish and then being color blind (a rare trait in females). They have a signature line—"We are two bodies and one soul"—that they repeated to me often. But it was also clear that Stepha's assertive manner overshadowed Annetta's compliant nature. Stepha was setting the agenda for where I would go and to whom I would speak. No one knows exactly how identical twins' matched behavioral dispositions get channeled differently, though variations in their prenatal conditions, parental treatment, and life events may explain these differences. Both twins accepted their contrasting roles, but sometimes Annetta seemed frustrated. Robby said that they quarrel often, not because of Stepha's controlling style, but because they think the same way and jump into conversations quickly. But their disagreements are short-lived. As Annetta's daughter Daphna said, "They are like magnets—where one goes the other is forced to follow."

These twins had covered the world: Yugoslavia, Czechoslovakia, Israel, Kenya, and Australia, mostly driven by persecution or by hostile regimes. Stepha led the way and Annetta followed, with one exception: Annetta was sent to Theresienstadt six months before her sister. Until then, and in the years that immediately followed, they were never apart.

Stepha and Annetta were born on February 4, 1924, in Subotica, Yugoslavia. Their mother, Therese, was thirty and unmarried at the time. The premature twins spent their earliest days in shoeboxes, wrapped in cotton wool. Black-and-white photos show Therese smiling at her little girls, her arms wrapped protectively around them. She was an attractive woman, plainly dressed. Her determined look reminded me of Stepha's.

The twins and their mother moved to Prague when the girls were three. There, Therese worked as a seamstress, then as a stenographer. The community did not help them: "My mother was a Miss, not a Mrs.," Stepha explained. But regardless of their circumstances, the twins have happy childhood memories, especially of their mother. And they attracted lots of attention because they looked so much alike. People joked that their red cheeks had been rubbed with the red paper used to wrap chicory, an ersatz coffee. Outgoing Stepha enjoyed the attention; introverted Annetta did not. Therese eventually married Artur Heilbrunn, a tour guide. The couple had a daughter, Elisabeth ("Lizinka"), who was six years younger than the twins. The twins adored her. Stepha recalled that Artur favored his own daughter, which may have made Therese "love us even more."

The twins and their family were highly assimilated; they were Czech compatriots and Jewish, but not religious. Nonetheless, their lives changed in 1938 when Hitler occupied Czechoslovakia. Jews were required to wear yellow stars and were banned from schools, stadiums, and theaters. Stepha and Annetta began training as nannies at a Jewish orphanage. Then, in 1941, Therese, Artur, and Lizinka were transported to Lodz (Litzmannstadt), a Polish ghetto. Stepha and Annetta, then seventeen, rushed to the exhibition hall where people were assembled. They tried to join their family but were sent away. They never saw their mother, stepfather, or younger sister again.

Stepha and Annetta continued working at the orphanage, believing that their family was safe. They were growing interested in men and had similar tastes, but Stepha was more demanding. "I took the boyfriends that Stepha didn't want," Annetta said. An exception was Egon Kunewalder, a former engineering student who managed the machinery in the orphanage. "He was arrogant and good-looking," Stepha recalled. Stepha and Egon were married in April 1942: "I loved him, but Annetta came first." A month later Annetta was sent to

Annetta (left) and Stepha at age twelve, in their childhood home in Prague. When the twins' mother, Therese, was ordered to leave for Lodz, she gave her friend Vera Pfefferova a small suitcase with this photo and others for safekeeping. (Vera was a Gentile married to a Jew.) Vera managed to find Stepha and Annetta when they returned to Prague in 1945 after surviving Theresienstadt and Auschwitz. She welcomed them into her home and gave them the photos. The twins still send gifts to her daughter, also named Vera. (Photo courtesy of Annetta Able and Stepha Heller.)

Theresienstadt because her last name, Annetta Heilbrunn, came earlier in the alphabet than her sister's, Stepha Kunewalder.

Stepha and Egon were transported to Theresienstadt six months later. Finding Annetta among the thousands of inmates would have been nearly impossible, but a woman at the railway station recognized Stepha as Annetta's twin and told her that her sister worked in the ghetto hospital. Egon was assigned as a policeman, a job for which he received boots and trousers. But with time, Egon grew increasingly pessimistic about their chances for survival. Both twins worked in the hospital, where their living conditions were "tolerable." But they were exposed to patients with infectious diseases, which kept them from attending the community's cultural activities. One such event was a children's opera, *Brundibár*, written in 1938 by the Czech composer Hans Krása. In 1942 Krása was deported to Theresienstadt, where officers ordered him to rewrite the opera for use in a Nazi propaganda film. The opera tells the story of a young brother and sister who must buy milk for their sick mother.[7] Their attempts to earn money by singing and dancing are thwarted by the organ grinder, Brundibár. Eventually, however, some children help them get the money they need. Annetta told me that in some of the camp's performances a talented little boy impersonated Hitler in a highly derogatory way; she was amazed that the actors got away with this. She hummed several bars from one of the musical pieces for me, and looked sad. These are the words as she remembers them:

> I am frightened of Brundibár,
> The man with the loud barrel organ
> Who gets money for his playing
> And has power over men.
>
> Mother is rocking a baby in a cradle
> And thinks how the children are growing up
> And soon will fly away like birds.
> Water flows, the years are passing
> Brundibár will be silenced
> We will sing with joy.

In December 1943 Stepha, Annetta, and Egon left Theresienstadt for Auschwitz—on the final transport. Annetta had not been assigned to go, but she joined Stepha and Egon voluntarily. They traveled for nearly two days in railroad cattle cars packed with people, and without food or water. I was uneasy asking the twins to relive this terrible time. They were nearly eighty years old and had established new, productive lives. But they willingly answered my questions—they wanted to be sure that others knew that the death camps were no myth.

When they arrived at Auschwitz, the males and females were sent to separate barracks. Egon and Stepha saw each other only occasionally before Egon was transferred to a different camp. But being twins saved Stepha and Annetta; survivor Perla Ovitch, one of seven dwarf siblings experimented on by Mengele, called it the "grace of the devil."[8] When Stepha and Annetta arrived at Auschwitz, someone shouted for twins to step forward. They did so, not knowing if this was good or bad. And for some time they didn't know. They were tattooed and sent to the Czech family women's barracks (frauenlager), where they slept packed together "like sardines."[9] But they complained that the "worst thing" was having no toilet paper, and they still wonder how they managed without it. Eventually they met Dr. Mengele.

"When we first saw Mengele he was good-looking and we were impressed by him. He pointed nonchalantly and he whistled an aria," Stepha recalled. When the twins were called to his laboratory they were X-rayed, photographed, measured, and given a gynecological exam. "It was unpleasant, but it wasn't frightening," Stepha said.

A camp document dated September 22, 1944, lists numbers and names of twins in Auschwitz II's family barracks: "72890 Annetta Heilbrunn" and "72919 Stefania Kunewalder" are on it; it is a requisition for blood.[10] The twins received a bizarre blood transfusion during their second visit to Mengele's lab. Blood from identical male twins was transfused into the young women's veins, one twin at a time. Both twins subsequently developed severe headaches and high fevers. Later, they learned that they were to be impregnated by identical male twins to see if twins resulted. Annetta was scared when she heard this, assuming that Mengele would have them both killed in order to look for multiple embryos. "But they never asked us about our periods," she remembers. "We had lost weight so we didn't have periods at that time."

Fortunately, the camps were liberated before the impregnation plan could be carried out. But Stepha and Annetta were forced to do and to see other things. They carried the bodies of prisoners who had died from illnesses, beatings, and other torments from behind the barracks and loaded them into trucks. They got through this ordeal by numbing themselves psychologically, by talking about ordinary things like cooking and recipes. Afterward, they washed their hands in cold water and chlorine, and they ate the extra bread they had been given for performing the task. It was hard for them to eat, but they wanted to survive. One day Mengele brought Stepha and Annetta to the gypsy camp. As they described it, Mengele loved music and was delighted when the gypsy children performed for him. The next day the gypsy camp was liquidated—everyone perished in the gas chambers.

To pass the time the twins avoided serious subjects and talked only about practical matters, mainly food. Stepha admitted, "I was startled by the complacency creeping on us and letting us live, and see the dying like something not real and impersonal."[11]

In late 1944 news that Russian soldiers would be liberating the camps caused Mengele to flee Auschwitz. By then, Stepha's husband, Egon, had been sent to Schwarzheide, another camp, where he died. Stepha didn't know that she had become a widow at twenty-one. In January 1945 Auschwitz-Birkenau was evacuated by a "death march" during which prisoners were made to walk along icy roads. The journey took Stepha and Annetta to the Ravensbrück and Malchov camps, in Germany. Annetta contracted typhoid in Malchov, but she recovered. And when Stepha's shoes got wet, Annetta tied straw and rags around her sister's feet so she could walk. One morning when no guards were around, the twins just left, taking bread and blankets with them. Days later, they received supplies and assistance from U.S. soldiers in Holzstadt. Eventually, they reached Luebeck, where they were given food and shelter until a truck transported them to Prague. "The most important thing was that we were together," Annetta said.

Stepha and Annetta reached Prague in 1945, at age twenty-one. People could tell from the numbers tattooed on their arms that they had been in the camps, but no one wanted to discuss it—and the twins thought that no one would believe what they said. They knew that their stepfather had died in Lodz, but they learned later that their mother and younger sister had died elsewhere.[12] They still looked for their faces in crowds. Stepha also heard that her husband, Egon, had either been beaten to death for stealing bread or had thrown himself onto the electrified barbed wire at Schwarzheide.[13] Out of guilt at their own survival Stepha and Annetta decided to become nurses. They could no longer help their mother, sister, and husband, but they could help others.

Both Stepha and Annetta were hopeful despite what they had been through. Their spirit was captured in an aging black-and-white photograph that sits on Stepha's shelves: The twins' heads are slightly tilted, their long brown hair is curled, and they are smiling. The picture was taken by identical male twins Jirka and Lada Salus, who had also been at Auschwitz. The two identical couples confused everyone when they went out together. They never discussed Auschwitz; instead, they focused on building new lives. In a letter to her mother's brother, Rudolph (Robby's father), Stepha wrote, "We both prefer to remember only the nice moments in our lives, the other times full of pain and worries we push back into a blank and it enables us to see life's beauty."[14]

In 1947, the twins celebrated their nursing school graduation on a boat on the Moldau River. That day Annetta met Jirik (Jiri), her future husband, when he asked her to dance. Jiri, also an Auschwitz survivor, told Annetta that he had recognized her from the camp. But she didn't believe him until he showed her the number on his arm. Then Annetta remembered him—he was a prisoner who had smiled at her on his way to collect corpses. Even then, she recalled, "a sparkle of a warm feeling was felt by a young woman in the midst of the darkness and despair."[15] Annetta and Jiri married and had a son, Michael, whom I met in Melbourne. Annetta believed that this child would be "the new root, shooting up from the ashes of all the lives lost in the Holocaust."[16]

The twins' dissatisfaction with Czechoslovakia's communist government made them leave for Israel in 1949, first Stepha and then Annetta with her new family. They worked as nurses, Stepha in Haifa and Annetta at Kibbutz Hayim Ichud. There, Annetta delivered her second son, Danny. I met Danny one afternoon in Annetta's home. His muscular build and jet black hair set him apart from the twins, though he and his aunt (but not his mother) have the same white streak across their foreheads. Danny actually has three names: Daniel, Amiel, and Yoram. Annetta liked the first name, but since Stepha preferred the last two, Annetta gave him all three. Danny joked that his mother prepares better dinners, while his Aunt Stepha makes better desserts. "The twins form a beautiful balance," he said.

Annetta's Melbourne home was smaller and more modest than her sister's, but both were filled with candy, fruit, and family photos. Annetta and I sat down together one afternoon to talk about the twins' life in Israel. Our conversation turned to the children. With Danny's birth, Annetta had two children and Stepha had none—Stepha was single after a second brief, unsuccessful marriage. Annetta recalled, "I was very willing to give Danny to Stepha." I was taken aback. I wondered how a new mother could casually give away her child. But for Annetta this was not a conscious decision; it was simply the way things should be. Giving away her son would have filled a gap in her twin's life (being childless) and eased a pain in her own life (seeing her sister childless). As both twins insisted, sharing meant giving the "bigger piece" to their twin. But as things turned out, Danny stayed on the kibbutz with his own family.

In 1953 the twins' cousin, Robby, visited them in Israel. Born in Yugoslavia in 1921, Robby had lived his late teen and adult years in Kenya, where his family had moved following Hitler's rise to power.[17] His father (and the twins' uncle), Rudolph, had conspired with the twins to find Robby a wife, but Robby fell in love with his cousin Stepha. A marriage proposal was not immediately forthcoming because Robby and Stepha had to resolve the genetic implications of being first cousins; close relatives are at greater risk for having genetically defective children than are unrelated couples.[18] But once they were comfortable with their relationship, Stepha moved to Kenya in 1954. "The best thing in my life was meeting, falling in love and marrying Robby," she said. But Stepha didn't forget her twin sister. In a letter to Rudolph, she wrote: "You are aware what they [Annetta and her family] mean to me and so far I cannot comprehend how I will suffer knowing that I cannot see and help them."

EXTRAORDINARY CIRCUMSTANCES

Having children was important to Stepha, but she had two reasons to be concerned about starting a family. Aside from her biological tie to her husband, she had had an ovary removed because of a cyst. Nonetheless, in 1955 both Stepha and Annetta delivered daughters (Naomi and Daphna, respectively), twelve days apart. Shortly thereafter, Annetta and her infant daughter visited Stepha in Kenya. Daphna and Naomi, the blonde cousins and genetic half-siblings, were often taken for twins. But it was a bad time for Annetta to visit her sister; she had left her two young sons on the kibbutz and their father, Jiri, was away on military service. Then in 1956 the Suez War delayed her return. But Annetta had been driven to see her sister, who was recovering from a miscarriage. Annetta's son Danny said that he had always accepted the fact that Stepha came first in his mother's life. But his father, Jiri, had a hard time knowing that he came second.

In 1959 Stepha gave birth to her son, John, now married and living in Brisbane. John was a good baby and life was going well. But political instability in Kenya forced Robby to move his family to Australia in April 1962. There, he worked in several businesses until 1975, when he became Australia's sole manufacturer and distributor of stump socks, garments worn by amputees. (After he retired in 1988, his son-in-law took over the business.) Stepha assisted Robby in this work, but she also sold Avon cosmetics to women in her neighborhood. When Annetta moved to Australia in 1963, she was often mistaken for her sister. Stepha coached her to smile back to avoid offending her clients.

Annetta's family had not wanted to move to Australia, but they went so that the twins could be together. Over the next twenty years Stepha and Annetta were busy working, raising their children, and babysitting their grandchildren. They rarely discussed Auschwitz, either with each other or with close friends. But the Jerusalem hearing gave the twins' past a new present.

According to their children, both twins had been noncommittal about attending the 1985 hearing in Jerusalem. They didn't need to discuss their experiences with other people because their intimacy gave them the support they needed. "They processed it even without words," said Danny. But their children persuaded them to go. So the twins went to tell the world what they had gone through—and also to fight rumors that the Holocaust had never happened. For Stepha, meeting other twins made it a "surprisingly pleasant reunion," and for Annetta it was "an opportunity to share memories." But both twins were stunned by the other twins' testimony—Stepha and Annetta had been in the family barracks, so they had never seen the twin children or heard about the experiments. When they were in Mengele's lab, there were no other twin pairs around (except when they underwent the blood transfusion). The hearing "opened the flow of nightmares and pain hidden for so many years in our lives," said Stepha.[19] Many Australians hadn't heard of the twins experiments until they saw *60 Minutes.*

The *60 Minutes* piece was seen by thousands of people in Australia, and suddenly the twins were recognized by passersby. I sat down one morning to watch the program with them. It was quiet in Stepha's family room. Annetta held her coffee cup tightly, while Stepha covered her mouth with her hand. Now they were hearing about what had happened, not telling it, and seeing scenes, not describing them. Stepha didn't cry—except on film when her testimony ended. "There were memories which one would rather forget, but is unable to," said Stepha. But I saw tears in Annetta's eyes. "Seeing this pulls a string that makes me cry," she said. "We never danced. And when I think that we had our birthday on the death march, then I cry."

As *60 Minutes* ended, all three of us gasped. There I was, standing between Stepha and Annetta, toasting them on their sixty-first birthday at the Jerusalem hearing. We had forgotten about that.

Stepha now lectures to students every Thursday at Melbourne's Holocaust Center, which was established in 1984. Holocaust studies are now part of the required school curriculum for fourteen- and fifteen-year-olds. She explains, "It's easier for us to go on knowing that others will remember." But she doesn't want to visit Auschwitz: "What's the point? I have the deceased in my heart."

Stepha's work distinguished her as a 1998 nominee for WIZO's (the

Women's International Zionist Organization's) Woman of the Year Award. Annetta is less comfortable addressing groups and has only occasionally accompanied her sister to public events. "Stepha talks for both of us—I bask in her fame," she explained. But Annetta's taped testimony, given in 1996 as part of Steven Spielberg's oral history project, is extraordinary in its insight and delivery. And both twins' written work—Annetta's poem "Is It Not a Dream Anymore?" and Stepha's memoirs, "Kaleidoscope of Memories"—vividly portray their joys and tragedies.[20] Their joint letter to Japanese children is a simple, heartfelt explanation of why the Holocaust should be remembered. The letter is displayed at Japan's Holocaust Education Center, in Hiroshima.

Both twins believe that Dr. Mengele is dead. Their acceptance of his death has helped them to move forward, and their older age while in the camp probably prevented them from seeing him as a "god," as did some younger twins who still believed he was alive. But there are still reminders of what the twins have been through. They feed extra bread to birds or use it to make dumplings rather than throw it away. Stepha uses utensils to eat finger food because she didn't have forks and spoons at Auschwitz. Warm baths remind the twins of cold water and chlorine. And there was pink flowered toilet paper in Annetta's bathroom.

I was amazed that Stepha and Annetta had volunteered for twin research in Australia, given what they had been through. But both of them think twin research is important for understanding human development. Stepha and Annetta have participated in studies looking at bone density and vision. Annetta told the physician, "Mengele would have been happy studying all these twins." He replied, "Your sister said the same thing."

Annetta had her tattoo removed in 1964, soon after arriving in Melbourne. She was tired of answering questions from passengers on trains. To one curious person she replied, "It's my boyfriend's phone number." It bothers Annetta that Stepha hasn't removed her tattoo. "It's not my shame," explains her sister. Annetta joked that Stepha didn't ride the trains so she had less reason to be self-conscious.

Stepha (left) and Annetta, a few weeks before their eightieth birthday. They are standing in Stepha's front yard. (Photo by Nancy L. Segal, January 2004.)

At Auschwitz they "relied on each other, supported each other, lived for each other—without words," said Annetta. Both twins now know that being twins saved their lives, though they didn't realize it at the time. Concentration camp experience drove some twins closer together, but it was not the driving force between these two women. "We were the way that we were," they said. "We would be close regardless of where we were or what happened to us." According to Robby, Stepha's letters to Annetta from Kenya described details "to the last iota." And Stepha relived the problems and experiences Annetta wrote about from Israel. But the relationship between them has changed over the years.

The twins' guiding principle had always been "give the bigger half to your sister." Today, the twins' children, grandchildren, and Stepha's husband, Robby, compete for the "larger half" and often win. But when I asked Annetta to describe their twinship now, she said, "We are entwined—like the title of your other book *(Entwined Lives)*." Are

EXTRAORDINARY CIRCUMSTANCES

they? The twins still share things in ways that blur the boundaries between them. Stepha recently engineered a liaison between Annetta and one of her former boyfriends; Annetta was widowed in 1981 and Stepha wanted to see her sister happy. Annetta's new friend compared the twins constantly, and even called her by the wrong name while praising her sister. But Annetta didn't mind. When two people are as entwined as these twins, they may see little difference between them. It's a family joke that the phone must ring differently when Stepha calls because Annetta senses when her twin is on the other end. Both women also believe that their twin understands them better than their children, other relatives, friends, and spouses.[21]

But Robby knows that Stepha and Annetta can irritate each other when they are together. They didn't always have this luxury, but recently they have argued over who has had what dream. Robby calls himself their "lightning conductor," deflecting their strikes and flashes. I saw Robby as the twins' team captain, giving them security, confidence, and comfort when they needed it. He managed them quietly—a look, a word, or a gesture could end a useless discussion or decide the evening's meal. Robby also knows how close the twins can be. He is not jealous of their relationship, even when they lapse into their native Czech, which he does not understand. He simply says, "No Czech."

Despite their bond, Stepha and Annetta are also aware of the possible downside to twinship. "Twins need to develop full personalities," said Annetta. Both of them think that twin children should have different classrooms, friends, and experiences. But most identical twins I know have relished their time together and do not feel that it hurt their individuality in any way. Of course, periods of separation can be helpful if one twin feels controlled or intimidated by the other. Annetta has seemed compelled to follow Stepha's lead, but that has occurred mostly since they've been adults. I wondered if Stepha and Annetta really believed that separate experiences are best for twins, given that their years apart were so painful. They concede that their hardest separation was from their mother.

Stepha and Annetta have celebrated their mother's birthday, December 15, nearly every year since they were seventeen, when she was sent to Litzmannstadt. They both say that their mother's words helped them to cope with adversity and to make wise choices: "Don't jump before you learn how to walk"; "Don't put off what you can do today because tomorrow is unknown"; and "When you are unhappy, look at others whose burden is larger than yours." Annetta, the more cautious twin, personifies the first piece of wisdom—she talks hesitantly about topics of which she is uncertain. Stepha, the more daring twin, personifies the second; she will speak on subjects of which she has only passing knowledge. The twins' sensibilities are contrasting but complementary. Annetta's daughter, Daphna, said that she starts fights with her mother and ends them with her aunt. And when the twins described the death march out of Auschwitz, Stepha recalled dates and places, while Annetta recalled emotions and feelings. Annetta's son Michael said that his mother can "hold back" his aunt, a quality that works in their favor. "We all need a safety mechanism," he said.

But the twins' attitudes do not deviate when it comes to family. "Their world was their kids and grandkids. My kids are only a part of my mother's world," said Jennie, Stepha's daughter-in-law. Naomi, Stepha's daughter, complained, "She [Stepha] wants to own part of us." Annetta's daughter, Daphna, was "amazed that mom and Aunt Stepha came out of their experience so sane." The twins say that their children and grandchildren are their "victories over the past."

On my last night in Melbourne I talked with Stepha until midnight. She insisted on adding an elastic band to my bathing suit, which she claimed didn't fit me properly. The night was peaceful and quiet in a way that helped us to speak freely. Stepha brought up Mengele. She recalled hearing that he had left Auschwitz to visit his son, Rolf, who was sick (Rolf is now a lawyer in Bavaria). "We all hoped that his son would die, it would have served him right," she said. But Stepha had a different experience with another Nazi officer whom she encountered when she returned from the latrine. The officer told her that he was also "imprisoned," forced to be away from his family and to follow orders he didn't like. She felt sorry for him. Neither Stepha nor Annetta feel hatred for Germans or for anyone else. This was also true of the other Mengele twins I met—perhaps positive views of human behavior gave all these twins enough optimism to tip the survival scales in their favor.

That last night Stepha also shared one happy memory from Birkenau. The camp had no trees, grass, or flowers. But behind her barracks, she and some other inmates saw a yellow flower, "the kind that you see everywhere." They all looked at it and thought they saw more. I couldn't help wondering if she meant more flowers or perhaps a bit of hope.

8

Twin Towers

They were "Brenda-Linda" to their parents and siblings. Their younger sister, April, had put their names together, and the label stuck. "They were like the glue on this chair," April told me, hitting the chair hard with her hand.

Brenda Conway and Linda McGee were born on February 19, 1961, to Edith and William Alexander. Edith was a part-time office cleaner and William was a building security worker in Manhattan.[1] When Edith brought the twins home she didn't remove their identification tags because she couldn't tell them apart. Growing up, Linda dreaded picture day at school because the photographer always returned just one set of photos, thinking they were the same child. But whether the twins were identical or fraternal has never been determined. They looked a lot alike in childhood, but their adult photographs show similar, though not identical, facial contours—they look similar and different enough to make me wonder.[2]

As young children Brenda and Linda were always together. Linda said, "We were like three children—there was our older brother, Stanley, our younger sister, April, and Brenda-Linda." She remembers the day that their dad brought home a bike, ostensibly for Brenda, but really for both of them. There was never any question that they would share it. April joked that she was "Brenda-Linda's victim—they did me wrong—they would take my doll's head off and deny that they did it. But they let me hang with them."

In high school, Linda and Brenda were a "package deal." They both made the basketball team, but if only one of them had made it, then neither twin would have played. And when they dated, each twin's boyfriend had to like her sister if he was to stay around. They also sang in the choir and worked together on church activities. As an adult, Linda applied for a job near where Brenda worked. The twins joked that if she got the position they would see too much of each other and get nothing done.

Linda married two years before Brenda, but they lived in the same apartment complex. "I was always at the bus stop when she came home," Linda said. Brenda's husband, Russell, accepted their twinship more easily than Linda's husband, Mike, probably because Russell had younger twin brothers. "Russell told Mike that it wouldn't change," Linda said. "But I think Mike got it eventually. At least Russell stopped complaining." Linda admitted that she and Brenda had a special bond not shared with their husbands.

As adults, Brenda and Linda were passionate shoppers; "shopping was our greatest pastime," Linda said. Finding bargains was even better, so the twins took off on shopping trips nearly every weekend. Linda's son, Michael, sometimes wondered where they found the money to shop so much. The twins also loved going to the theater and eating out, just the two of them. But as close as they were, they had different personalities and styles. Brenda was outgoing and flamboyant—she did the talking for the two of them, and she was always cutting or dyeing her hair. She also liked wearing brightly patterned socks that got attention. Linda is quiet and conservative—she let her sister do the talking, and in all their years together she cut and colored her hair just once. Linda said that she was "shocked" when Brenda wore her patterned socks to church. But Linda finds herself wearing them lately.

I met Linda in April 2002 during the taping of a television program on twins.[3] She is a striking African-American woman, nearly six feet

Linda McGee, in the summer of 2002, ten months after her twin sister, Brenda, died in the World Trade Center attack. I met Linda in New York City, several months after we filmed the twins program for *Berman & Berman*. We sat in a coffee shop and talked for hours about her loss. When the shop closed, we moved to another one. (Photo by Nancy L. Segal, June 2002.)

tall and slender, with long straight hair and a delicate smile. When we met, she was friendly but slightly reserved. She spoke slowly and deliberately about her twin sister. Linda was forty years old when Brenda died. She handed me a picture of Brenda—it showed a young woman in a bright red blouse, wearing pearl earrings and a gold necklace, staring as intently as Linda seemed to. It was then that I noticed Linda's necklace with the names *Brenda-Linda* in gold, connected by a row of hearts. A friend had given it to her for Brenda's memorial service on October 13, 2001, one of many funerals held for victims of 9/11. As part of the service Linda read the poem "When Tomorrow Starts without Me," written by Erica Shea Liupaeter. A church member had given her a copy.

Linda pieced together the ordinary details of the ordinary weekend preceding the World Trade Center attack. On Saturday, the twins had gone to Philadelphia for a shopping trip. On the way back to New York, Brenda's daughter Danielle hurt her ear so they stopped at a hospital emergency room. The twins talked from nine o'clock in the evening until five o'clock the next morning while Danielle was waiting to

EXTRAORDINARY CIRCUMSTANCES

be treated. Linda admitted that the twins' social skills suffered because she and Brenda spent so much time together.

Once Danielle was released from the hospital, the twins headed to their homes, seven miles apart. But they met later at their church where their mother, Edith, was pastor. Linda and Brenda always sat in the same row. Later that Sunday evening the twins spoke on the telephone as they did most nights, while watching the same program on TV. They finalized their plans for the following Thursday: Brenda would pick up two tickets on Tuesday, September 11, for a show at the Beacon Theater on Broadway.

Linda, a third-grade teacher, got to work on Monday morning, September 10, and found a phone message from Brenda. Brenda, a systems analyst at Marsh and McLennan, worked on the ninety-seventh floor of the World Trade Center's north tower.[4] But there was a thunderstorm that night and the twins' grandmother had always warned them that it was dangerous to use the phone in bad weather. So Linda decided that she would call Brenda on Tuesday. On Tuesday morning, September 11, as Linda's students were settling down, she overheard a conversation in the hallway about the World Trade Center attack. She couldn't leave school immediately, so she turned on the television in her classroom. Eventually, Linda left the building and headed to her mother's house with her son, Michael. Family members were already gathering. Linda thought, "Brenda will have some story to tell when she gets home." But she didn't like the look of the tower falling.

Linda's son, Michael, described the scene in his grandmother's house: "At first it wasn't real serious. We talked and we played movies and computer games—but my mom didn't really join in. We waited for 'Auntie' to call. But as the time passed, our anxiety went up and it got quiet." Linda's mother recalled, "At first I took it light. I figured Brenda got out. I didn't panic. But the next day we hit the streets with pictures." By Friday there was no news and the family presumed that Brenda was dead.

A week later the telephone rang in Brenda's home and her son,

Mandell, answered it. The person on the other end sounded like his mother. He switched on the speaker phone and he and his sister, Danielle, looked at each other. "We had a bit of hope because people were still being found," said Danielle. It was their Aunt Linda.

I heard Linda's story twice that day, privately in the studio and publicly on the set. She seemed fragile, but under the lights she was in full command.[5] "If someone all of a sudden just cuts off your leg you would be in pain for so long," she explained. "Eventually you'd learn how to walk, but it wouldn't be the same. And some days you may look down and say, 'What happened to my leg?' And that's how I see it. I think eventually I'll learn how to function, but it still will never, ever be the same." She added, "I have a lot of good days and some bad days. I must admit now, I do have a little more better days than before."

Photographs of Linda and Brenda were shown throughout the televised segment—as little girls, as teenagers, as wives, and as mothers. These scenes were followed by footage of Linda staring at the hole where the twin towers once stood.

There is something unsettling about single twins, perhaps because we see them as a unit: they were born together, and so we expect them to stay together, to grow old together, and to die together. Twins have these same expectations. Twins from intact pairs do not mix well with "twinless twins," and some even avoid them. None of the hundreds of twins at an annual twins' gathering in Oklahoma City attended the special session for bereaved twins.

Fortunately, a weekly support group was set up exclusively for twin survivors of 9/11.[6] These bereaved twins were Linda's strength: "The twins can't find the words either, but they understand." Linda mentioned one survivor, Greg Hoffman, whom she thought of as a kind of "new twin": "When either of us talks the other one nods. We just get it." This implicit understanding bound them together, much like the understanding that each one had shared with their own twin brother and sister.

Most people did not lose twin siblings on September 11, but Linda was not alone. We now know that about forty people lost their twins in the attacks on the World Trade Center and the Pentagon, and in the crash of United Flight 93.[7] We also know that bereaved twins (identical and fraternal) grieve more for the loss of their twin than for almost any other relative, with the exception of spouses and children.[8] Most people celebrate twins' interconnected lives, but few pay attention to the end of that relationship. Acknowledging this loss is vital, especially for the twinless twins whose best therapy is connecting with others like them.

Over the years I have heard many stories of twin loss.[9] The twins' personal experiences give depth and definition to the notion of the twin bond. Their stories are about relationships cut short and plans unfulfilled, but with an added dimension: They often feel lost on birthdays and at other joint celebrations, and they remain living reminders of their missing twin. Linda's loss was about all these things. She thinks about the vacations that she and Brenda will never take. "But we will do that musical," Linda insisted. (Brenda had written several plays that were locally produced and had wanted to put one to music.) Linda's loss was also compounded by the fact that news of the attack was always in the media.

Over the next few months and years Linda had more bad days than good days, despite her statement to the contrary when I first met her. She had taken a leave of absence from her teaching job because, as she told me, "remembering thirty-one students' names and preparing lessons was becoming overwhelming. And I couldn't express myself in front of the class." But she returned to college to study psychology, kept up e-mail contact with the twinless twins, and joined a 9/11 sibling support group. Over time, Linda gained confidence as a public speaker. She was proud of how she handled questions at a memorial event at her old high school. And she was excited about a children's book she was writing on how Brenda overcame a childhood learning disability.[10] As a child Brenda had had trouble recognizing words—she would read the name Barbara and think it was Brenda. "Overcoming difficulty is my passion," Linda told me. But there were days when she didn't get out of bed or leave her house. News of suicide bombings in Israel "brought it all back."

Like many bereaved twins, Linda looked for ways to keep her sister's memory alive. At the annual church picnic she wore a T-shirt with Brenda's picture on it, and the word "Twinternity" printed across the front; she created this word to mean "we are twins for eternity." She also helped organize a memorial boat ride for Brenda, one year and two days after her death. Linda once said, "My friend [Brenda] was always with me. We had a unique twin bond, but now it's broken." Most twinless twins would say that the bond is broken or missing but not gone. This theme is captured in a poem that Linda wrote and read on that occasion:

> Our future proceeds in new directions
> We face new tomorrows
> View new visions
> Dream new dreams
> Journey on as a new person
>
> As some may wish at a wishing well
> Over candles on a birthday cake
> Or on a falling star
> Our bodies ache longing to hear from you
> To touch you, to see you one more time
>
> Yet we find endurance in our memories
> Strength from your spoken words
> Power in the God we serve
> Remembering you is a never ending story
> Deeply etched in our hearts and minds forever.
> We cannot remain paralyzed by the question why
> It is too complex for our minds to comprehend
> Professors can't teach it
> Textbooks can't teach it

Webster can't define it
The thousands touched can't express it.

Time alone can't heal all wounds
They must be stitched with love
Covered with the ointment of prayer
And wrapped with bandages of unity
Then the wounds will eventually heal
But we will always be left with a scar of remembrance.

Although badly wounded we must go on
We have more lessons to learn
We must attempt to pass other difficult tests
We have to seek strength in life's complexities.
We have more good times to experience,
More memories to create,
And a destiny to fulfill.

So one year later we can endure sad time by the grace of
    our God
We're able to smile even when tears are falling
We know that this brief separation clouded by sadness
Cannot be compared to an eternity together rejoicing in
    gladness.

Twincerely, Linda (9/13/02)

More than one hundred friends and family members showed up for
the boat ride and released dozens of balloons in Brenda's name. "People from Brenda's office said I look just like her," Linda remarked. This
was hard to hear. But Linda admitted that her birthdays were the biggest challenge; they were, in her words, "worse than holidays because
they are so personal."

Brenda and Linda's birthdays used to be three-day affairs: a day
spent with their family, a day spent alone together, and a day spent on
"recovery." Their last joint birthday party in 2001, called "The Twins'

40th Birthday Bash," was a large celebration at Brenda's home in the Bronx. The next day, the twins rode the train to their favorite restaurant, where they celebrated by themselves. February 19, 2002, was Linda's first birthday alone. On that day she "shut down" and told everyone not to call her. She sat at home as the phone rang continuously, but she let the answering machine pick up. She has celebrated her birthday that way ever since.

As time passed, some victims' remains were being discovered.[11] Linda and her mother each provided a blood sample for DNA analysis. Finding Brenda could bring closure and solace to Linda and her family—strangely, it would also settle the question of whether the twins were identical or fraternal. But Linda is afraid of finding her twin. "Someone I know was told that they had found his sister's leg. I can't deal with anything negative now." But Linda felt some consolation at the unveiling of Marsh and McLennan's memorial plaque in midtown Manhattan. The names and signatures of the 295 deceased employees are engraved in glass and stone under their printed names. "It was 'her'—Brenda signed her name slanting backwards and when I saw it with my niece, we said 'yes!'" Linda also posted a poem on the wall of the Family Visiting Room on Liberty Street, overlooking the World Trade Center site:

> Memories of our past
> Often replay in my mind
> We shared a relationship
> Unlike any other kind
>
> Always there for one another
> Year after year
> It's really hard to believe
> That you are no longer here.
>
> I do have the joy of knowing
> You will always be my twin

Although we are apart temporarily
We will be reunited again.

Linda (Twin to Brenda)

But memorials can't provide lasting comfort or satisfying answers. "I am no longer Brenda-Linda. But who is Linda?" she asked. Surviving twins face the difficult task of redefining themselves, as individuals and as twins. This requires reworking relationships with parents, spouses, children, colleagues, and oneself. As an individual, but mostly as a twin, Linda was unprepared for losing Brenda when she did: "It all boils down to the twin thing—one or both of us never let go." She described a set of identical male twins in her last class: "They reminded me of me—they would always look up to see where the other one was." She added, "I fear for them. I never felt like this before. Now things are totally different." Some of Linda's family relationships have also changed.

Linda's husband, Mike, wants things to be like they were before. "But they never will be, I am a totally different person," Linda said. Just as Mike "didn't get" what Linda's twinship was about, it may be hard for him to "get" her loss. Linda and her family spent the first Thanksgiving after 9/11 at Brenda's home, and it was "awkward—there were too many memories." Still, Linda has stayed close to her niece and nephew, Danielle and Mandell, though she has changed from their "Totie" (aunt) to a kind of mom. "But it's not like I'm suddenly stepping up to the plate," she said. Linda's daughter, Shantaé, said that she and Danielle sometimes "switched mothers" when they got together. Not surprisingly, Danielle told Linda, "I see my mother in you." And while Danielle misses her "mother/daughter hangout days," she can hope to recapture them through Linda.[12] When Linda advises or scolds Brenda's children, they tell her, "My mom would say the same thing."

Linda was reluctant to speak with reporters at first, though now she shares her feelings candidly. But she still grapples with the unreality of her situation. She stifles impulses to call Brenda when something in-

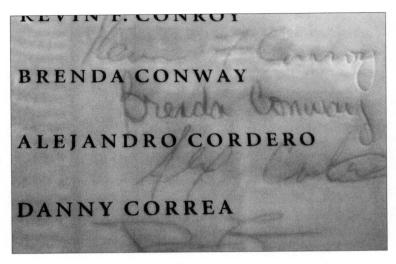

KEVIN F. CONROY

BRENDA CONWAY

ALEJANDRO CORDERO

DANNY CORREA

Marsh and McLennan's stunning memorial to its 295 employees lost on September 11, 2001. Completed in the summer of 2003 by artist Richard Fleischner, it is built from stone, glass, and bronze. The memorial stands in a small, enclosed plaza outside the company's headquarters in midtown Manhattan. (Photo by Nancy L. Segal, January 2004.)

teresting or funny happens; this may be why she is writing a piece called *What We Didn't Say*. But Linda feels no hatred or anger toward the terrorists who blew up the World Trade Center because, she reasons, they died also. Recently, she appeared in *Hype Hair* magazine as a "Shining Star"; her winning essay about Brenda identified her as a "model of strength, courage and compassion."[13] Photographs show Linda looking gorgeous after her free beauty makeover and hair styling. But Linda was not the twin who changed her looks or attracted attention; Brenda was. Perhaps several years ago the tattoo on Linda's arm would have seemed out of character, but the simple message it bears, *Twinternity,* is part of her new identity.

A lot has changed. About two years after 9/11, Linda returned to the restaurant on Boston Road where she and Brenda ate chef's salads. She has also revisited the drug store where they would lose each other in the aisles and end up laughing as they tried to reconnect. And she has

EXTRAORDINARY CIRCUMSTANCES

seen shows at the Beacon Theater. Thinking about going to these places is more overwhelming than actually being there. But she can't shop like she used to. "Now I rely on catalogs," she said. Linda can't name her most difficult memory of her sister. But it must be the day that she saw the unpacked bags of clothes in Brenda's closet, the ones Brenda had bought in Philadelphia three days before 9/11. Brenda hadn't found time to put the things away.

Linda's only uninterrupted activity since 9/11 has been attending her mother's church services each Sunday. She expects Brenda to be sitting in their usual row, though she is getting used to seeing her empty seat. When it comes to twins, some beliefs, habits, and expectations are expressed as automatically as a blink or a sneeze—and Brenda-Linda had been at it for forty years.

In all our conversations Linda was spirited and talkative, so it was hard to think of her as the "quiet twin." But in life, twins often exchange roles or adopt different ones, perhaps to maintain a psychological balance. Now Linda is forced to be verbally assertive without her more outgoing sister. And Linda loves talking about Brenda. I have seen this before; surviving twins leave my office reluctantly, as if afraid that their twinship, re-created in the telling, will fade. "We had our own little twin world," Linda said.

Saturday, September 11, 2004, was the third anniversary of the attack on the World Trade Center. On that day, Linda and her family went to the site and to the memorial garden. The next day they had a commemoration service at their church, and Linda signed copies of her newly published children's book, *B Is for Brenda*. Her niece, Danielle (Brenda's daughter), had recently given birth to identical twin girls, Diamyn and Destiny, and according to Linda, they are like Brenda-Linda all over again. In her words, "that made the day extra special."

9

A Good-News Story

Kirk and Allyson MacLeod faced big decisions in spring 1998. Having spent years teaching and working on behalf of their Keswick, Ontario, congregation, they decided it was time to think about starting a family. But their hopes faded after Allyson's two miscarriages, the second one at twenty weeks. At age thirty-one, Allyson could still become pregnant, but her previous experiences made the outcome uncertain. Torn between in vitro fertilization and adoption, she and Kirk chose adoption since a successful outcome seemed more likely. Because Canada's policies favor the rights of biological parents over those of adoptive parents, Kirk and Allyson chose international adoption.

By January 1999 Kirk and Allyson had picked China because the high standards of care in its orphanages promised healthy babies. Furthermore, their region offered excellent cultural programs for Chinese children. Both Kirk and Allyson dismiss the notion that they were motivated out of a noble desire to save a child. "We just really wanted a family," they said. It would take lots of paperwork, payments, and patience before that happened, thirteen months later.

Another Canadian couple, Mike and Lynette Shaw, from Amherstburg, near Windsor, began thinking about adoption in June 1998. They had been mourning the loss of their seventeen-day-old son, Jonathan Christopher, from *truncus arteriosus,* a condition resulting in a malformed heart and other anomalies. Some cases have a genetic origin, while others have no clear cause. Jonathan Christopher's condition was most likely genetic. The Shaws were afraid that another child of theirs, especially a male, could be born with this disorder, so they decided to adopt.[1] The couple already had two biological children, Heather, four, and Eric, three, but they wanted another child quickly. "We were relatively young, thirty-one years old, and we wanted to be young parents to our children. We also wanted to minimize the age gap between Eric and our third child," Lynette explained.

By early 1999, Mike and Lynette had chosen China for the same reasons as Kirk and Allyson, but Mike was more outspoken. "Russian adoptions take longer, there are palm greasings, and some kids show the effects of their mother's drinking. Chinese kids are a lot healthier," Mike said. Like Kirk and Allyson, they learned that it would be a long time before they had their baby.

For the next thirteen months, Kirk and Allyson and Mike and Lynette met frequently with social workers and with other families adopting through the same agency. Twenty couples met initially before they were reduced to two groups of ten, depending on their assigned baby's province. The two groups were organized into four subgroups with five couples each, on the basis of the child's orphanage. They would keep this arrangement when they traveled to China. The five couples in each subgroup became friendly, and Kirk and Allyson and Mike and Lynette were in the same one. Kirk and Allyson were excited about having their first child and had read a lot about Chinese culture; Mike and Lynette were used to being parents, but since the loss of their son they were also focused on receiving their newest child.

The arrangement of the couples into smaller clusters proved to be more than administrative minutiae. On Christmas Eve 1999 the adoptive parents received photographs of their daughters-to-be. A five-way family picture exchange, via the Internet, followed. Kirk and Allyson and Mike and Lynette were independently struck by how similar their future daughters looked. In order to get a closer comparison, Mike put the two photos together on the computer screen. "The resemblance was uncanny," he said. "But when we saw that both girls' birthdays were June 26, 1999, we really began to wonder. Were the children twins, or was the same baby mistakenly assigned to both of us? I wondered if Kirk and Allyson saw what we saw." Mike waited a few days before contacting the other couple, giving them time to react, but when no e-mails arrived he asked them directly. Kirk and Allyson had noticed the girls' similarities and had been asking themselves the same hard questions as Mike and Lynette.

The two families contacted the adoption facilitator in Ottawa, and she agreed to look into the matter. She assured them that the two babies were unrelated and that any similarities between them were coincidental. "China's policy mandates that twins found together be kept together, so the girls could not be related," she explained. But outcomes don't always reflect official policies. Kirk and Allyson and Mike and Lynette weren't persuaded by what the adoption facilitator had told them; and though the families didn't know it at the time, other Chinese twins had been separated at birth.[2] The families had to wait and see.

In February 2000 the two couples flew to China to meet their babies for the first time. The prospective parents waited by the elevator on the twenty-fourth floor of the Golden Source Hotel. The tension was "unbearable"; the flashing lights above the elevator indicated an approaching car that suddenly reversed direction before finally beginning the important ascent. When social workers exited holding the five babies, they had their answer: Two children were indistinguishable except for their pink and yellow pajamas. Mike said, "We knew immediately that one was ours and one was theirs." The families had prepared for this eventuality during their long flight together. They had more to discuss on their return trip, but the big plan—nurturing the girls' twinship— had evolved without question. From then on, both families would be involved in major decisions concerning the two girls. One small incident already suggested that the families could agree: Allyson and Lynette had unknowingly picked identical outfits for the twins.

But should the girls be raised together? The possibility that one family would raise both twins was never discussed at that time. It crossed the minds of the four new parents, but not seriously, and since DNA tests hadn't been done, there was a slight chance that the babies might not be twins. Regardless, I believe this was too difficult a question for the families to think about, or even to acknowledge. Raising the girls together might have been an option while they were still in China, before they returned to their separate homes, but deciding who would take both twins would have been emotionally devastating. Moreover, the couples had also been quietly told that if they didn't take the babies as planned, then the girls would be returned to the pool of potential adoptees. The couples who would then get them might not suspect that they were twins.

Kirk and Allyson and Mike and Lynette had worked too hard and had waited too long to give up their daughters. Now they focused on the lifestyle changes that would take place as a result of their accidental connection. Their main goal was letting their respective daughters—Lily MacLeod and Gillian Shaw—be twins.

Lily and Gillian lead the shared lives of ordinary twins and the separate lives of close cousins. They know typical parent-child relations and exotic interfamily connections. Does each twin have one set of parents, or two? Two sets of grandparents, or four? I tried to find out from Lily's parents when I met them in May 2002 in Oshawa.

Two-and-a-half-year-old Lily bounced into the hotel lobby dressed in pink, her favorite color. A matching ribbon was tied around a skinny pigtail that stood straight up from her small head. The long hallway was a child's paradise, and Lily lost no time turning it into a running track, grabbing smiles like batons from whomever she passed. She had enough energy and charm for two children.

Both Kirk and Allyson are ordained ministers, but Allyson has been a full-time mother since Lily arrived. Both parents hold master's degrees in divinity from the University of Toronto. Kirk, age thirty-four, was a proud and protective dad—he was upbeat and friendly toward me, but his warmth escalated when he held his daughter's hand and walked alongside her. Allyson, age thirty-five, laughed repeatedly at whatever Lily said or did. She kept looking at Lily as if she could hardly believe that this little girl was hers. Kirk and Allyson looked as though they were still getting used to being parents. They were very eager to talk about how Lily and her twin sister, Gillian, had become part of their lives.

Kirk suggested that we have lunch outside the hotel. I sat in the front seat of their van and answered Lily's questions about who I was and what I was doing. When she called me "Doctor See-gool," her parents beamed.

Kirk insisted that I tell a "good-news story" about the twins and their adoptions, though we both agreed that dividing twins is *not* good news. A lone sock or a lost glove is bothersome because the pair works in ways that each part cannot. Human twins are neither socks nor gloves, but when one twin is absent, things do not seem quite right.

The restaurant's atmosphere was relaxed, making it a good choice for families with children. Lily interrupted her parents often to ask them questions or to show them her drawings. She demands lots of attention, a trait that she shares with her twin. Lily was still too young to understand what her parents were telling me—how and why they got her.

Lily and Gillian were in a Chenzhou orphanage, in China's Hunan province, but they may have been born elsewhere. No one knows why the girls' mother abandoned her twin daughters, but they were probably among the thousands of unwanted female babies born under China's One-Child Policy. This 1980 policy was intended to curb population growth, but cultural traditions favoring males discriminated against females; thus wanting a son could mean giving up a daughter.[3] Female fetuses were forcibly aborted and female newborns were often killed. Some infant girls were abandoned in places where they would likely be discovered, such as a lively city or a market square. A relative, maybe the mother, might watch to see that they were found; once discovered, these babies were generally taken to orphanages.[4] Relinquishing their daughters was heartbreaking for most families. Some pregnant women or their infant girls were hidden or sent away so the women would not be harassed, fined, or even sterilized. I wondered:

Are male twins born under China's One-Child Policy allowed to stay together? Are female members of male-female twin pairs abandoned, especially if their families have older daughters? Families with twins are supposedly not penalized for the extra births. Still, it's hard to get reliable answers to such questions because the One-Child Policy has been variously enforced across locations.

Lily and Gillian were found in different places, so they didn't arrive at the orphanage together. Once there, they were called Lian'er (lotus flower) and Shuang'er (twin or double). Their names betray a curious hint of things to come: Once the adoption process was under way, Lian'er's adoptive parents, Allyson and Kirk, wanted a name for their future daughter so they could pray for her and for her birth mother. One night Allyson had a dream and knew that they would name her Lily. Shuang'er's name was suggested by the double fold of her eyelids (considered a lucky charm), not by her status as a twin.

In fact, Lily and Gillian's twinship was never officially acknowl-edged during their eight months' stay in the orphanage. Why this was so has never been determined—Mike speculated that because the girls had been found separately, the orphanage staff did not consider them twins. Or maybe the orphanage couldn't afford the DNA testing that would have proven their relationship. But what administrators denied, the nurses quietly acknowledged: Lian'er and Shuang'er were identical twins. They were kept in separate rooms because they were nearly in-distinguishable; Allyson said that the twins' only unique feature was a small growth on Shuang'er's little toe.

I reminded Allyson of her first e-mail message to me, in December 2001, when the twins were two and a half. "I have come to realize that as uncommon as twins raised apart may be, reared apart and yet grow-ing up to know one another as a twin is perhaps even more uncom-mon," she had written. Raising twins together is a formidable venture for most parents, but raising twins in parallel is uncharted territory. There are no how-to books on the subject, so Kirk and Allyson and Mike and Lynette are still writing their own scripts.

I met Mike and Lynette Shaw in March 2003. Mike is an account manager for Bell Canada, a job he took out of high school. Mike was open about voicing his opinions, which he did with humor and flair. He was also proud of his family and protective of their happiness. Lynette trained as a dental assistant after high school and now works in that field. She was warm and friendly, but less assertive than her husband. Lynette was intrigued by Lily and Gillian's similarities, but she seemed bothered by the attention the twins attracted, sometimes at the expense of her two other children.

Both couples were eager to tell their story. Although they have become accustomed to their unusual situation, they still wonder why their girls' twinship was denied by adoption officials. They also marvel at how close the twins came to never being twins. Their girls' lives as virtual singletons were reversed by a photo exchange, but any number of events could have derailed their reunion. What if pictures had not been available in advance? Would they have noticed the twins' resemblance at the hotel if they hadn't anticipated it? Maybe, but maybe not. What if Lily and Gillian had not been assigned to couples in the same group of five? Would they have met at some future date? Possibly, but we can't know for sure. Could the orphanage nurses have conspired to ensure that Lily and Gillian would meet? All four adoptive parents have thought about these issues.

Kirk and Allyson's religious faith leads them to conclude that God wanted two families to be blessed. They understand, but are awed by, the interest that their story receives. Mike and Lynette's faith tells them that God chose people who could handle certain situations, in their case, the loss of a son and the adoption of a separated twin. "I do not believe in fate," Mike said. "You can create plans, but you never know what will happen. There can be that weave in the road." Mike also says that the last two years were like "an infomercial," in which customers get gifts with each purchase: "We thought we were just getting a skillet, but we got all the other equipment, even the vegetables!"

Both families are astonished by the twins' parallel development. "The girls have very similar voices, cries, and giggles . . . so much so that both mothers go running at the sound of them," Allyson said.

When Lily took her first step, Allyson went to her computer to e-mail Lynette—but Lynette had e-mailed first with the same news. The twins' reactions at a gathering of Chinese adoptees also set them apart; eight of the ten children played in the pool, but Lily and Gillian sat outside. They eventually went in the water, but Allyson thought they wanted to be alone together for a while. The twins' parents also said that clowns and Santa Claus scare them, which Kirk attributed to the costumes. "Both girls have a sensitive spirit, so maybe the masks hide an angry face—this is at the heart of Lily and Gillian," he explained. On Halloween, both twins independently dressed up as ballerinas.

As happy as the twins have made their parents, they have their try-ing sides. "We were shocked that Gillian could be so aggressive," said Lynette. "Our other two children, Heather and Eric, never acted like that. We thought, well maybe it's because she has an older brother and sister. But Allyson says the same thing, and Lily is an only child. Both girls have picked on other children and have shown their fits and tem-pers, although these behaviors have started to disappear." Lynette's words show the power of two in deciding why children act as they do. Social explanations are easy to find when kids act alone, but when identical twins act alike, especially when they are raised apart, genetic explanations come closer to the truth.

Some families are like transformers, a child's toy that takes on new shapes and identities when pushed into different positions. Whether through adoption, artificial reproduction, divorce, or remarriage, ordi-nary relations can be overridden by uncommon attachments. Mike and Lynette said that Lily was a novelty to Gillian's older siblings, Heather and Eric—a credible version of their little sister, but one who didn't compete for parental attention or the last cookie. Eric likes them both, but Heather thinks that Lily is a little nicer than Gillian because Lily doesn't live with them. Maybe Heather was still upset at having to stay after school one day after telling her teacher that Lily was coming to visit her family; when her teacher asked who Lily was, Heather ex-plained that she was "sister's sister."

The twins know each other's parents as "aunt" and "uncle," yet these labels hide the significance of the children in the adults' lives. Allyson said, "I find it difficult to leave my daughter's twin, as if leaving part of her behind. I want to scoop her up, but I'm not part of her daily life." Lynette agreed. "I think it's tougher for us than for the kids," she admitted. Both sets of parents weigh in on important decisions, such as visits, media appearances, and even my interview with them. Kirk and Allyson had once planned to move nearer to their own relatives on Canada's east coast, but that would have increased the distance between the two families. "We did not want to be more than a day's drive from Gillian," Allyson said. Another unknown involved the twins' grandparents, each of whom had acquired a new grandchild— or grandchildren? Would they send one present on birthdays and holidays or two? The situation was a little hard for the grandparents at first, but now they think of the other family's twin as a second granddaughter, and they all correspond.

All the adults are extremely interested in tracking the twins' relationship with each other. They watch the girls closely because they don't have the luxury of seeing them together all the time.

Allyson remembered, "One day Lynette called to see if Lily was okay. Gillian had dreamt that something terrible had happened to Lily." The twins were two and a half, probably too early to tell if they sensed a special quality about themselves, an elusive something that set them apart from others. No twin knows the moment he or she becomes aware of a second person who was always there, though by four or five most twin children know that they are twins. Maybe Gillian's dream suggested a dawning sensibility, a concern for another companion who was like her. I also wondered if this understanding affected Lily's reaction to a photo of her with her sister: "It's Lily and Lily," she said.

There was little question in their parents' minds that Lily and Gillian were identical twins, but they wanted to be sure. I arranged for the girls to have DNA tests when they were nearly three. When the results were known, Kirk and Allyson felt "completely elated and desperately sad." They were happy knowing that Lily and Gillian were truly

EXTRAORDINARY CIRCUMSTANCES

Gillian (left) and Lily, nearly four, say good-bye to each other after a family get-together in Oshawa. This was the first time I saw the twins together. Both girls were just getting over the chicken pox. (Photo by Nancy L. Segal, March 2003.)

sisters. But they were upset knowing that the girls who were born together had been separated. Mike and Lynette were pleased, but their reaction was tempered by the responsibility thrust upon them. "We are realists," Mike explained. "The results were great for the girls—now I know that my daughter has a sister. But this story is not candy-coated. I am being selfish in saying this: if the girls had not been related then I could carry on with my own family as before. But now there is a commitment to another child and another family. When Lily and Gillian are together they get lots of attention, and I have to think of my other two children. It's a hard balancing act every day."

Lynette recalled the time a stranger said that Gillian was a beautiful little girl. "I have two beautiful daughters," Lynette had replied. Because her family lives in a small neighborhood, everyone notices

Gillian, and because of her they get special treatment at Chinese restaurants. Lynette's subdued tone suggested a mix of pleasure for Gillian and concern for Heather and Eric. Mike recalled that when they first took Gillian out in public, an elderly lady stared at them, as though wondering how Caucasian parents could have an Asian child. "I still don't know what happened," Mike said to her sarcastically.

On June 26, 2002, Kirk and Allyson made the 250-mile trip to Windsor for Lily and Gillian's third birthday celebration. "Lily and Gillian got along like two peas in a pod," observed Allyson. "Obviously, now that they can communicate it's less frustrating for them." I saw a picture panorama from the party, which showed the twins opening gifts and gobbling treats. I saw them arm in arm, smiling and sitting by Mike and Lynette's pond. They seemed like ordinary twins growing up together. In one picture Gillian was comforting Lily, who was momentarily overwhelmed by the new relatives surrounding them.

After dinner the parents started talking, then realized that the twins had left the table. They were curled up together in the small bed Lynette had prepared for Lily, and they were talking quietly. Lily and Gillian had come a long way since their first meal together at age one, when they had stared at each other, perplexed. "I flashed to the future," Allyson said. "We have hoped that this was how it would be, that the girls would want to spend time alone together." Lily's picture had been tacked to the refrigerator in Gillian's home, but it was in tatters because Gillian carries it with her when Lily goes home. And when Gillian visits her sister's house, Lily "goes off the walls" with excitement. I believed this when I saw the girls together.

I saw Lily and Gillian together in March 2003, in London, Ontario. The twins, nearly four, stared at each other when they met at the hotel entrance. They hadn't been together for several weeks, so maybe they had to get used to each other again. Then Lily yelled, "Yippee!" Heather had her arm around Gillian, so perhaps Gillian felt somewhat restrained.

We went to a large room with a big table. I talked with the parents but kept an eye on the twins. The girls drew pictures, watched a videotape, and ran around with Heather and Eric. They seemed comfortable with each other—they tickled each other, argued, moved apart, and came together, like most young twins.

The parents were still amazed by their girls' similarities and awareness of each other. Both twins were thirty-nine-and-a-half inches tall and weighed thirty-five pounds, though Lily's face was fuller than her sister's. Both were slow, picky eaters, and their shirts were too short for their longish bodies. Both twins had asthma, and they had caught chicken pox one day apart, leaving them with matching pox marks—probably a legacy of their similar immune systems. Both girls were also clear speakers and used the same words, drawing them out slowly, as in "ac-tu-al-ly." And they often put their hand defiantly on their hip, or patted someone's face with their hands when they didn't like what was being said. They also tossed their hair by flicking their head and hand, behaviors they developed independently. When Lily said or did these things, her uncle Mike called them "Gillian expressions."

Best friends sometimes use or invent the same words and gestures, but friends have time together to share and develop them. Lynette and Allyson said that when they see their daughter's twin, even after several months' absence, the girls' similarities make their "spines shiver" and their "jaws drop."

The girls' characters were becoming clearer as they approached early childhood. "They both have a strong, independent streak—our challenge will be to tame their personalities, not to break them," Allyson said. And they are "entertainers"; they like to dance, and they demand attention. They also like teaching each other. "But they are both so hyper when they are together, maybe they'd be better off apart," one parent said, but in jest. When the families visited Disneyworld, in Florida, several weeks before I saw them, Lily cut into a restaurant line: "Be glad she's not a twin," the waiter remarked.

Allyson recalled a time when Lily worried because she, not Gillian, had gotten a pony ride. "They have quickly associated themselves as sisters," she said. Best friends might show this kind of concern for each other, but young children's friendships can be short-lived, whereas Lily and Gillian's attachment was enduring. During their Florida trip the families stayed in a three-bedroom home, where the twins slept apart. When Allyson finished reading Lily a bedtime story, Lily ran to Gillian's room to kiss her good night. "It seemed so natural," Allyson said. "And when I asked Lily who her best friend was, she said 'Gillian' in an impatient way, like saying, 'Come on ma, isn't it obvious?'"

"I want you to come home with me," I heard Lily say to Gillian when it was time for them to leave. Lily kissed her sister good-bye and Gillian rubbed the spot on her cheek. Then they hugged each other. The girls' good-byes are getting harder—Lynette said that Gillian is "down" after Lily leaves and wonders why Lily's family can't live closer. And when Allyson told Lily that they would be seeing Gillian over the 2003 Christmas holidays, Allyson said, "Out of the blue, Lily started crying. She said, 'I want to live closer to Gillian, I want to be there now. This is awful, why did it have to happen?'" It is unclear if Lily fully understood why she and Gillian had been separated, but it is clear that Lily missed her.

Both twins now know how their parents got them and brought them to Canada. But when they are older, they will be asking more complicated questions. Some of those questions will not have answers because information on their early lives is limited; their adoptive parents can only wonder what really happened to the twins in their earliest days. Were they sick? Were they abandoned? But the four parents know that having the twins and watching them grow up together matters more than having this knowledge. Lily has not asked about her past, but Gillian has wondered if she will "meet the lady whose belly I grew up in." Unlike Lily, Gillian has two adoptive siblings who look nothing like her. This fact, coupled with the frequent visits made by the Shaws' relatives, may make Gillian more conscious than Lily of biological connections.

Many Caucasian parents adopting Chinese children are concerned with creating a birth heritage for their children and instilling pride in the Chinese culture.[5] Kirk and Allyson celebrate three new holidays— Lily and Gillian's birthday, Chinese New Year, and "Gotcha Day" (February 27)—the day that Lily became their daughter. They are "so thankful to China." They want their daughter to appreciate her culture, so Lily will attend community programs for Chinese children when she turns five; she is already showing interest in drawing Chinese characters. Kirk and Allyson also plan to spend a year in China when Lily is older. But for now, they are delighted that four of the nine children in Lily's class are Chinese, two of them adopted.

Mike and Lynette have not added the Chinese New Year or "Gotcha Day" to their celebration day list, but they remind Gillian of these events. Classes in Mandarin are available for young children in their neighborhood, but they won't be sending their daughter. Lynette explained that Gillian gets lots of attention and that she and Mike want Gillian to be part of the Canadian culture: "It's hard for Heather and Eric to understand why Gillian gets special things. We want the kids to know that they are equals." Lynette and Mike are willing to take Gillian to China to see her birthplace, but they do not feel an affinity with that country. They prefer to have Gillian appreciate Chinese history and culture without becoming immersed in them.

Lily has started to understand that she looks more like some other people than her parents. When Lily was three, she and her father passed an Asian woman on the street. Lily said, "She is Chinese." Kirk asked her if he [Kirk] was Chinese, and she replied, "No, dad." And when Lily said that she liked being Chinese, Kirk thought that was "cool." Lily is also friendly with the clerks at the local grocery store. Recently, she whispered to Allyson, "Is she [one of the clerks] Chinese?" Allyson said she didn't think so, and even though she told Lily not to ask, Lily asked anyway. "Excuse me, are you Chinese?" The young woman said that she was Cambodian. Lily replied, "Oh, Cambodian. I'm Chinese and we have the same kind of skin." When I met the families in March 2003, Lily gave Gillian a Mulan doll. These twelve-inch figurines were inspired by the 1998 Disney film *Mulan,* based on an ancient Chinese poem about a female warrior.[6]

Gillian also has a growing sense of looking different from her parents and siblings, who are mostly blonde and blue-eyed. Lynette said that Gillian jokes about looking like her mother on some days and like her father on other days. And when she passes an Asian person, she might say, "Look, mama, another one. I'm not the only one who is Chinese." Gillian is just one of two Chinese students in her school of three hundred, so she is noticed—and students ask Heather and Eric how Gillian could possibly be their sister. Heather and Eric have turned these potentially annoying questions to their advantage through their school's adoption awareness program, by speaking about their Chinese sister.

The families hope that the twins continue to enjoy each other's company. "If Lily and Gillian want to live together some day, it will mean we have succeeded," said Allyson. Signs suggest that the twins' relationship will continue, but the future is never certain. Differences in their lives—Lily has no siblings, Gillian has two; Lily's family is Presbyterian, Gillian's is Catholic; Lily's neighborhood is ethnically mixed, Gillian's is homogeneous—seem unimportant now, but they may be important later. For example, both families are Christian and religious, but as Mike said, there are different undertones to their faith.

Mike said that one of the best things to come out of adopting Gillian has been his family's "new family." Kirk agrees with Mike, but he added that "their relationship was forged, not by choice, but by necessity." The families get along well, and there have been no rivalries between them over their daughters' accomplishments or activities. Of course, the twins' developmental similarities keep parental competition in check, but that could change as Lily and Gillian get older.

Many separated twins never find each other, and those who do mostly meet as adults, bitter over their lost childhood years together. The two fathers, but not the two mothers, spoke about the twins' hypothetical rearing by one family. They raised this question on their own, without prompting. Kirk and Mike were less involved in the twins' daily care than Allyson and Lynette, so it may have been easier for them to consider the situation unemotionally, if only briefly. But this topic could only be broached safely when rearing the girls together was no longer possible.

Kirk confessed, "We would have taken them both, and we know that Mike and Lynette would have, too." There was a slight hesitation in his voice, a hint that one couple might have given up one of the twins so they could have been raised together. Mike said, "Even if one family had been gallant enough to give one up it would have been a legal nightmare."

It seemed pointless to pursue this question since it went beyond the events as we knew them. We all believed that adopted twins should be raised together whenever possible, but that sometimes requires a perfect world. And we all knew that these families had not separated the twins; they had brought them together, trying to right a regrettable wrong. The parents, in love with their daughters, would not want them abandoned again.

Lily and Gillian seemed destined to grow up apart. Although they are not growing up together as ordinary twins, they are growing up together as exceptional ones. Kirk wanted me to write a good-news story. And so I have.

IV

EVERYDAY WONDERS

Families with identical twins easily create new parent-child and sibling relationships for which we don't have names. This process happens when twins and parents of twins date, marry, and have children. The children of identical twins are "half-siblings," not just cousins, since each has a genetically identical parent. And their identical twin aunts and uncles are their "parents," biologically speaking.[1]

New reproductive technologies that allow infertile couples to conceive are partly responsible for these new family arrangements. A "twin-like" half-sibling set was created when a Michigan husband and wife conceived naturally—at the same time that a surrogate mother was impregnated with the husband's sperm. A California couple had four "twin-like" half-sibling sets: a surrogate mother impregnated with the husband's sperm had male-female twins (David and Dina), and three months later the man's wife delivered a naturally conceived identical male set (Steven and Sam). Pairing each identical boy with his older half-brother and half-sister creates two copies of the "same" half-sibling set (Steven-David, Sam-David; and Steven-Dina, Sam-Dina). The possibilities for generating these exceptional families seem endless, but the opportunities nearly ran out for thirty-four-year-old identical twins Marcy and Tracy, from Santa Cruz, California.

Tracy and Marcy lived closely matched lives. They lost their first tooth, chose their college major, decided to marry, and tried to have children at about the same time. But after Marcy had given birth to a son and a daughter, Tracy was still childless. Tracy and her husband, Brian, tried getting help from fertility specialists, but nothing worked. In fact, their attempts could not succeed because Tracy had contracted a rare, mysterious illness—Valley Fever—that made pregnancy dangerous. But Marcy and Tracy's identical genes gave Tracy an unusual chance at motherhood, one that most women don't have. Today, Tracy has a daughter, Marcella (Ella), and Ella has the same biological connection to Tracy and Brian that she would have had if she had been conceived the old-fashioned way.

Thirty-four-year-old identical twins Craig and Mark Sanders of Houston also shared a special relationship. And they wanted wives who would understand it. They met identical twins Diane and Darlene Nettemeier in August 1998 at the annual Twins Days Festival in Twinsburg, Ohio. Craig was attracted to Diane and Mark was attracted to Darlene, and vice versa. A double wedding followed about a year later.

This marital arrangement might strike some people as inappropriate or even perverse. Each person's in-law is a genetic duplicate of his or her spouse, something that could cause rumors, especially since all four twins live close together. But such reactions are less likely to occur in people who have seen the two couples together. Instead, their story tells us how unique and individual even identical twins can be. Indeed, all four twins insist that they could not have married anyone other than their spouse.

Craig and Diane and Mark and Darlene came together by choice. But I met another set of four who began naturally and were just as enlightening. They were three-and-a-half-year-old Canadian quadruplets Nicky, Benny, Matthew, and Michael.

The quads were conceived without reproductive assistance by thirty-six-year-old Mandy Scarr and her partner, thirty-nine-year-old Rob Crosmas. The set of four consists of six possible "couples," but unlike the Sanders, some of the Scarr-Crosmas "couples" are friendly and some are less so. In fact, the friendly partners were matched behaviorally from birth, while the less friendly partners were not.

EVERYDAY WONDERS

Watching the quads one weekend was an educational adventure into the roots of human social behavior and organization. And watching Mandy and Rob take care of their kids gave me a look at the emotionally and financially wild venture of raising multiple multiples—along with two older daughters.

Scientific mysteries are evident all around us, especially in families with twins, twin-like partners, and triplets plus. In a time of increasing social fragmentation, twins are staying together, reminding us that it is hard to replace the social and emotional benefits that families provide.

10

Selfless Love

They are "Marce" and "Trace" to their family and friends, "Moon" and "Treen" to each other. Identical twins Marcy and Tracy were born in San Jose on April 24, 1967, to John and Patti McEnery. John was twenty-four and Patti was twenty-three at the time. The couple already had a two-and-a-half-year-old son, John. As John joked, life was "great, then these two gorgeous twins came along, the attention shifted, and I've been trying to get noticed ever since!"

The family moved to Aptos, California, when the twins were in the first grade. John recalled the time that five-year-old Tracy broke her collarbone and couldn't go in the water. "Marcy shadowed her and protected her," he explained. "Since Tracy couldn't go swimming, Marcy wouldn't go either." According to their mother, "Marcy was always a little more outgoing and pulled Tracy along when they were little." This pattern repeated, sometimes with variations. If one twin did better in school or in sports, the other one felt bad. "We have always felt more for the other one than for ourselves," Marcy said.

The twins both married when they were twenty-five and began trying to have children two years later. Marcy had a daughter, McKenna, and a son, Tom, Jr., but seven years later Tracy was still childless. Her infertility was puzzling and heartbreaking. Marcy said, "I have to do this [have a baby] for you." Tracy said, "Great, I'll let you."[1]

Six-pound fifteen-ounce baby Marcella (Ella) McEnery Winterhalder was born on January 24, 2002. Tracy didn't have the baby herself, nor did she donate her egg to her sister or to another surrogate. Still, Ella had the same biological relationship to Tracy as all babies have to their mothers. And Tracy's husband, Brian, was Ella's biological father, even though he wasn't present at her conception. How was this possible?

The answer to that question lies in the creative use of the twins' identical genes: Marcy was artificially inseminated with Brian's sperm. Neither Marcy nor Tracy could say which twin thought of it, but the plan was there, waiting to be tried, and both twins knew it. In May 2001, Marcy conceived Ella—then she handed her over to Tracy eight months later, in the delivery room, with their families watching. Tracy had been a mother for a year and a half when I met her.

Tracy and her family occupy the lower floor of an apartment building that sits close to the ocean.[2] The windows in their apartment afford gorgeous views of the beach and sky. Tracy's house epitomizes the California lifestyle—open, airy, and casual.

Tracy was waiting on the front lawn when I arrived. She is five feet four-and-a-half inches tall, with short, stylish blonde hair and brown eyes. She is athletically built, partly from years of running on the beach with her twin sister. She wore a long-sleeved lavender T-shirt with "Good news will come to you from far away" printed across the front. The shirt was a gift from Marcy, who found this message in a Chinese fortune cookie. After Ella's birth, Marcy discovered the T-shirt and gave it to Tracy. Tracy loved it.

Marcy and her two children, seven-year-old McKenna and four-year-old Tom, Jr., drove over from their home in Aptos, just five minutes away. (Marcy and Tom have two homes, one in California and one in Oregon, where Tom is still working.) McKenna is blonde and brown-eyed like Marcy, and Tom is red-haired like his dad and gets freckles in the sun, just as his dad used to. Then, ceremoniously, Tracy carried one-and-a-half-year-old blonde, blue-eyed Ella outside. Marcy pronounced her "a perfect combination of Tracy and Brian." Ella's two cousins ran over and patted her. Marcy said that her children sensed

EVERYDAY WONDERS

they were like siblings to Ella, since their mother had "carried Ella in her tummy."

Tracy brought the three children upstairs, so I had several minutes alone with Marcy. Marcy was a half-inch taller and five pounds heavier, but still a stunning reproduction of her sister. I confused them many times that day, even though small differences in their expressions and demeanors were soon apparent. Marcy, for example, seemed slightly more confident, determined, and self-assured than her sister. But their similarities overwhelmed their differences. Both twins brought energy, enthusiasm, and excitement into Tracy's living room when they told their story. As with dance partners, their expressions and gestures were well matched. We talked about what it meant to be a twin.

Tracy and Marcy traced their awareness of their twinship to early childhood, insisting that their attachment was "always there." They attended separate classes in elementary and middle school, so they had some experiences apart from each other. Marcy said that they argued in junior high school over "girl stuff—clothes, shoes, personal items. We slammed doors and grabbed each other's hair. But I don't remember that too clearly." People ask them if they are, or were, competitive, "but I don't get this," Tracy said. The twins rarely dated in high school and college. Boys asked them out, but they didn't pay attention to which twin was which. According to Tracy, boys wanted to date "one of the twins. They didn't get to know us as individuals. We said 'no way.'" Instead, the twins opted to spend their time together. "People thought we were stuck up," Marcy said. But in fact the twins were so close that they didn't feel a need for boyfriends. As Tracy explained, "We were like spouses—she was my significant other in that sense."

After graduating from high school in 1985, Marcy and Tracy attended the University of California, at Santa Barbara. They roomed together except in their sophomore year, and they took the same classes until their junior year, when Marcy majored in sociology and Tracy majored in psychology. That same year they went to Rome together for a study abroad program. Always athletic, the twins played a variety of sports. And though they each had their own favorite activities, their interests and achievements mostly coincided.

Back home after graduation in 1989, Tracy worked toward a teaching certificate, while Marcy worked for a real estate license. One night while they were at a local restaurant, Marcy met her future husband, Tom. She knew him slightly, as they had attended the same high school and had some common friends. Both twins were there that night, but Tom talked to Marcy first. "Tracy is attractive, but I don't know why I was more attracted to Marcy," Tom explained. "Maybe it's because Marcy is more outgoing and I like that. She bought me a drink—then it was all over!" Marcy, for her part, was immediately attracted to Tom.

Marcy and Tom dated throughout that summer, but Tracy didn't have a boyfriend. "I was a bit envious of their relationship, but it was exciting for me that she had someone," Tracy said. "I was on my own, I was a 'third wheel' to Marcy and Tom, but not really because Marcy made me feel welcome." Marcy "felt bad" that Tracy didn't have a boyfriend because "it's wonderful to love someone." Things stayed that way for nearly a year, and while a boyfriend could have derailed some twinships, it didn't upset this one. The twins' relationship succeeded because Marcy cared about Tracy's feelings, and because Tom felt strongly about the importance of family. "If Marcy and Tracy had not gotten along, I would have been really upset," he said.

Nine months after Marcy met Tom, Tracy met her husband, Brian, at a mutual friend's wedding. She asked him to dance, he called her the next night, and they have been together ever since. Brian had also attended the twins' high school, one year behind them. "I met Tracy before I knew Marcy," he explained. And while I knew Marcy was taken, I felt an unexplainable attraction to Tracy. She is more low key than her sister." It turned out that Brian and Tom had grown up across the street from each other, and Tom had been close to Brian's older brother.

For the next few years, Marcy and Tom and Tracy and Brian lived together in a house they called "The Love Shack." The twins liked each other's partners, but they admit that they are attracted to different types of men. They agree on "cuteness," but Tracy likes quieter types than her sister. Tom is a tall, lean redhead who co-owns a business with his brother, managing tax-deferred real estate exchanges. Brian is a tall, lean brunette (whose head is now shaven) and licensed paramedic. The twins' brother, John, commented that Tom is more outgoing and "easier to read" than Brian, who is more reserved and independent.

The twins married in 1992, Marcy in July and Tracy in October. "We were on the same track," said Marcy. "And marriage was the next stop." They were each other's maid of honor, and each twin said that her sister "never looked so beautiful." But they would see each other less often after Marcy's ceremony, because she and Tom moved to Salem, Oregon, five hundred and fifty miles away, where Tom's business had relocated. They visited each other often, however, and they joked that their husbands felt "unnecessary" because the twins were always on the phone with each other.

Marcy and Tracy began trying to have children at the same time, two years into their marriages. They wanted their children to be the same age so they could raise them together. Both of their husbands also wanted children; Tom and Marcy had thought about having three.

Marcy delivered her first child, McKenna, in September 1995. But Tracy was childless. "I was not surprised at first," said the twins' brother, John. "You think you can plan having children, but it's not that easy. We have four kids, but there were three miscarriages in the middle." Time passed, however, and the family noticed. Tracy dreaded her cousins' phone calls because they were often about a new pregnancy or delivery. "Tracy never resented Marcy," the twins' mother said. But according to Tracy's brother, John, "family functions were tough—occasionally, you got engrossed in a family moment with your child, but then you thought about Tracy and what she was going through. You felt a little guilty because she wasn't able to feel that way. She may have wondered if she would ever have that kind of moment with a child of her own—or if a child of hers would be left behind because there wouldn't be any same-age cousins."

"Marcy's first pregnancy was awesome, but I was still not pregnant," Tracy said. After two more years of trying, Tracy and Brian underwent extensive medical testing that resulted in a diagnosis of "unexplained infertility." Tracy then began in vitro fertilization (IVF), a process by which a woman's eggs are extracted, then mixed with her partner's sperm in a petri dish to form embryos, which are then implanted in her uterus.[3] "This gave me a mission," Tracy said. "I felt I was doing something to help myself."

This was also the time that Marcy made "the hardest phone call I had to make, to tell Tracy I was pregnant for the second time." Tracy insisted that "it was such a happy time," but both twins' joy was tempered. Marcy explained, "I knew she felt bad and I felt bad for making her feel bad. But the great thing about us is that I let her know it was okay to feel that way."

Tracy had five IVF treatments over the next few years, which included several egg/sperm/carrier combinations. The first two trials, in 1996 and 1997, used the conventional mix of Tracy's eggs and Brian's sperm, but both were unsuccessful. Given that Brian's sperm were found to be normal, the doctor thought the problem might be with Tracy's eggs. This possibility inspired Marcy to donate her own eggs to be mixed with Brian's sperm and implanted into Tracy at the start of cycle three. So in 1998, Marcy started hormone treatments to stimulate egg production. Interestingly, she produced the same small number of eggs as Tracy had previously, causing the doctor to shake his head in wonder that she had became pregnant on her own. Embryos were implanted, but one month later the results proved negative. This left the twins with what they thought was their final plan: Tracy's eggs would be fertilized with Brian's sperm and implanted into Marcy. "I would never have asked this of Marcy," Tracy said. "But she came to me and she said we will do it like this." However, their husbands had to agree—both men did, though Tom and Brian knew that the twins' minds were made up by the time they gave their opinions.

"Tom was reluctant at first," Marcy admitted. "When I approached him it was not a question, it was a statement. I said, 'I need to do this for her and for me. I hope you are on board.' And he said he knew he couldn't stop us." But Marcy knew Tom was being realistic. "He worried about complications even though my other pregnancies were easy. And he worried about an emotional attachment I might feel to the child. But he saw my struggle over what Tracy had gone through and he understood." She continued, "I was in so much pain because I could not enjoy what I had unless Tracy was also enjoying it. Even though I had two children and Tracy had none, I felt infertile because the other attempts had failed."

Tom recalls being "a little bit shocked" when he heard the plan: "It was surprising to think our lives would take that turn. We had thought about having a third child, but we weren't set on it. But helping Tracy was a great experience." The twins' brother, John, said that Tom was wonderful throughout Marcy's pregnancy: "If there was anything 'behind the curtain,' you didn't sense it. But it would be a lot to deal with."

Tracy said that Brian felt "great" about what they were doing. "Being a paramedic, he came to this with a logical, medical mind," she explained. "He told me he would love to see me pregnant, but if it was not meant to be then Marcy was the best choice since she has the 'same' body." Brian recalls having two reactions to the plan. "What a great deal!" he thought at first. But then he asked, "Do we really want to put Marcy through all that? Then I was convinced that she wanted to do it, so after thinking about it and doing some research, I was excited." But Tom and Marcy wondered if the twins pushed Brian too hard.

To their brother, John, the twins' plan was a natural and spontaneous act: "I wouldn't hesitate to lift a heavy package for one of my sisters. Marcy's carrying a baby for Tracy was a huge gesture, but it would be like my lifting a package for one of them—a foregone conclusion." Their mother, Patti, thought the idea was "wonderful."

But the result of this attempt was no better than the previous ones. This was puzzling because Tracy produced eggs that did not differ in quality from Marcy's. At this point, Brian was afraid of jeopardizing his wife's health and begged her to stop. Tracy wanted to keep trying, however, and had exploratory surgery to see exactly why she couldn't get pregnant.[4] The results were shocking. Tracy had *coccidioidomycosis,* or Valley Fever, a lung condition common in the southwestern United States and northwestern Mexico.[5] Tracy was baffled as to when or how she contracted the disease. She had a cyst on her ovary and the "worst case of scar tissue" her doctor had ever seen. The scar tissue covered her abdomen and blocked her fallopian tubes, so that "nothing was working right." Pregnancy was out of the question because the type and amount of medication Tracy required to control the disease could be fatal to both a pregnant woman and her fetus. Thus Valley Fever was both the cause of her infertility and the reason she had to stop trying to have a baby.

Marcy continued trying "to get pregnant for us." She did this by inseminating herself with Brian's sperm, via the "Turkey Baster Method," using a hand-held syringe. Doctors refused to perform intrauterine insemination, or IUI, using a catheter because of legal concerns—what if the pregnant mother decided to keep the child?[6] Then the twins' luck changed.

No one knows how or why it happened, but in February 2001 Marcy received a call from attorney Shelley Tarnoff, telling her that Dr. Christos Zouves, from Daly City, California, had changed his mind and was willing to perform the IUI. Dr. Zouves had been Tracy's infertility doctor during her failed IVF attempts, so he knew the twins well. They called him because "we thought he would be our only chance to get what we wanted done." He eventually agreed because the twins "had such a unique bond . . . they were a wonderful team."[7]

Marcy and Tracy were ecstatic, even as Marcy walked alone on the beach, asking herself, "Do I really want to do this?" But she knew that her answer was yes. Again, both husbands were consulted, and as before, Tom was hesitant but agreeable and Brian was enthusiastic and grateful. Tom said, "If we had not had our own kids, it would have made all the difference—all the difference in the world."

Soon it was May, and Tracy called Marcy to wish her a happy

Mother's Day. It was not a happy holiday for Tracy, but she should have looked more closely at a fortune cookie message she had found earlier: "An emptiness will soon be filled."

"I was alone in the house," said Marcy. "It was two weeks after the procedure. When I woke up my breasts felt tender so I thought this might be a sign. So the next day I went to the store, bought the kit, peed on the sample, but didn't look. Instead, I took a shower. When I finally looked, the result was positive. I tried calling Tracy, but she wasn't home and I didn't want to call anyone else. I was so excited I wanted to tell her myself."

Marcy reached Tracy later that afternoon. "You'll be celebrating Mother's Day next year," she told her. "Call everyone and tell them you are pregnant." In a way, she was.

"This feels so good, and I get to feel it for nine months—no, I get to feel it for a lifetime," Tracy wrote in her diary. Tracy accompanied Marcy to all her medical appointments over the next nine months and lived with her in Oregon during the final month of the pregnancy. When the baby came, Tracy felt like her own body had given birth. As for the delivery room, "Who wasn't in it?" Tracy joked. The crowd included the twins, their spouses, their brother and sister-in-law, their parents, Tom's parents, and Brian's mother. They had all invested emotionally in Tracy and Brian's struggle and had watched Ella's conception plan take shape. Everyone wanted to be there for the conclusion.

During the delivery, Tracy was on one side of Marcy, Tom was on the other side, and Brian assisted in the delivery. Tom said that Brian's participation was Marcy's idea, "and although admittedly it was a bit strange, I think that it was a great thing to have him so involved at this moment. Being right there is something no father could ever forget."

Marcy wanted Ella placed on Tracy's tummy so that her sister would feel like a new mother right away. But Tracy insisted that Marcy hold the baby first as her true "auntie." Tracy called her sister "selfless—Marcy didn't want it to be about her." Tracy also recalled that "there was a lot of champagne and tears and hugs by everyone." According to Tom, "the look on Tracy's face [when Ella was born] is

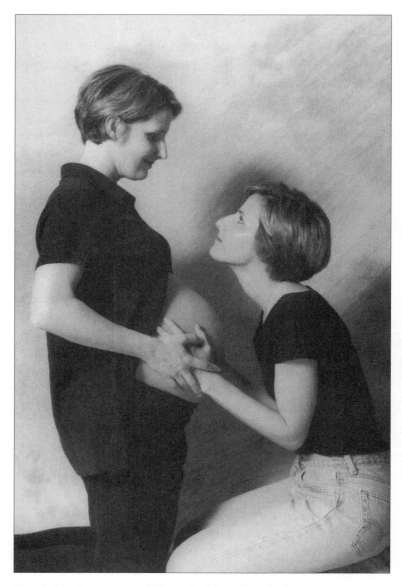

"I took this picture at our old house in Salem. Tracy had come up to stay with us for the final month of the pregnancy, so it was probably right around eight and a half months. I remember that moment very vividly—we had taken a few pictures and were laughing a bit. Tracy kneeled down, put her hands on Marcy's stomach, looked up at her, and was suddenly overcome with emotion. I knew that we had a great picture." (Photo and reflection by Tom Moore, Marcy's husband.)

something we will all remember forever." Tom also traded glances with Marcy: "Her face told me everything I needed to know. Marcy wanted that moment for Tracy just as much as Tracy herself wanted it. It was a great thing that had just occurred, and I was extremely proud of my wife."

What these twins accomplished comes as close as possible to being the "real thing." It's not quite the real thing because behavioral differences between identical twins, such as eating or drinking habits, could affect a developing fetus. Still, DNA testing could never tell that Marcy had conceived and carried the baby. In fact, what Marcy did is equivalent to what many twice-married women do: have children with different husbands.

What did Marcy think about this pregnancy compared with her other two? She said that she was "nervous" in the beginning, eager to pass the critical twelve-week mark. Most expectant mothers have these

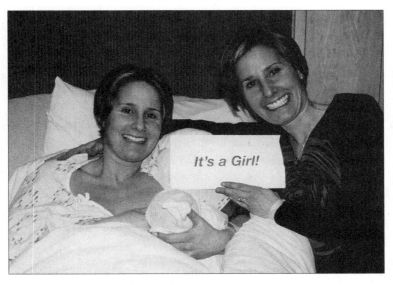

Marcy (left) and Tracy with baby Ella in between, just moments after she was born. (Photo by Marie McEnery, the twins' sister-in-law.)

concerns, but Marcy was not an ordinary expectant mother; she was an extraordinary expectant aunt: "I was never the mother. I knew that when the infant was out it was Tracy's." And that's how it was—and is. But Marcy does feel extra close to her niece "because," as she explains, "I carried her."

Maternal hormones predispose new mothers to take pleasure in infant care. Baby Ella was not good at nursing, so Marcy's breasts were pumped and the twins took turns feeding her, passing bottles back and forth. According to Marcy, "We had a great thing going." In hindsight, they agree that bottle feeding Ella was probably a good thing, since it helped dampen Marcy's possible feelings of attachment. Two weeks after her daughter's birth, Tracy left Oregon to go home to California. This was the only emotionally trying time for Marcy, whose body and brain expected a baby to nurture. "Like any great anticipated event, it was a letdown when it was over," she admitted, "and being away from Tracy and Ella was hard. I cried." But with exercise and rest her physical and emotional health returned. Marcy and Tom also worried that their own children had been shortchanged because Marcy's pregnancy had taken time away from them. "But the kids' reward was seeing their new cousin," Marcy said. Meanwhile, Ella was making Tracy happy: "It's fate. I couldn't have children, but I have a twin and that made it possible. That's what it means to be so close."

Ella's biological connection to Tracy and Brian did not, however, override Oregon's family laws. Marcy explained that pregnant women's husbands are considered to be the fathers of their children, so Tom had to sign his paternal rights over to Brian. Then Tracy had to adopt Ella because her own eggs were not used for the conception. The easiest way to do this was for Tracy to become her step-parent. Brian didn't have to adopt his daughter because he had donated the sperm.

But do legal realities override emotional ones? Marcy said, "I never felt like Ella's mom. And she doesn't look like my kids, so that helps." But other people noticed the special bond between aunt and niece that Marcy had hinted at earlier. "Tracy shares Ella with Marcy," said John. "If Ella cries Tracy and Marcy are equally likely to comfort her. It's not just maternal instincts—it goes back to the sharing thing and how Marcy feels about Ella. Tracy allows this to happen."

Marcy also shared her niece's real name, Marcella. "I knew my twin would give me a girl, I dreamt about it," said Tracy. "And I wanted to give her a version of Marcy's name." Marcy wears a Tiffany bracelet charm shaped like a heart that Tracy gave her two months before Ella was born. The heart was blank then, but now the name *Marcella* is engraved on one side; the other side says, "I hold your name, you hold my heart."

"Tracy's back!" said friends and relatives when they saw Tracy and Ella together. With Ella's birth, Tracy and Marcy each resumed their daily lives, but the twins were still living apart. Recently, Marcy and her family moved to Aptos, close to Tracy and her family. "Tracy and I had always dreamed of raising our children together," Marcy said. McKenna and Tom, Jr., seem to sense something unusual about Ella's birth, but they "don't really know how the whole thing worked," said Marcy. "They understand that Aunt Tracy had an 'owie' in her tummy and couldn't have children—so I offered to help."

Tracy and Marcy don't think about Ella's birth every day, but when they do they remember that having her wasn't easy. Tracy said, "I couldn't talk about this if I didn't have Ella. She's such a good baby, she fills my heart every day." Tracy looks forward to the time when her daughter will understand the remarkable circumstances surrounding her birth. Tracy has drafted a children's book that will tell a twin surrogacy story with a happy ending, using kangaroos as the main characters. Some day it will be fascinating to hear what Ella thinks about it all.

Marcy and Tom's generosity is striking. How many husbands would agree to such a plan? How many women would enter a pregnancy as an aunt, not as a mother? Most of the twins' friends thought that Ella's birth was "cool," and Tom said that he would have agreed to the same procedure if Marcy had been the childless twin. "More people in our situation would do this than they realize," Tom said. But given Tom's worries over Marcy's well-being after "giving away (for lack of a better

Tracy (left), holding Ella, and Marcy with her children, Tom, Jr., and McKenna. According to Marcy, Tom and McKenna sense something unusual about Marcella's birth, "but they don't really know how the whole thing worked." (Photo by Nancy L. Segal, July 2003.)

term) this child"—even knowing it would be in their lives—keeping the end result in mind was essential. In the end, Tom sipped champagne and voiced no regret that the baby wasn't his.

Looking back, Brian said that Ella's birth was *not* too good to be true; it happened because everyone wanted this baby. "Being a paramedic has opened my eyes to how different people can be," he said. "Some people were closeminded when I explained my situation to them, but they were thinking like armchair quarterbacks—they didn't understand Marcy and Tracy's bond. If Marcy wanted to do this again, why would I deny her that fulfillment?" In fact, everyone who knew Marcy and Tracy were delighted by Ella's birth, and most saw it as an understandable outcome of the twins' close relationship.

I wondered if Brian had felt emasculated by the way his daughter

EVERYDAY WONDERS

was created. "No way—after all, Marcy got pregnant, didn't she?" He added, "When I look at Ella, I see my own child."

I was sure that Ella was the happy ending to the twins' story, but I was wrong. Tracy and Brian had considered adopting a child to give Ella a younger brother or sister. But Marcy hinted that she might repeat the insemination to have another baby for Tracy and Brian. If Marcy and Tom were to have a third child of their own, he or she would be six years younger than their son, Tom Jr.—in their opinion, not a good age gap. And having a third child seems less important to them than having a second, biological child for Tracy and Brian—and a sibling for Ella.

I heard about this idea from the twins before their brother, John, did. John was surprised when I mentioned it, but only momentarily, because he hadn't considered it before. He noted, "It would be just another day in the life of those twins . . ."

And it was just another day in the life of those twins. In September 2004, Tracy wrote to say, "By the way . . . Exciting news you may want to add to your book . . . there's a new baby on the way! Marcy is pregnant and carrying our baby again . . . What a gift they have given us, and twice!"

The baby was due April 24—Marcy and Tracy's birthday.

POSTSCRIPT. On April 28, 2005, I received an e-mail message from Tracy: "We had a girl on April 21, and she's beautiful. Her name is Gianna Patricia. She weighed seven pounds four ounces—a little bundle of happiness. Marcella is so excited to have a sister. Somehow, that's just how I knew it would be, two girls, just like Marcy and me! Now I can watch them grow and think about the two of us. It's perfect."

11

Marital Math

It was a weekday morning in February 1999. Thirty-four-year-old identical twins Craig and Mark Sanders from Houston, Texas, were taking their usual jog before heading to the office. The athletic, dark-haired twins asked each other, "How is it going? Are you in love?" They were referring to their girlfriends, twenty-eight-year-old identical twins Diane and Darlene Nettemeier, from Aviston, Illinois. That same morning, blonde, blue-eyed Diane and Darlene were driving together to St. Louis, where they worked as legal secretaries.

Craig and Mark knew that if one of them was ready to propose, they would both have to do so and at the same time. Both twins said they were ready. So they designed a marriage proposal website on their shared laptop computer. They decided to place the computer in a top-floor suite of the Florida hotel where all four twins would be vacationing a few weeks later. Craig and Mark felt that proposing in the same big room, via the web page they had created, would let them propose together while maintaining each couple's privacy. They would have flowers, candles, and soft music in the room for the big night—March 5, 1999—seven months after the twin pairs met.

When they arrived in Florida, Craig and Mark told Diane and Darlene that their dinner reservations were for seven o'clock. But the men suggested that they first go to the hotel's top floor to see the view.

Diane and Darlene resisted because neither likes to be late, but Craig and Mark got them to agree. When they entered the suite, Diane and Darlene heard a "cracking noise," which was the sound of a bat hitting a ball, a feature of the computer's screensaver. Craig and Mark both designed websites for professional and college athletic teams, so the sports motif made sense. But Diane and Darlene were suspicious.

The four twins gathered around the computer. Moving the mouse opened a screen with two links: *Diane* and *Darlene*. Darlene, who is more outgoing than Diane, clicked first. Her link brought her to a screen bordered by small red hearts, with the question, "Darling Darlene, will you marry me? Click here if *yes;* click here if *no.*" Clicking *yes* would bring a picture of a diamond engagement ring; clicking *no* would bring the message, "No, seriously . . . (maybe you misunderstood the *question?*)" But Darlene clicked *yes,* and when she did, Mark took her to one side of the room, knelt on one knee, and asked her to marry him. Then he put a diamond engagement ring on her finger. Meanwhile, Diane clicked on her link and answered *yes* to the same question. Craig gave her an engagement ring identical to the one that Mark had given Darlene; it had even been cut from the same stone. The jeweler told the twins that it was the first time in thirty years that he had sold identical engagement rings. The only difference was that the jeweler etched the letter *C* inside Diane's ring and *M* inside Darlene's so that the women wouldn't mix them up.

The couples celebrated their engagement with a lavish dinner. Craig and Mark had really made dinner reservations for eight o'clock, so they arrived on time.

Coordinating marriage proposals may seem unusual to non-twins, but twins think about things differently. Mark explained that Darlene and Diane are even closer than he and Craig. He was sure that Darlene would have worried if he had proposed to her privately—what if Diane had not received the same offer from Craig? In that case, Darlene might not have said yes. Craig and Mark were both convinced that proposing to Diane and Darlene together would improve their chances for success, and they were right.[1]

I met Craig and Mark and Diane and Darlene when they stopped by my lab in 2001. It was the third time I had seen identical married couples, a special class of unions that are like *quaternary marriages*.[2] I was fascinated by the sight of two identical couples, more so than by the sight of two identical pairs; twin couples are less common than twin pairs, though the frequency of twin-twin marriages is unknown.[3] These families raise fundamental questions about who we marry and why—as well as what makes us happy.

I was struck by the comfort and fit the twin couples shared as they sat around and talked. All four of them used collective pronouns (we, us, ours) when they described their homes, jobs, and vacations. And everyone's in-law was a genetic replica of his or her spouse, making the families familiar from the start. In fact, Diane looked puzzled when I asked her about her "brother-in-law." When I explained that I meant Mark, she said, "Oh, he's immediate family." Unlike most identical twins who marry non-twins, these four were relieved that they didn't have to fight their spouse to have time with their twin; each knew without explanation that their spouse's twin would be important in everyone's life. It was an intimacy that others could envy.

I was curious about several things. First, how did each twin know which member of the other twin pair he or she was attracted to? Craig, who was the leader in his twin pair, had married Diane, who was the follower in hers. They seemed happy, but could the opposite pairings have happened just as easily? And did the wives think that their husbands were "interchangeable?" Second, Craig and Diane had brought along their children, two-month-old identical twin boys Colby and Brady. Darlene was four months' pregnant with her first child, a girl. Were Mark and Darlene jealous of Craig and Diane because they had twins? It is generally believed that, unlike fraternal twins, identical twins don't run in families, though some studies suggest that they might.[4] Regardless, most people would assume that what happens to one identical couple also happens to the other. Did Craig and Diane

EVERYDAY WONDERS

and Mark and Darlene think of each other's children as their own? Finally, what were the advantages and disadvantages of marrying twins?

There was no time to pursue these questions the first time I met the couples. In order to understand the twins' relationships, attractions, and lifestyles, I visited them in March 2004 at their homes near Houston. Going between the two houses was easy because they are connected by a common backyard.

I started on Friday morning at Craig and Mark's office, a two-room suite in a suburban office building. The twins now devote full time to their website, *twinstuff.com,* which posts news and information about twins and sells twin-themed birth announcements, clothing, and equipment. The twins also founded and direct Twinstuff Outreach, and they run the annual Texas Twins Round-Up.[5] Craig has also been teaching high school part-time, something Mark is considering doing as well.

When I arrived at their office, I was surprised to find that Mark was alone. Seated at Craig's desk, Mark explained that his brother was home taking care of Colby and Brady, who had colds. But Craig was never far away because the twin brothers instant messaged each other all morning; Mark updated his twin on new orders and Craig updated his twin on his twin sons' health.

Mark was dressed casually in a sport shirt and slacks. At age forty, he still had the same thick dark hair I remembered from several years before. And while he had retained his athletic build, he had put on a few pounds. Mark was a delighted father of two daughters, two-year-old Reagan and ten-month-old Landry. He was friendly but sometimes reserved, as if protecting a piece of himself. Mark also has a cool sense of humor, such as when he joked that the first names of his children and his twin's children, Colby and Brady, turned out to be the last names of prominent Republicans.[6] "But none of us are Republicans," he insisted. Then he told me about growing up as a twin. Craig, Diane, and Darlene were just as enthusiastic and thoughtful when I spoke with them later.

CRAIG AND MARK. Craig and Mark Sanders were born on February 22, 1964, in East Orange, New Jersey. They were the youngest of seven children. Their mother, Lenni (Lenore), a marketing manager, had been married twice, first to Michael Sovern, with whom she had three children. After they divorced, Lenni married Ronn Sanders, a bookstore owner who had two children. Then Lenni and Ronn had Craig and Mark. "We were like the Brady Bunch, except that my mom had two more kids," Mark said.

"They were adorable," said Doug, the twin's half-brother, who is three years older than Craig and Mark and who lived with them until they were seven. Doug Sovern is a reporter for KCBS radio in San Francisco. He and the twins have the same mother, but Doug looks more like his father—he is shorter than the twins and seems more intense and driven. His first conscious memory was of the Beatles' appearance on *The Ed Sullivan Show,* and his second was of Craig and Mark coming home. "I was incredibly happy to have more kids to play with," he said. "I thought that my mother had taken someone else's baby because there were two."

DIANE AND DARLENE. Diane and Darlene Nettemeier were born on August 16, 1970, in Trenton, Illinois. Darlene is forty-five minutes older than her sister. Their parents, twenty-four-year-old Sharon and twenty-eight-year-old David Nettemeier, had no idea that they were having twins; they already had a four-year-old daughter, Tina. Sharon said that when the twins arrived she was excited, but shocked, and wondered how she would manage. But she did. Sharon was a "stay-at-home mom" until her girls grew up, and her husband, David, was a truck driver. Sharon had dressed her girls alike as children, something Darlene enjoyed but Diane (who is less outgoing) did not because the attention made her uncomfortable.

Diane and Darlene have always been each other's "built-in best friend." They were never apart growing up except when Darlene was hospitalized at age six for seizures. They were so close that their mother worried they might never find husbands.

CRAIG AND MARK. Craig and Mark left New Jersey for Virginia, then Wisconsin, before moving back East to New York at age seven. Their father, Ronn, died when they were five, and their older half-siblings eventually moved out. Because their mother worked, the twins relied on each other a lot. They were "latch-key kids" in a rough part of the Bronx. According to Mark, "You had to be tough to survive, but we were unique—we were two small twins and we were cute so people didn't pick on us much." The twins had friends, but not as many as most kids. This is not unusual; many identical twins are so compatible that they don't need other companions. The twins' half-brother, Doug, said that Craig and Mark were shy as kids: "But they loved each other. They were an insular team, joined at the hip."

The twins went to high school in California, where they moved when they were thirteen. There they discovered a flair for debating and became president, at different times, of the speech and debate team. And they enjoyed sports, an interest they pursued throughout their public relations careers. They were competitive with each other, but not jealous—when Craig scored higher on the SATs and when Mark was named Student of the Month, the other twin was just "a bit upset." They also discovered girls, though neither had a serious girlfriend in high school or at UCLA, where they attended college.[7] But Craig and Mark sometimes talked about how much fun it would be to date twins.

DIANE AND DARLENE. In high school, both Diane and Darlene took classes in typing and secretarial skills, then lived and worked together after graduating. Neither twin had wanted to go to college. Darlene got a job first, as a legal secretary in St. Louis, but when there was a vacancy in her office, Diane filled it. Diane and Darlene actually liked the hour's drive each way between Aviston and St. Louis because it gave them time to talk.

Darlene said that she and Diane hadn't dated much in high school or in their twenties because their closeness "scared guys away." Like Craig and Mark, they both thought it would be fun to date twins, but meeting twins in their small town was unlikely. People often told them that because they were so close they would have to marry twins, or at least brothers.

CRAIG AND MARK. After graduating from UCLA in 1986, Craig and Mark both got public relations internships in the University of Houston's Athletics Department. Then they separated for five years, when Craig took similar jobs in New York City, first for the Mets baseball team, then for a cable television station. Mark said that during those years the twins "devoured the Internet—Craig egged me on, but I needed no egging." In 1996, the TV station folded and Craig returned to Texas. The twins discussed new career plans. According to Mark, Craig suggested that they form a joint website development company. Mark agreed and came up with the name: TwinSpin Design. The business, which they launched in 1996, was a success; eventually, an Austin-based company bought them out and hired them to run the Houston office. The twins worked exclusively on TwinSpin Design until the dot.com crash, at which time they turned their attention to their personal website, twinstuff.com. Now they work together every day and see each other every night.

"I am a bit uncomfortable saying I love him," Mark said. "But I worry if Craig is out and is late coming home. If the bond were gone, what would happen?" Mark admitted that he has relied on Craig more than he should: "Maybe Craig leads by example—lots of times I let him take charge." But Mark is content with this situation. Maybe he feels secure when his brother calls the shots. This is how it has always been. As Doug explained, "When they were riding tricycles, Craig decided which way they went."

Mark admitted that he takes his twinship for granted. He and Craig are very close, and though they argue often over silly things like forgetting to shut the door or deciding who should walk the dog, their arguments end quickly. Their dog, an Australian shepherd named Shadow (which Craig and Mark owned before they were married), lives with Mark and Darlene; Diane was attacked by a dog and is scared of them.

Craig named their dog—"Shadow" came from a question asked by a former acquaintance, who, seeing Craig alone, asked, "Where is your shadow [twin]?"

DIANE AND DARLENE. Diane and Darlene have grown closer since moving away from their family in Illinois to live in Texas. "I know it's odd, but we never fight now," Diane said. Darlene admitted that it was an "adjustment" working in different law offices; they had enjoyed working together in St. Louis. They looked so much alike, Darlene explained, that one of the lawyers in St. Louis didn't know for several months that there were two of them.

Darlene talked more than Diane when the twins were together, but they both talked a lot when they were apart. Darlene is the more dominant twin, and Diane seems comfortable deferring to her sister.

The twins' division of mental and emotional labor, tacitly acknowledged by them and by many identical pairs, helps divert jealousies and conflicts. We don't know exactly where these roles come from, but birth order, birth size, and serendipity probably factor in. It would be wrong to think of these contrasting roles as *differences;* mostly they are slight variations of the twins' matched personalities and temperaments. Early twin studies found that identical twins were more alike in some ways when they were apart than when they were together, perhaps because they could act more freely on their own.[8] Later studies failed to support this finding. In my own work I have seen slight changes in identical twins' behavior when they are apart, as though once separated they are more like themselves. Mark was lively, outgoing, and confident when he talked to me alone, but he was quieter around Craig. And Darlene was more assertive than Diane, but mostly when they were together. Perhaps twins' subtle behavioral changes elude current personality surveys, which are intended to pick up on what people do most of the time. An outside observer watching twins would most likely notice their slight behavioral changes, caused by who is present and what is happening.

Later that day, Mark and I picked up his two daughters from child care. I waited in the car and watched Mark come back, holding both girls and pushing a stroller. Reagan was a lively little girl with a shy smile, and Landry was a quiet baby with an intense stare. Mark spoke gently to both of them as he fastened them into their safety seats. He called himself and Craig "at-home dads"; they are responsible for bringing the children to and from day care because they work nearby, whereas their wives work downtown. Craig and Mark also enjoy preparing meals. They like being involved in these domestic tasks, maybe because they are living the life that they always wanted. "We married late, at thirty-five," Mark said. And because their father died when they were young, they may take parenting extra seriously.

Mark and I headed to the twins' homes, located in a large housing development. Each twin has keys to the other's house, and though they "barge in during the day," they ring the bell at night. Their doors are rarely locked, however, and the twins and their children wander freely back and forth through the shared backyard. (There have been mornings when Craig and Mark have called each other on their cell phones to discuss the day's business, then wandered into the yard and unknowingly continued their telephone conversation while standing only a few feet apart.) The two houses are not identical because the company that built them doesn't allow adjacent homes to be the same. Each house was constructed according to the couple's specifications. Craig and Diane selected a model with red bricks and a downstairs master bedroom; Mark and Darlene chose a house with tan bricks and an upstairs master bedroom. Diane and Darlene had wanted an intercom between the two houses, but their husbands had refused. It wasn't just the cost. Mark explained, "I value my privacy more than the others."

Having separate homes was a step up from the twins' first four months of marriage. Owing to construction delays, the newlyweds lived together in Craig and Mark's former house. "It was cramped; none of us liked it," Mark said. But he complained mostly about the limited bathroom time.

Mark and I stopped briefly at his home before visiting Craig's. Toys were all over the floor of the large living room and family room, and there were lots of family pictures on the walls, mostly of both twins' children. I looked for two wedding portraits, one of each couple, but there was just one. Maybe this was a way to establish privacy.

When Craig opened the door I saw another Mark. Like his twin, Craig was dressed casually in a polo shirt and jeans. The only distinguishing physical feature I saw was a slight downward turn of Craig's mouth—and Craig is right-handed, whereas Mark is left-handed, a difference that occurs in 20 to 25 percent of identical twin pairs.[9] But unless the twins were smiling or writing, they were virtual duplicates of each other, and I confused them many times. Like Mark, Craig was friendly, personable, and slightly reserved, but he had a more commanding presence at times. Craig showed the same physical affection and gentle manner toward his children that Mark had shown toward his. Even when his twin sons were fighting upstairs, I overheard Craig ask, "Are you playing nicely, boys?" (Given that they were screaming at each other, Craig was most likely showing the same sense of humor I had seen in Mark.)

The twins say that their homes are different, but they looked similar to me. (True to form, identical twins often exaggerate their minor differences.) Craig's home is more "child friendly" that his brother's, however; the living room is wider and brighter, so the two families spend most of their time there. Craig and Diane (but not Mark and Darlene) had several books from Lucy Fitch Perkins's children's series on twins around the world.

Craig's earliest memory of being a twin was watching *Sesame Street* on television seated next to "someone": "I didn't think I was different from my other brothers and sisters, except that there was this person who I played with. Many people strive for love and friendship, but twins have this bond from birth." Craig also talked about the twins' joint business. "I let Mark do the graphics and I do the text or come up with the concept," he explained. "Mark is more willing to listen to me than vice versa."

I wondered how the twins' relationship with each other had affected their experience of meeting, dating, and marrying their wives. This particular story begins when Craig and Mark and Diane and Darlene met at the annual Twins Days Festival in Twinsburg, Ohio, in August 1998.[10]

Each year since 1976, twins, triplets, quadruplets, and their families have gathered in Twinsburg for a weekend of look-alike contests, talent competitions, and social events. Recently, psychologists, physicians, and economists have gone to Twinsburg to gather data from the several thousand twin pairs (mostly identical) who attend; I set up a research booth on twin-family relations at the 2000 festival. The atmosphere at this event is upbeat because everyone understands that they share something fundamental and positive. Twins dress alike and act alike, feeling more like themselves here than any place else.

Diane and Darlene were returning to Twinsburg for the fifth time. Their grandparents lived two hours away and had encouraged them to attend. Diane and Darlene say that they didn't go to Twinsburg to find dates; they went to have fun. But the festival draws lots of male pairs— and Diane and Darlene sometimes worried that they might be attracted to twins who lived in another city or state.

Like Diane and Darlene, Craig and Mark had always thought it would be fun to go to Twinsburg. They didn't go to the festival to meet women, and they didn't know that some quaternary couples had come together there. But according to Craig, once they saw all the fun everyone was having, "we made a more conscious effort of at least finding out if female twins we were meeting were single." Like Mark, Craig admitted that he and his brother had dated infrequently: "I was not a Romeo or a Casanova, but I did date a little more than Mark." He added, "I never thought we had to find girlfriends at the same time." But they did.

Twinsburg was a working weekend for Craig and Mark—the Houston Astros had just acquired Randy Johnson from Seattle, so the twins spent time updating the team's website. But on Saturday night while Craig was working, Mark went to the lounge, where "a big social scene" was unfolding. Male twins whom he and Craig had challenged at the "Golf Scramble" were talking to Diane and Darlene. "These guys were there to hit up on girls, so I thought I would save them," Mark said. "I started talking to them. I got along great with both of them, but I couldn't tell them apart. They asked me where my twin was, so I left to get Craig." Craig was instantly attracted to Diane. Mark said, "Craig made it a point—he wanted to talk to Diane." And Craig agreed. "I had an attraction to Diane," he said. "They looked different—Diane has sweeter, gentler features, but I am not sure what attracts people. I guess it's a physical thing; but once we started going out it became a personality thing. It would have been that way if I had met them separately." Craig will never know that for sure.

The two twin pairs had brunch together the next morning. Diane and Darlene dressed up "like for a date—I was impressed," Mark said. "And people in the restaurant smiled at us, the two identical couples, and asked us if we were married. It was a good omen." But Mark still couldn't tell the women apart. "Craig talked to Diane," he explained, "so I talked to Darlene—he instigated it. But it wasn't like I had the 'leftovers,' I was more than happy to talk to Darlene." The brunch lasted only ninety minutes because Craig and Mark had to return to Houston. En route to the airport, Craig asked Mark if he liked one twin better. Mark couldn't tell them apart, but he said that he liked the one he had talked to (Darlene). According to Mark, Craig said, "Good, because I like Diane. So you e-mail Darlene." Mark explained, "I trust him."

Craig and Mark had written down the twins' e-mail addresses, but they were identical except for the three-initial prefix: *dln* and *dan*. Fortunately, they knew the twins' middle names—Ann and Lynn—and reasoned that Diane Ann and Darlene Lynn "sounded dumb," so their names were probably Diane Lynn and Darlene Ann. Without previous discussion, they began their messages the same way: "I hope I am writing to . . ." They got it right, and Diane and Darlene answered. According to Darlene, after the brunch the sisters had asked each other, "Is this it?" Diane had thought that Craig was cuter and Darlene had thought the opposite, which Darlene decided was "luck or destiny." A week later, Craig and Mark sent them cards, teddy bears, and balloons for their birthday. And they exchanged lots of e-mails.

The four twins decided to meet in September in St. Louis. This time Mark could tell the women apart; he noticed Darlene's deeper dimples and straighter hair. The twins exchanged more e-mails in October, then met again in Las Vegas in November. It was Mark's idea for the two couples to do things separately and to meet occasionally. Mark and Craig's half-brother, Doug, was "stunned" when he heard about their trip to Las Vegas: "It seemed unlike anything Craig and Mark had ever done."

Mark said that after their Las Vegas weekend he and Craig had "decided separately, but had discussed how things were going with Diane and Darlene." They agreed that things were "getting serious." So they invited the sisters to Houston for New Year's Eve 1998. Then they went to Aviston, around Valentine's Day 1999, to meet the Nettemeier family.

Later that month, Diane and Darlene returned to Houston to appear with Craig and Mark on TV.[11] Craig joked, "We took them from being farm girls to talk show celebrities." The program's producer had hoped that Craig and Mark would propose to their girlfriends on the set, but they didn't. "We weren't ready then, but we knew that we would be ready in March when we went to Florida," Mark said. They were. The two twin pairs were married eight months later, on November 13, 1999. The wedding invitation—the first official decoupling of the twins—lists Darlene and Mark at the top, so Diane and Craig said their vows first. The ceremony had been videotaped, and we would watch it later that night.

Diane walked into the kitchen while I was still talking to Craig. She looked a lot like she had when I first met her. She is five feet four inches tall, blonde, and trim with a solid build. She looked a little tired but seemed to wake up when her twin boys ran to hug her. Darlene and Mark and their children showed up a few minutes later. Darlene is a different version of Diane, not a reproduction the way their husbands are. Her hair is parted on the left side and falls over her fore-

EVERYDAY WONDERS

head, while Diane's is parted in the center and brushed back. Darlene seems more businesslike than Diane. For example, she filled out the forms I sent her and answered my e-mails more quickly.

It was easy to forget whose house we were in. Darlene and Mark were as much my hosts as Diane and Craig. And their children ran around freely, probably because they played there often, perhaps more often than at their own home.

That night the twins and I watched their wedding videotape, "The Double Wedding." It included photos of both twin pairs growing up, scenes from their weekend trips, and the ceremony itself. Diane and Darlene looked gorgeous in their identical gowns and hairdos, which they wore "to avoid being compared"; Craig and Mark wore slightly different tuxedos and were listed as best men as well as grooms, which was confusing at first. Guests tossed Doublemint gum at the dance that followed, and they ate slices from one cake with four figurines at the top. Mark and Craig's half-brother, Doug, called the wedding "the biggest thing that ever happened in Aviston—three TV crews covered it."

More interesting than watching the wedding tape was watching the twins watch it. They stared at their childhood pictures and at their individual interviews, conducted before the ceremony. Diane thought that she sounded nervous, but I thought that she sounded great, and Darlene told me that she had a smile on her face all day. Craig and Mark came across as excited, happy, and amazed by what was happening. There is an enchanting, almost magical quality about their wedding, probably because of the enormous interest that identical twins generate, highlighted by the sight of the double couples in love. Even though both pairs had joked about marrying twins, they had found mates who would allow their twinship to flourish. It was probably a more serious hope than any of them had realized.

I watched the twins again when we played tapes of their appearances on several talk shows.[12] When one of the hosts asked if it "gets annoying" when people stare at them, Craig said, "not really," and Mark nodded slightly. Then Mark explained how the twins met, and Craig said that he had preferred Diane from the start. Darlene's face didn't change, maybe because she has heard this story often. The topic of mate selection—each twin's insistence that they never could have married their spouse's identical twin—never came up. I raised this issue with all four twins a lot.

Mark, who confused the sisters at first, said, "Only after I started to know Darlene I became more attracted to her because, spiritually, we are more alike. I am the younger, less dominant twin in my pair and Darlene is the older, more dominant twin in her pair. I like the fact that she takes charge, and Diane is happy to let Craig take over. But we all get along." Darlene said that she "knew right away that Mark was the right one."

Everyone agreed that each twin had ended up with someone who was similar to his or her twin sibling. Maybe these marital relationships worked because they replayed features of what was important and familiar in everyone's life. The four twins also insisted that the reverse pairings (Craig with Darlene, Mark with Diane) would have been disastrous. According to Darlene, "Craig and I are more alike. We'd butt heads because we would both take charge." Their views support recent twin studies.

Research shows that identical twins do not pick similar types of spouses, suggesting that who we love and marry is decided more by romantic infatuation and chance than by clear rules or reason. In one study, very few people who were married to an identical twin said that they could have "fallen for" their spouse's co-twin.[13] This is surprising given that identical twins usually like the same people. Perhaps when it comes to mates, subtle between-twin differences are important.

Both pairs included a more dominant twin and a more submissive twin, and all four were convinced that only certain marital pairings were possible.[14] But what if Craig had met Darlene alone, and Mark had met Diane alone? On her own, Diane may have been more outgoing, as Mark had been when I saw him alone at his office. At first Mark had had difficulty telling Diane and Darlene apart, but it was their physical resemblance that threw him. More important, what if Craig had not returned to the Twinsburg social hour with Mark? One twin I know was attracted to her twin sister's future husband, but she happened to be on the other side of the room when her sister met him first.

Another unanswered question is why some couples have identical twin children and other couples don't. According to Craig, Darlene wanted to be pregnant first. "She was older," he explained, "and Diane said 'okay,' so we waited a year. But Diane became pregnant first, in October 2000, after only one month of trying. When we told Mark and Darlene, they were ecstatic for us." But there was more to come. In November Diane and Craig returned to the doctor for Diane's first follow-up visit. Diane's doctor always knew that she was a twin, but she didn't know until then that Diane had married a twin. And though the doctor didn't suspect multiples, she said, "Let's see how many are in there." According to Craig, just a few minutes later she announced that it was twins. "But she said it so matter-of-factly that we didn't take her seriously," he recalled. "Then, when we saw the ultrasound, we were shocked." Craig continued, "I thought that meeting twins, marrying twins, and living near my twin was destiny, a dream. And having twins was destiny, too, one more step along the way."

That night, Craig and Diane felt some trepidation; they told Mark and Darlene that they had "news to share." Mark said that he was "ecstatic and in a state of disbelief" when he heard about the twins. Craig recalled Darlene saying, "Don't tell me it's twins." Diane said that Darlene was happy for her, but sad that they weren't pregnant together. This may be one of the few times that Diane "decided" things, though they were beyond her control.

Identical twins don't usually run in families, so Craig and Diane beat the odds. But because the two Sanders families are visible in the "twin world," Mark and Darlene probably felt that everyone would expect them to have twins, too. Craig said, "We have always been careful that no one should raise this [issue] with them." Doug recalled that at first the family teased Mark and Darlene about having twins, then thought better of it. Darlene got a little weepy remembering that time: "It was hard because Diane was having two and I couldn't have one."

Darlene finally became pregnant two months after Diane, but she miscarried. She would eventually get pregnant two more times, but both couples weren't destined to have twins—Darlene and Mark have two non-twin daughters, Reagan and Landry.

All four children are endearing, but the novelty of identical twins gives them an edge in a crowd. Not surprisingly, Brady and Colby, who are always dressed alike, get a little more public attention than Reagan. (Landry is too small to mind much, though Craig thinks that the baby is slighted.) At age three, the twin boys and Reagan are often mistaken for triplets; they are full siblings, genetically speaking, and they are only six months apart. But they may look less like triplets as they get older. Diane thinks that as Landry gets bigger people may think that Darlene's daughters are twins. Darlene plans to dress them alike for special occasions, but not every day.

Craig loves watching his boys play. "Their level of interaction is amazing—they remind me of Mark and me," he said. I have heard other adult twins say the same thing about their twin children, grandchildren, nieces, and nephews. Mark says he isn't jealous that Craig has twins because "twins are a handful." He added that any jealousy on Darlene's part disappeared when she had her own children, though he did admit that having girls made things easier since his brother had boys. "Another boy might have been an odd man out," he said. I suggested that Mark's daughters are a unique non-twin addition to this family, but he disagreed: "Having twins is unique no matter what."

The two families have attended the Twinsburg festival every other year and will continue to do so. No doubt, other twins will fuss over the twins who have twins—they will stand out even from the twin crowd. I wonder what Mark and Darlene will think, or if Reagan and Landry will eventually resent these vacations. Mark recalled that his older half-siblings felt jealous when he and Craig got attention that they didn't get. Diane belongs to the local mothers of twins club, but she attends meetings infrequently, and she dresses her twin boys alike only because she was raised that way; she herself didn't like the atten-

Back row (left to right): identical couples Craig and Diane; and Mark and Darlene. Front row (left to right): the "genetic full siblings"—Colby, Reagan, Brady, and Landry. "One big happy families" is how one of the couples put it. (Photo by Nancy L. Segal, March 2004.)

tion as a child. As I passed through Diane's kitchen, I saw a notepad that read, "World's Greatest Mom of Twins."

All four twins feel very close to their nieces and nephews; Diane and Darlene think of each other's children as their own, but their husbands are cautious on this subject. "I occasionally feel like Colby and Brady are my kids," Mark said. "I am definitely there when their parents aren't around and they need my help. But I do not overstep my boundaries." Craig said that each couple does a lot for the other couple's children, but pays more attention to their own kids. Mark also said that the children can identify their own parents 95 percent of the time. "They do not understand the twins married to twins thing," he explained.

Craig and Diane and Mark and Darlene have merged their new life with their old life and they seem happy. Their situation exemplifies the advantages to living with extended family. Both couples have "built-in babysitters," allowing them to enjoy a night out knowing that their children are cared for by "an extra loving aunt and uncle." Craig and Mark still co-manage their website and record sports statistics for professional games on weekends. When Craig stayed home to take care of his twin sons, he knew that Mark would run their business smoothly. And Diane and Darlene know that if one of them gets delayed at work, they will still have a ride home, without resentment.

Saturday morning is a laid-back time for the twins, as it is for many families. When I arrived at Craig and Diane's house at 9:30 A.M., Reagan had already wandered across the yard for waffles. Diane showed up wearing a T-shirt and pajama bottoms—she had been taking care of her twins and hadn't had time to get dressed. Darlene was already there, and Mark came over with Landry. Diane and Darlene do their Saturday errands together while their husbands watch the children. The three of us went to Home Depot and to Sam's Club, both giant discount stores. The twins consulted each other on what to buy as we went through the aisles, and they helped each other load and unload packages from the car without asking. They also knew that while their husbands would be working at a Women's Professional Basketball Association event that night, they would not be alone.

I wondered if the twins saw drawbacks to their lifestyle, but Diane and Darlene insist that they see none. Marrying twins was probably the only way that each could have a family as well as each other. Mark, who had raised privacy concerns earlier, said that he and Craig (but not Darlene and Diane) take sides when their children fight, with each father believing that his brother's kids started it. Although he and Craig have no special friends of their own because they work together, he insisted, "it's nothing that keeps me up at night." Craig said that "there are no downsides to the relationship aspect [of my twinship], but if I want to get away I can't because we live together and work together—however, I can't imagine that I would totally want to be away. It's not a real downside." Nonetheless, he looks forward to a time when each couple can take an adult vacation alone, leaving the children with the other family.

Mark and Darlene have decided not to have any more children for now, but Craig and Diane are hoping for a daughter. When I asked Craig how he would feel if they had twins again, he said that their story would not be more remarkable. "Life in the media spotlight is over," he said. But a second twin set in this family would be extraordinary, and the media would love it. Craig smiled and raised his eyes as he finally admitted that he'd love another set. "But I'd take just one child, too," he added.

People only see the unusual sides of these two families—the identical twin pairs falling in love, the identical couples living next door, and the nearly identical lives that they lead. But for Craig and Mark and Diane and Darlene, their situation is part of the background, surfacing mostly on birthdays and anniversaries. Being twins is all they have known, so marrying twins probably feels natural to them. Mostly, all four twins face the same challenges at home and at work as everyone else, except that they are more likely to be stared at.

Mark and Craig always wanted separate homes. They have known children who were born to quaternary twin couples who suffered because they were raised in the same household. These individuals were confused over which "parents" to listen to and unsure about whose home they lived in. Craig and Diane and Mark and Darlene hope that their children will not have these problems; some day we may know what they think about their identical parents, aunts, and uncles.

As I was leaving for the airport, Craig and Mark's mother, Lenni, asked, "Wouldn't it be something if Brady and Colby married twins?"

12

Quad Boys Are Fine . . .

On October 3, 2003, I took a train from Toronto, Ontario, to Cobourg, a town of 16,000 people one hour away. The passenger next to me said that the town of Colborne (just outside Cobourg) is famous for the Big Apple Restaurant, which serves an assortment of delicious apple-based delights. A giant replica of the fruit sits beside the restaurant and is visible from the highway that runs past it. But my mind was focused on a different attraction: the unique multiple-birth experience waiting for me in the smaller town of Brighton. I would spend the weekend with the "Quad Boys," three-and-a-half-year-old Nicky, Benny, Matthew, and Michael. I would also meet their sisters, Jade, eight, and Tifanee, twelve, as well as their parents, Mandy Scarr, thirty-six, and Rob Crosmas, thirty-nine.

Quadruplet births are rare, occurring in approximately 1 of every 1,000,000 natural conceptions and deliveries.[1] The rapid rise in assisted reproductive technology (ART) since the late 1970s elevated that figure to 1 in 800,000 in 2001.[2] In fact, there has been a 400 percent increase in higher-order multiple births (defined as triplets, quads, and quints) since 1980.[3] Most higher-order multiples are fraternal, having developed from separately implanted embryos resulting from in vitro fertilization. The tendency of women to delay childbirth until after age thirty-five has further increased the rate of fraternal multiple births, though less so than ART.[4] The Scarr-Crosmas quads were exceptional in several ways, making them the scientific crème de la crème of higher-order multiples.

Born on January 26, 2000, this Canadian quartet was conceived naturally—their mother, Mandy, was thirty-two at the time, three years below the age of risk for fraternals. She actually delivered two identical twin sets simultaneously: sturdy, fair-haired Nicky and Benny, and delicate, brown-haired Matthew and Michael, an event thought to occur in only 1 of every 24,000,000 births.[5] Simple rearrangement of these little boys yields four fraternal twin pairs—Nicky and Matthew, Nicky and Michael, Benny and Matthew, and Benny and Michael. As such, they are a researcher's dream, allowing physical and behavioral comparisons between genetically identical and non-identical same-sex sets exposed to shared intrauterine and home environments. Apparently, Mandy released two eggs that were separately fertilized to produce fraternal twins. Then, sometime during the next two weeks, each zygote (fertilized egg) split to produce identical twins.

Scientists have been divided over whether identical and fraternal twinning are related or unrelated events.[6] Another controversy concerns possible genetic influences on identical twinning: We know that genes can play a role in fraternal twinning, but the rare occurrence of identicals and fraternals in one family, let alone in one pregnancy, suggests that the two types of twins could be genetically influenced *and* linked in some families.[7]

The quads are a medical marvel, but there is a tragic wrinkle in their story. Nicky, the firstborn, was diagnosed with spastic quadriplegia, or cerebral palsy (CP), when he was four months old.[8] According to Judy Scarr, the twins' maternal grandmother, "When Nicky was in the neonatal intensive care unit, he looked like he was in the Bahamas, he was too laid back (floppy) for a normal baby." From the time Nicky was born until he came home two months later, he was more irritable than his brothers. His eyes were noticeably crossed and he was colicky. At three and four months Nicky's arms and legs grew stiff and his feet pointed downward. His body was very rigid. It was then that Mandy's physician, Dr. Elizabeth Asztalos, visited their home. "We have something to discuss," she said. "Nicky has CP, doesn't he?" Mandy asked. "Yes," the doctor said. "Well, I knew that already," Mandy replied. She and her partner, Rob, had done quite a bit of research on the physical risks of quad births. She was upset but not crushed. "I had no time to be devastated," she explained. And that was true—besides Nicky, three newborn quads and a four-year-old daughter were crying for attention.

Two identical twin pairs, four fraternal twin pairs, one quadruplet set, and a disabled child in one reproductive gamble raise lots of questions. But answers are not always available.

Ever since Mandy contacted me in the summer of 2002 for information about her children, I have been intrigued by her story. I had many questions for her as well: How did she and Rob react to news of a multiple-multiple pregnancy? What were their greatest parenting challenges? Did each child prefer his identical co-twin to his two fraternal co-quads? How did their elder daughters, Jade and Tifanee, handle the attention that multiples inevitably attract? And how did the presence of a child with cerebral palsy affect everyone's daily life?

In fall 2003, when the quads were three-and-a-half years old, I suggested to Mandy that I visit her family for several days. She and Rob were very receptive to this idea; they had read widely about multiple-birth pregnancies and believed that their home was the "perfect environment" for a study.[9] But Mandy was also blunt: "I am not going to cook or clean or do anything different for you; you can eat pizza with us in the kitchen. You are going to see what always happens in this house. And bring earplugs." Terrific, I thought. That's just what I want.

As the train pulled into Cobourg, I spotted Mandy's big gray truck in the parking lot. Having visited hundreds of families with twins, I am used to oversized vehicles outfitted with matching car seats and littered with toys, tissues, water bottles, candy wrappers, and loose change. Mandy had told me what she looked like so I would recognize her—short and heavy-set with dark hair worn in a bun—and I did. She brought three of the quads and her daughter, Jade. Mandy wore a baggy white T-shirt, red plaid pajama bottoms, and comfortable shoes, and instead of a bun her hair was pulled into a half ponytail. "I don't care what I look like," she had warned me. "By the end of the day things are spilled all over me. Even without the boys, I wouldn't go to the beauty parlor." But she admitted that raising quads left her with little private time, the only real source of contention between her and Rob.

The ride to the quads' home took thirty minutes. I sat in the front seat next to Jade, with Benny, Matthew, and Michael strapped into car seats behind us. I turned around occasionally to study the three boys. Benny was on the far left, Matthew was in the middle, and Michael was on the right. This was a familiar configuration—Matt and Mike, one set of identicals, seemed to inhabit a separate world. And, though not intentionally, they let others know it by their close physical proximity, their carefree spirit, and their congenial play. They spoke in similar soft tones—unintelligible to me, but perfectly understandable to each other—and shared a "zoned-out, go-with-the-flow" attitude, according to their parents. Matt and Mike were oval-faced, slender, and fair-skinned. In fact, they were virtually indistinguishable except for a small mole on Matt's left cheek. Their soft curly hair reached almost to their shoulders, so I was surprised to learn that they had just had haircuts. "Their long hair is lovely, it fits their artsy personality," Mandy explained. I pride myself on being able to tell twins apart, but I would confuse Matt and Mike many times that weekend.

Benny was a striking contrast to his two brothers. His face was round, and his straight blond hair was short and slightly spiked. Nicknamed "Benny, the Bull Dog" by his parents, he was athletic and dark-skinned, and short hair fit his solid build. He was more fidgety than his brothers, eager for freedom from the confines of his car seat. I wondered how much he would resemble Nicky, his presumed identical twin, who was at home. DNA testing on the twins had not yet been done, but Mandy was "99.9 percent sure" that the quad boys had come in two sets of two.[10] Even their belly buttons, ear lobes, and penis shapes were matched within pairs, distinctive between pairs. Later, she showed me a chart with the scribble "MC/DA x 2," medical shorthand for two pairs of monochorionic/diamniotic twins, consistent with identical twinning.[11] A fused triplet placenta (Nicky, Matt, and Mike) and a separate single placenta (Benny) were noted.

More than once, Jade interrupted my observations of Benny, Matt, and Mike with stories about her special passions: animals and camping. Mandy had explained to her that this was my weekend with the quads, but old jealousies linger. "Do we really need more kids?" Jade once asked. This is a common complaint among older siblings of infant multiples, because being babies *and* twins guarantees that the multiples get lots of attention. By contrast, when single children come after twins, their younger age gives them a competitive edge.

It struck me that Benny carried a tough burden—prenatal fate had christened him the constant reminder of what his identical twin brother Nicky might have been, if not for the whims of prenatal life. "During the pregnancy, it felt like Nicky was grinding into my pelvis," Mandy said. Matt and Mike also carried emotional weight. Their play, their chatter, their joy in each other's company would ultimately remind Benny of what his twinship with Nicky might have been like and what he had missed. At age three-and-a-half, the boys were too young to grasp these aspects of their situation, but the seeds were being sown. The three brothers only sensed that Nicky was different from them and that his presence affected everything they did. Mandy observed, "We are more like families with CP children than families with quads."

The Scarr-Crosmas home sat about forty yards off the main highway. The family had lived there since the quads were eight months old. They owned several acres of land and eighteen different animals. Mandy joked, "We have too many animals *and* too many children," but her tone hinted that one (or both) remarks was probably true. She also explained that Jade and Tifanee were daughters from previous relationships—Jade was hers and Tifanee was Rob's. Jade lived with them, while Tifanee lived with her mother twenty miles away and visited each weekend. Both girls were strongly attached to the quads, though Jade occasionally felt like a wallflower at her four half-brothers' parties. In contrast, Tifanee seemed more involved with the boys—I

EVERYDAY WONDERS

would see her hugging and playing with them more often than Jade did. This is understandable; Tifanee was not raised with the quads so she never vied with them for parental attention. She was also eight years older.

The first room we entered was supposed to be a garage, but it housed an iguana named Igor, a snake named Cornelius, and various other living and non-living things. What really grabbed my attention, however, was a large circular rack that held more than thirty small sweatshirts, coats, and jackets—it was the kind of item you see only in department stores. "Quantity" was something I would see a lot of over the next few days. For example, Mandy urged me to help myself to whatever food I wanted from the cupboard and refrigerator. The first time I did I was overwhelmed—the food closet was like a minimart, jammed with boxes of granola bars, crackers, fruit juice, and other snacks. Everything in the house seemed to come in multiples.

Then I saw Nicky. He was propped up in his wheelchair next to the kitchen table, with his father's big arms around him. Nicky was a near replica of Benny, leaving no doubt in my mind that the two boys were identical twins. Nicky had Benny's same blond hair, solid build, oval face, and dark skin, but he was not the same. Nicky wore a baby bib and was being fed by his father. In between swallows, Rob wiped the drool off his son's face with a yellow towel. Nicky's eyes were still crossed, but just slightly thanks to corrective surgery. Despite the marked developmental differences, I could see that Nicky and Benny were made from the same DNA. The two identical sets created a kind of Noah's ark before my eyes.

Rob, the quad's father, had dark curly hair that was mostly hidden under a Toronto Maple Leafs hat, which he wore the entire weekend. At our first meeting he wore a white sweatshirt, blue jeans, and sneakers. He was five feet eight inches tall and 180 pounds, and he seemed like a giant papa bear beside his four cubs. He was warm and welcoming toward me, and completely comfortable with my presence in his home. Of course, he was used to having people around—he and Mandy had received help from more than forty friends and volunteers when the quads came home. I studied Rob and Nicky closely—Rob had a particular affinity for this child, evident in the ease with which he held him and spoke to him. And Nicky seemed happiest and most relaxed when his father was nearby.

Nicky's face broke into a gleeful smile when we arrived. He is a mentally alert child who hears and sees exactly what his brothers do. He cannot speak clearly despite weekly speech therapy, but he occasionally produces recognizable sounds—his versions of "ball," "Nancy," and "I love mummy" delighted the adults, though they were not always recognizable to me. To the extent that Nicky shared Benny's athletic sensibilities, I could imagine his unhappiness at not being able to run around and play. Mandy read my thoughts. "It would be so interesting to see Nicky without CP—especially since Benny is so athletic and Matt and Mike can't run without tripping." Perhaps the family looked to Benny as a way to identify Nicky's potentials and frustrations. Unfortunately, Nicky has not achieved the developmental milestones his parents had hoped he would—he cannot sit and will most likely remain dependent on caretakers.

I distributed the chocolate Halloween lollipops I had brought for the boys. Benny, Matthew, and Michael yanked off the wrappers and went to work on their treats. Rob removed the wrapper from the fourth pop and held it to Nicky's mouth. The children quieted as children do when their attention is keenly focused. I used this time to talk to Mandy and Rob about their relationship, their decision to have a child together, and their news of Mandy's pregnancy—especially when they learned she was carrying more than twins.

Mandy Scarr and Rob Crosmas have never been married, to each other or to their previous partners. Both grew up in Oshawa, Ontario, fifty miles from Brighton. Mandy had a certificate in parks and recreation and a diploma in urban tree maintenance from Sir Sanford Fleming College, in Haliburton. She had done tree-trimming and related work for the Oshawa Parks Department for seven years before having the quads. Since then, she has only had time for occasional gardening. Rob earned a diploma in mechanical engineering technology from Durham College, in Oshawa. He now designs measuring equipment and car parts. He met Mandy six years ago when he played in a local baseball league and Mandy came to watch. They dated and eventually lived together in a house they both owned. Their decision to have one child, maybe two, came partly from their wish to get away from notions of "your child" (Tifanee) and "my child" (Jade) and to have a more traditional family. It also came partly from Rob's sense that he had missed out on raising his daughter, Tifanee; and he wanted greater involvement with his own children than his parents had had with him. Mandy and Rob agreed that a boy would round out their all-girl brood.

Once they decided to have children, Mandy got pregnant quickly. Her stomach grew so fast that by three months she was wearing full-term maternity clothes. An ultrasound taken at four months showed triplets. "I see three fetuses," the doctor told her. But he said nothing about their health status or condition, leaving Mandy terrified—the thought of having three babies at once was overwhelming, but the lack of information was worse. Even scarier, he gave her a sealed letter for her family physician, which she opened immediately after leaving his office. It was a referral to Women's College Hospital in Toronto, a high-risk gynecological clinic.

Mandy called Rob to tell him he would be the father of three. "Gotta go," was all he said, and hung up. But Mandy wasn't worried; she guessed that he was simply stunned. And he was—Rob knew that triplets would mean moving to a larger home and losing Mandy's income since she would have to stay home with the kids.

Several days later, Rob and Mandy headed to Toronto for the next series of ultrasounds. After three hours, the technician announced, "It's a boy." Then she said, "It's another boy." Then she stopped speaking. When she was unable to get a stable reading on the third fetus, Rob lost patience and left to take a smoke. What no one realized at the time was that the technician was getting different (but stable) readings on babies C and D, not unstable readings on baby C. Eventually, the entire staff was consulted and a fourth fetus was confirmed. Neither

Mandy nor Rob was especially upset. As Rob explained, "Triplets were a big deal, they changed everything. Quads just added to it." Perhaps only parents of higher-order multiples can grasp this sort of reasoning. But then, most parents who conceived naturally are surprised that they ended up with multiples in the first place.

Mandy and Rob still ask themselves, "Why us?" Fraternal twinning runs in families, mostly on the mother's side. Rob's maternal uncles and Mandy's paternal aunts are fraternal twins. But there was another clue of which Mandy and Rob were unaware: Research has shown that parents of twins (both identical and fraternal) are more often left-handed or ambidextrous than their own same-sex singleton siblings.[12] Rob is ambidextrous, whereas his sister, Lezlie, is right-handed. (Mandy and her brother, Jeff, are both right-handed.) One of Rob's twin uncles, his mother, and his maternal grandmother are also left-handed. However, the causal link between left-handedness and twinning is unknown.

Mandy, meanwhile, had her own quadruplet theory: Before she knew she was pregnant, she had spent several hours tossing hay in her parents' barn, after having worked a twelve-hour day for the Parks Department. "It felt like a thousand degrees in there," she said. "Maybe the heat caused the two fertilized eggs to divide." Researchers have not yet determined the events behind identical twinning, though delayed implantation (attachment) of the fertilized egg in the lining of the uterus has been linked to identical twinning in rabbits.[13] I find it amazing that this vital bit of information has been so elusive, despite years of study. Mandy and Rob also have an explanatory joke—Mandy released two eggs, and Rob's sperm "blew them apart."

Mandy stayed in Women's College Hospital for the rest of her pregnancy. At twenty-eight weeks and six days, her blood pressure rose dangerously, making delivery of the quads imperative. They were delivered the morning of January 26, 2000, by Cesarean section: Nicky at 11:47, Benny at 11:48, Matthew at 11:48:30, and Michael at 11:49. Five staff members monitored each child. Once delivered, each baby was held up for Mandy to see. "I just got a quick look at baby A's leg, and I

EVERYDAY WONDERS

think I missed baby C," she recalled. Mandy didn't touch or see her infants for two days because they were rushed to incubation units. But when she did, "It was awful. They looked like little birds. They were covered with tubes and wires. Maybe it's not bad with one infant, but it's too much to deal with when you have four." Everyone but Matt had needed transfusions and had shown heart murmurs. And when Mandy held Benny for the first time at one month, his nurse said he had had a brain hemorrhage two weeks earlier.[14] Actually, Benny had craniosynostosis (premature fusion of some cranial bones, preventing skull expansion); he didn't need surgery, but he has a ridge on his skull that will need cosmetic repair. All this left Mandy sobbing uncontrollably.

"We sent no birth announcements because this was not a celebration of happiness," Mandy explained. "They were born too early, they were not sufficiently 'baked,' and we were scared we would lose them." Then, soon after the delivery, Mandy's blood pressure rose again and her lungs filled with fluid, sending her on a scary visit to the emergency room. Rob worried that he would go home alone with the four boys. I remember the intense media attention surrounding the "miraculous birth" of the McCaughey septuplets, in Iowa, in November 1997. But the difficult physical and emotional consequences of such multiple births are less often acknowledged. Like Nicky, two of the McCaughey septuplets have cerebral palsy. Higher proportions of twins than non-twins are affected with this condition, owing to their more precarious birth situations.[15] Of identical twins with cerebral palsy, only about 40 percent have co-twins who are also affected, demonstrating that birth events may differ between twins.[16] Increased birth trauma in twin deliveries may also partly explain the higher frequency of left-handedness among multiples relative to singletons.[17] The quads included one lefty (Nicky), one "switch-hitter" (Mike), and two righties (Benny and Matt).

I looked at the quad boys, all of whom were of course oblivious to events preceding their birth and delivery. They were polishing off their lollipops and becoming restless. Rob led them to a family room upstairs to watch a Disney movie. He carried Nicky. Moments later, I caught a glimpse of the three boys seated on the long sofa. Matthew and Michael sat together, displaying the incredible match of their profiles and postures. When I mentioned this to Rob, he recounted his "Stephen King–like experience." When Matt and Mike were two, they were seated together on a rocking chair. When Rob looked up at them they turned toward him at exactly the same moment, their heads cocked at exactly the same angle. Suddenly they turned away and began rocking as if on cue. "I was actually afraid of them," he said.

Benny sat on the end of the sofa, looking like a third wheel next to Mike and Matt. Rob held Nicky on his lap nearby. The odd thing about Nicky and Benny was that their resemblance was so changeable—with Nicky in his wheelchair or on his father's lap they looked alike in general, but different in detail, mostly in expression. They had the same physical build and facial features, but Benny looked alert and focused, whereas Nicky stared vacantly with his mouth open or, more often, with a big grin. When they were napping or playing on the floor, however, Nicky and Benny could be mistaken for each other. While they slept, their expressionless faces masked the differences that were apparent when they were awake. And when they were playing, events could trigger the same response, causing their separate faces to blend into one, even if momentarily.

Nicky and Benny were not just physical matches. Mandy noticed that when Nicky was upset, it was Benny who patted his head—Matt and Mike were "less interested" in consoling their brother. Nicky also seemed happier being with Benny one-on-one than being with all three of his brothers. In fact, many of these patterns were evident when the quads were only one-and-a-half years old. I believe this is partly traceable to each identical pair's similar and compatible behavioral styles, based partly in their common genetic makeup. Mandy and Rob have watched Nicky and Benny go from happy to sad in seconds—one harsh word devastates them. They will sob and push down their lower lip. Matt and Mike, however, are fairly oblivious to harsh tones. If reprimanded, they probably wouldn't care so long as they could go off and be together.

I have always believed that twins reveal most about human development when they are just being themselves. So it was with the quad boys—Matt and Mike and Nicky and Benny (albeit, to a lesser extent) were pairing off in ways that seemed tied to their genes, despite being raised in close quarters.

With the quads occupied by the movie, Mandy gave me a tour of their house. It was large. The kitchen, dining room, living room, play area, and bathroom were downstairs. Five bedrooms, a family room, a playroom, an office space, and a second bathroom were upstairs. There were several television sets (one big-screen), sound systems, and a high-speed networked computer; Mandy had insisted on these comforts knowing that she would be home a lot with the boys. But the tour's crown jewel was the children's clothes closet—its shelves were bursting with shirts, shorts, pants, sweaters, pajamas, socks, and underwear, all neatly stacked and labeled. I wondered if Mandy ever dressed all four boys alike, or just the identical pairs, as she did that weekend. "You try finding four size fours," she snapped.

Matt and Mike share a bedroom, as do Nicky and Benny. But because Nicky wakes up several times each night, he usually sleeps with Rob and Mandy. Until recently, Matt and Mike slept in separate toddler beds, but ended up sleeping together in Matt's bed. Now, with their new bunk beds, Mike climbs down to the lower level to sleep with his brother. "Mike goes to Matt more than Matt goes to him," Mandy observed. Judy, their grandmother, thinks it's because Matt, always the bigger of the two, has been more stable and content than Mike, and the first to master new tasks and skills. Identical twins' minor differences are often exaggerated by caretakers who are trying to keep the children's identities straight. Such distinctions are not unusual in identical twinship, however, and may actually strengthen the bond since the twins' roles become clearly defined.

I wondered if the two identical twinships had dictated the sleep-

A typical Saturday morning in the life of Rob (left) and Mandy, surrounded by their "Quad Boys" (left to right): Mike, Benny, Matt, and Nicky. (Photo by Nancy L. Segal, October 2003.)

ing arrangements. Actually, Mandy had tried disentangling the pairs to downplay what she called the "twin thing." But separating them proved to be a disaster, because Matt and Mike were "good sleepers" whereas Benny and Nicky were "nighttime screamers." Moreover, Matt and Mike never napped, while Benny and Nicky napped daily. Matt and Mike also had a great time talking and laughing together after dark. I wish I could have peeked in on them. According to their mother, as early as six months of age, they would lie on their stomachs with their hands underneath and "bump their bums" up and down until they fell asleep.

Matt and Mike's sensitivities to clutter were also vastly different from Benny's—Matt and Mike were messy, dropping things on the floor and not noticing what they left behind. But Benny, besides being the "bull dog," had been nicknamed "Mr. Clean." He organized drawers and stacked toilet paper rolls. He let Mandy know when cabinets were left open. Mandy also said that holding Matt and Mike was totally different from holding Benny and Nicky; Matt and Mike ran their noses along your shoulder like puppy dogs, whereas Nicky and Benny liked to cuddle. "Who would have believed such things could be genetic?" she asked. "And who better to tell us than two sets of identical twins?"

"My life is on my nightstand," Mandy explained, inventorying the pile next to her bed as a way of showing me what her life is like behind the scenes. I saw an apple core, dental floss, a stone, a magazine for parents of special needs children, hair ribbons, a crumpled tissue, and dinner recipes she has not had time to prepare (though she does cook simple meals). She laughed, as she has learned to do since the boys arrived: Nicky plus three means that whatever she or anyone else can do is determined by his physical therapy sessions, medical appointments, or mood. Unlike most mothers of multiples, she can't anticipate the day when she will reclaim her private time.

Mandy's house was incredibly neat and clean, considering that one child of eight and four children under four lived in it. She had both paid help and volunteers to make this possible. But most significantly, Mandy believed she was "perfectly suited" to caring for quads. She knew she had high energy and impeccable organizational skills—the latter evidenced by obsessively maintained notebooks, diaries, photo albums, and desk calendars documenting her pregnancy, delivery, Nicky's medical appointments, and the other boys' activities. I also explored her "chest of no return," a crate containing piles of memorabilia—the quads' baby bracelets, stuffed animals, and newspaper articles, all destined for scrapbooks each boy would eventually receive.

Mandy belongs to Triplets, Quads, and Quints, an organization supporting mothers of multiples, but like many other members, she has no time to attend. As we entered her small office, I saw eleven telephone messages waiting to be played. I pointed this out, but she waved her hand as though this wasn't unusual. (The number stayed at eleven for nearly my entire visit. I also saw two kitchen calendars turned to June and September, even though it was October.) And Mandy has her daughter, Jade, to worry about. In an attempt at equal time for quads and non-quads, Mandy volunteers one day each week at Jade's school.

Jade also has a pony and a donkey, but her push for my attention in the car suggested that this was not enough.

Mandy and Rob have just taken their first vacation alone since the boys were born—a week in Thunder Bay—and Mandy expects that their next vacation without the children is four more years away. With the exception of Nicky, the boys have gotten easier as they have grown older. "If Nicky were okay, I could do this on my own," Mandy insisted.

The pizza Mandy had promised me arrived, and everyone gathered around the large kitchen table. It was a great opportunity to observe eating habits in action. Matt and Mike have always been picky eaters. They were given small pieces from the two giant pies, and they ate them slowly, watching what their twin brother was doing. Until recently, they would chew meat and spit it out; even now they eat it cautiously. Their counterparts, Benny and Nicky, approach food with gusto, eating anything and everything. Benny ate bigger pieces of pizza than Matt and Mike and seemed to take bigger bites. Rob fed small bits of pizza to Nicky, who can only handle small, easily chewable pieces. But Nicky seemed happy with his meal. Afterward, Rob ate his own dinner standing by the sink while washing dishes. Jade and Tifanee appeared and ate their food quietly; because of the nature of my visit, the girls stayed together for the weekend, apart from the rest of the family. Mandy rarely sits at meals; she usually skips breakfast and eats snacks, one reason she has gained thirty pounds since the boys came home (she had gained fifty pounds during her pregnancy). But she did join us at the table that night, perhaps the one concession she made to my being there.

The boys stayed at the table for a while after dinner, and I continued to watch them. Matt was playing with a miniature car until Benny snatched it from him. When Mandy demanded that he give it back, he threw it on the floor in Matt's direction. "Mike would have handed it to him," she said. According to Mandy and Rob, this scenario was typical of ongoing intraquad relations. Matt and Mike's greater affinity for each other than for Benny agrees with research showing greater closeness between identical than fraternal twins.[18] What is impressive is not that these differences existed, but that they emerged when the boys were just two years old. It could be argued that Mandy and Rob treated the children in ways that encouraged these different loyalties, but in fact they had tried to shuffle the pairs through bedroom assignments that failed. For the record, Matt and Mike had one contentious battle during my stay. "I don't want Mikey in the playroom," Matt sobbed. But the incident was soon forgotten. The accumulation of events, not single occurrences, most faithfully captures the nature of twins' social behaviors and preferences.

It approached 9:00 P.M. and the end of the first day of my visit. Mandy stayed with me downstairs, while Rob got the boys ready for bed. Mandy talked about how much the kids love their father and how much she loves the fact that they do. She hinted just slightly that Rob is more involved than she is with fun things like bedtime stories, one explanation for his popularity with his boys. But she insisted that she and Rob are absolutely committed to each other and to raising their children, despite not being married. They have had stressful times, but they always manage to figure things out. "You are talking compromise to the max," she said.

I noticed Mandy's "good mom ring," a silver band with a row of diamonds that Rob gave her when the quads came home. Rob called it "the last crazy thing we could afford." His salary is sufficient, but he manages finances carefully because free diapers, clothing, food, and other products from baby and childcare companies are generally reserved for five babies or more. In fact, Mandy and Rob had received relatively few such perks. In the past, only Nicky went to preschool because they couldn't afford to send all four boys. Nicky was chosen to go because he was withdrawn and would cry when someone outside the family tried to care for him; Mandy and Rob believed he would benefit from the social experiences school provides. This year they could afford to send two children and decided to send Benny, whose hospital assessment indicated that he is less emotionally mature than Matt and Mike. Mandy felt that school would help him as well. As it turned out, the school building was considered unsafe, so neither boy went. The current plan is for all four boys to attend a free public kindergarten in the near future.

The family's financial situation is further compromised by Nicky's medical care; soon, they will need to buy him a lift that costs $20,000. Mandy and Rob explained to me that though they wonder where the money will come from, they trust that things will work out. Then, on a lighter note, Rob recited his original song "The Quad Boys," sung to the tune of "She's a Lady," by Tom Jones:

> There is Nicky in his chair
> And there's Benny with spiked hair
> They are the Quad Boys.
> And there's Matthew always kickin'
> And there's Michael always lickin'
> They are the Quad Boys . . .
>
> (Refrain)
> They are the Quad Boys . . . Whoa, whoa, whoa
> They are the Quad Boys
> Talkin' about the little Quad Boys
> And the Quad Boys are fine . . .

Mandy drove me to the hotel where I would spend the next two nights. Before she left, she scribbled "6:15" on her hand to remind herself when to pick me up the next morning—she had no time to find paper. When she arrived the next morning she was wearing the same baggy T-shirt, red plaid pajama bottoms, and shoes she had worn the day before.

The kitchen was quiet when we arrived at her home. Soon, Benny and Matt appeared in their pajamas and Mike appeared without his— he had had an accident in bed, the first one in a year. Benny gave him a rough time over this. "I peed in the toilet!" Benny bragged. Mandy washed Mike, gave him clean clothes, then prepared breakfast cereal for the boys. By the time this was finished, her mug of tea, largely untouched, had cooled to the point of being undrinkable; this had also happened the day before. Rob carried Nicky downstairs for breakfast wearing the same white sweatshirt, jeans, and hat from the previous day. He fed Nicky small mouthfuls of warm oatmeal. Then, with Nicky on his lap, he chatted on the phone with his sister while the other three boys ran around him. Every once in a while he reprimanded them gently.

"What's the best 'quad story'?" I asked Mandy. There were two. She and Jade had brought the boys to Wal-Mart on a shopping trip when Benny eyed *Bob the Builder* underwear. He enthusiastically ripped off his pants to try them on. On a different day they were shopping at Sobeys, an upscale Canadian supermarket. Benny, Matt, and Mike spotted Styrofoam pool noodles and began using them as swords. "Every day is an adventure, a roller coaster ride to somewhere," Mandy explained. Quadruplets are not more mischievous by nature than singletons, but there are more of them, making them harder to control— especially in public and with Nicky around.

Parents of multiples are used to bizarre, funny, and often thoughtless comments from curious onlookers. Mandy shared several choice remarks with me: "Four children! Are they quintuplets?" "Wouldn't he [Nicky] have been a cute kid? What a tragedy!" "How did you manage to have four at once?" But Mandy and Rob had quick replies ready: "Yes, quintuplets." "He *is* a cute kid." And "Sex!" Many parents wear emotionally protective shields when venturing outside with their children. Mandy and Rob wore several layers.

At 10:30 in the morning, everyone but Rob (who stayed home to work) went apple picking at a neighbor's farm. The owners, John and Ina, and their son had known Mandy and Rob and their children for several years, so no one stared when Nicky, bundled up against the wind, was wheeled in and out of the apple orchards. This rural community offered Nicky the warmth and protection that was lacking in Cobourg's less personal shops and malls. I took many photographs of the quads, picking apples off the ground and putting them into bags.

Mandy didn't seem to mind my taking pictures of Nicky, here or else-where. Perhaps she appreciated the attention he received, or maybe she was just used to it. I later learned that my first hunch was correct. When we watched Benny, Matt, and Mike playing in their "fort"—a white cedar tree with an elaborate network of branches—Mandy ad-mitted, "This is what breaks my heart, this would have been so great for all the boys. And this is why Nicky and Benny are often left out of pictures—they are without their twins."

For lunch, Mandy put together multiple tuna sandwiches with assembly-line proficiency. So I was all the more amazed when she said she was in "down mode"; to me she was clearly in "up mode." Matt and Mike refused the sandwiches and insisted on having cereal instead. But Benny sat at the table and, looking straight ahead, finished his sandwich with "authority." After lunch, Rob and the boys watched a movie and visited with relatives who had dropped by, while Mandy drove me to town to copy documents. Then she cooked chicken on the outdoor grill, while holding an umbrella over her head because of the rain. She has help from Jade and Tifanee, but she's afraid of making the young daughters into "little mothers." Jade (who had lost a tooth), Tifanee (who was slender), and Mandy (who made meals) comprise the next verse of "The Quad Boys":

> There is Jade with no teeth
> And there's Tifanee with no beef
> They know the Quad Boys.
> And momma's always cookin'
> And then she's always lookin' after Quad Boys.
>
> (Refrain)
> And the Quad Boys are fine . . .

Later that night, Mandy reiterated that she has the "perfect person-ality" to raise quads. I think this assertion comes from her growing awareness of how hard the task is, plus the evidence that she is able to do it. There has apparently never been a day when things were too much for her. But she is very aware of the downsides and says she could talk anyone out of fertility treatments, which often lead to multiple births. "Over two is too many," she explained. "I would like more time to hug each one." I wondered if she would do it again, knowing what she knows now. She said she would because things turned out all right—all the boys lived. But she did not feel this way until they were three or four months old. In the beginning, Rob was less involved in their care because of his concerns for Tifanee. But that changed quickly. And at the moment, Rob was giving the quad boys their bath. The organization of this daunting task was sheer perfection.

Mandy and I waited in her bedroom for the first boy to appear. In walked Benny from the bathroom, wrapped in a large towel, his hair damp. Mandy cleaned his ears with a cotton swab, put on his pajamas, brushed his hair, and settled him into their large bed. Matt came in shortly after that, then Mike, and the routine was repeated. Benny didn't object to having his hair brushed, but Matt and Mike fought it like tigers. Last to emerge was Nicky, carried in by Rob, and the after-bath ritual repeated once more. Benny, Matt, and Mike lay next to each other facing the foot of their parents' bed, while Rob and Nicky lay in the opposite direction. Mandy left to check on Jade and Tifanee, while I sat on the floor at the foot of the bed. It was story time.

I listened as Rob mesmerized the children with his original stories of pirates, witches, alligators, frogs, and beanstalks. Bedtime stories were a nightly ritual in this house. Watching the boys happily immersed in their father's tales of adventure and suspense blurred my memories of the day's whines, fights, and fidgets. I think it did for Rob, as well—and I assume this was why Mandy and Rob would have had this family all over again if given a choice. The boys were getting along with one another and were fully engaged, shouting out details that Rob would use in his stories the next night. You could see how much the boys loved being part of story time. I imagined them grown up, reminiscing about the times they fell asleep in their parents' room, listening to their father's stories. I recalled the final verse to "The Quad Boys":

> And the phone's always ringing
> And the daddy's always singing to the Quad Boys . . .

> (Refrain)
> They are the Quad Boys . . . Whoa, whoa, whoa
> They are the Quad Boys
> Talkin' about the little Quad Boys
> And the Quad Boys are fine . . .

When Benny, Matt, and Mike fell asleep, Rob carried them to bed, then returned to lie down with Nicky, who was still wide awake. A second ritual began. Rob threw a small green ball up against the ceiling, catching it each time. Like his brother Benny, Nicky thrived on fast action and so was particularly interested in this game. With each toss of the ball, Rob called out a letter of the alphabet and Nicky repeated it, though not always clearly. Still, each sound brought an enthusiastic response from his father. Mandy said Nicky was at his best at night, possibly because he was most relaxed at this time. In fact, Nicky stayed quiet and attentive, fully engrossed in this marvelous interchange. If Nicky got bored, then Rob let him grasp the ball himself. But if Rob stopped throwing the ball, Nicky grew noisy. Some of his behavioral changes were so subtle that I missed them until Rob brought them to my attention. The process continued for an hour every night. Sometimes Rob had the TV tuned to a sports event and would watch it between tosses, though he didn't that night. This father-son game was gratifying and touching to see—and a thrilling end to my visit.

Mandy picked me up at the hotel the next morning to drive me to the train station. Only Benny and Matt were in the back seat. It seemed unusual to see Matt without Mike, but they had left the house before Mike noticed. "I didn't want everyone with me," Mandy muttered. She wore a different pair of red plaid pajama bottoms but had on the same white T-shirt from the previous days. She seemed to be wearing a

EVERYDAY WONDERS

bit thin at this point—after all, she had had me to think about all weekend, in addition to her usual worries. In fact, she had shifted the quads' Saturday visits with volunteers to Sunday on my behalf. And she planned to garden later that afternoon.

We dropped Benny and Matt off at the house, picked up Jade and Tifanee, and headed to the train station. En route, we stopped at the Big Apple Restaurant in Colborne, where I purchased one of the famous apple pies I had heard about. But my experience with the quads was far more memorable. I had been given a rare look at the genetic and environmental scenarios that drive scientific twin data. Rob and Mandy were running a superb natural experiment on the second floor of their home. Both parents were astute observers of behavior, surprised but impressed by the similarities and differences within and between the pairs. I was not surprised when Rob said that he got his "genetic education" from his children; most parents of multiples interpret their "data" wisely, keeping their minds open to what their children show them just by acting naturally.

Mandy and Rob were extraordinary people and parents. Suddenly faced with enlarging their family by 200 percent, they turned their initial shock into informed acceptance. They read about multiple birth deliveries. They adjusted their life to accommodate a child with special needs. And they stay dedicated to each other and to the awesome task that they share. Neither Mandy nor Rob romanticized the process. Memories of the boys' uncertain survival and early health problems were still fresh. Once the quads came home, dividing their time fairly among them and finding sufficient finances were constant challenges. But Mandy and Rob know they have a unique cluster of kids—and, to their credit, they often sit back and enjoy the quads' growth and development from their ringside seats.

After the boys were born, Rob had a vasectomy to prevent further pregnancies, single or otherwise. But given that Nicky sleeps in their bed between them, Mandy joked that the operation was probably unnecessary.

I wondered what the quad boys were doing as I wrote their story.

Was Benny battling Mike over a favorite toy? Were Matt and Mike bumping their bottoms up and down? Was Nicky entranced by watching Rob bounce a ball off the ceiling? I also thought about their future—about the day Benny would notice his broken twinship, and the moment when Matt and Mike could offer understanding. I wondered if Benny would become an athlete, and if Matt and Mike would ever cut their hair. I wondered if medical advances would allow Nicky to walk and talk, to feel more on board the "ship of quads." And I wondered about the new adjustments Rob and Mandy would make—as parents and as a couple—as the boys got older. None of this can be known right now. But I was certain of one thing: that no matter what, "the Quad Boys are fine."

POSTSCRIPT. I touched base with Mandy in April 2005. Nicky had had an operation to relieve some of the spasticity in his legs. He still couldn't join the soccer team with his brothers, but Mandy and Rob bought him a uniform anyway and designated him the water boy. Mandy told me all this while drinking stale decaf coffee. "It's like an ice cap," she said. "It's been sitting here for a while." She did cheerfully say that she was wearing new Mickey Mouse pajama bottoms.

Afterword

I'm lucky—twin stories and twin studies multiply and change all the time, so working with twins never gets boring. It only gets better.

I remember how exciting it was when the Human Genome Project finally mapped all 30,000 human genes—albeit 70,000 fewer than expected.[1] Some day we may know why Jack and Oskar read books back to front and liked sneezing loudly in elevators. And we may know why Melanie's mutism is more pronounced than Mira's, and why Andru feels male and Audrey feels female. We may also learn why Tom is gay, while his identical triplet brothers, Owen and Frank, are not, and why Owen and Frank have multiple sclerosis and Tom does not. But tying specific genes to specific behaviors is a daunting task because personality, health, and sexuality are affected by many genes and many environments. The twins' stories have endings we won't know for some time.

But the most spectacular twin-related development was one that no one anticipated: the 1996 birth of Dolly, a cloned Scottish lamb.[2]

Dolly's birth raised lots of hotly debated questions about what would happen if human cloning became real. Although that's not likely to happen soon, if ever, the controversies have continued, often fueled by speculation over the re-creation of deceased children and the realization of Aldous Huxley's *Brave New World*.[3] Researchers have, however, made progress in cloning some animals. Cloned cats and other pets, once just possibilities, are becoming viable options—the first cloned cat, named "CC," arrived on December 22, 2001.[4] *Genetic Savings and Clone,* a company dedicated to duplicating exceptional animals, launched a "Nine Lives Extravaganza" in February 2004, with plans to present its first (nine) cat clones in December 2004. The latest is "Little Gizmo," a clone of a mixed-breed Siamese named "Gizmo." However, the $50,000 cost of the procedure is prohibitive for most people, and success rates are low; CC was the only survivor out of eighty-seven cloned embryos that were implanted, and by August 2004 *Genetic Savings and Clone* claimed to have cloned just two kittens, Tabouleh and Baba Ganoush.[5] Moreover, few people would agree that a cloned cat or dog could really replace their beloved pet. And no one would say that a cloned child could really replace a deceased son or daughter.

Critics of human cloning have argued that it would negatively affect family relationships. What would it be like for a father to raise his "delayed genetic twin" son? This situation, posed by the National Bioethics Advisory Commission (NBAC), raised fears that cloned children would suffer a "diminished sense of individuality" and "degradation in the quality of parenting and family life."[6] The NBAC was not the only concerned party; the writer Kenan Malik said that a "child conceived in this fashion will be the genetic twin of the person who was the cell donor." Law professor Leon Kass and philosopher Daniel Callahan were quoted as saying that "cloning confuses identity . . . by making the clone both twin and offspring of its older copy." Contributors to the volume *Clones and Clones,* for their part, made many references to "twins," "genetic twins," and "later twins."[7]

What surprises me is that no one looked at what twin studies have told us about individual development and family life. After all, identical twins are naturally conceived clones, so who better to inform us? What twins say and do could go a long way toward calming the cloning controversies.

So what *would* it be like for a father to raise his "delayed genetic twin son"? That's a good question, but it's asked in the wrong way, because *clones are not identical twins*—only the reverse is true. In fact, clones don't have a lot in common with twins. For one thing, clones would be conceived at different times, have separate prenatal environments, and belong to different generations, whereas twins share all these things. A dad born in 1950 would have seen the Beatles debut on *The Ed Sullivan show,* watched *Leave It to Beaver* on black-and-white TV, and typed papers on an IBM Selectric, while his cloned son, born in, say, 2010, might assume that the Beatles were bugs, think that Beaver was an ordinary rodent, and wonder what a typewriter was for. In fact, when I cite *Leave It to Beaver* to my psychology students as an excellent example of seeing the world from a child's perspective, most of them have no idea what I'm talking about.

Clones and donors would also develop in separate wombs. Their respective surrogate mothers would probably have been put on different diets, different medications, and different exercise programs, all of which could affect fetal health. But, paradoxically, clones and donors might be more similar in birth weight than identical twins because they wouldn't compete with another fetus for nutrition and space.

The molecular biologist Lee Silver has also talked about "delayed genetic twins," and we have had lots of interesting discussions about why I prefer the term "intergenerational clone." When I heard him discuss cloning on ABC's *Nightline* in 2001, I listened carefully—but he never said "delayed genetic twin." He e-mailed me the next day and said, "Believe it or not, you crossed my mind while I was talking on the show . . ."

Critics also suggest that clones might stand out in crowds because they would look exactly like their mother or father. This is hardly the case—clones and donors would be "hidden" because of their different life stages.[8] If a donor dad walked down the street holding the hand of his two-year-old cloned son, no one would notice. Look at a photograph of yourself when you were two and then look in the mirror—would anyone notice if the older and younger you walked down the street hand in hand? In contrast, identical twins grab people's attention at any age, and no one would suggest that we keep them apart.

Furthermore, there is no evidence that twins suffer from looking or acting alike. In fact, every year, at festivals all over the world, thousands of twins (mostly identical) gather to celebrate being twins—just like Craig and Mark and Diane and Darlene. The coveted prizes go to the pairs who look most alike.

A possible clone-donor advantage that has been overlooked is the greater mutual understanding and empathy these pairs would enjoy, relative to ordinary children and parents. This is because their identical brains might lead them to have similar reactions and feelings, as often happens with identical twins.[9] Tony and Roger, identical twins who met for the first time in their twenties, gave each other perfect Christmas presents—identical sweaters with matching socks—because each twin knew what his brother would want.[10] But when Roger opened his present he was shocked: He wondered if his wife had forgotten to mail his gift to Tony. Moreover, most twins seek each other out when they are upset because they know they will be unconditionally supported, accepted, and loved. Didn't Agnes call Audrey when she decided to change sex? And didn't Audrey fly to Oregon to be with her twin because she sensed that "something big" was happening? Too many teenagers complain that their parents don't understand them, but cloned teenagers might not.

Besides twins, some fathers and sons, mothers and daughters, and brothers and sisters share interests, outlooks, and appearances, circumstances they seem to like. Actress Blythe Danner and her actress-daughter Gwyneth Paltrow are a good example.

In one article, accompanied by a picture of Blythe Danner with her arms wrapped around her daughter Gwyneth, who is leaning against her, Danner said, "Watching a child come into her own is one of motherhood's greatest pleasures, especially if the blossoming talent takes after yours."[11] Paltrow insisted, "I'm *so* not like her at all—but we're so similar in so many ways." They like the same books, eat the same organic foods, use the same cosmetic products, and follow the same environmental issues. Danner also said, "She [Gwyneth] doesn't get carried away with this [acting] hoopla. I thinks she gets it from me." Maybe we should study these naturally occurring pairs to try to understand what cloned child-donor parent relationships might really be like.[12]

But would parents have unrealistic expectations for their cloned children? Wouldn't they encourage them to take over the family business—or make certain that they avoided their parents' worst mistakes? Probably, but most parents I know have these same thoughts and hopes for their sons and daughters.

Most people also assume that a clone and his or her donor would be less alike than identical twins since they wouldn't be born together. This "truth" was stated several times at a symposium I attended in 2002.[13] But no one really knows how alike clones and donors would be, compared with twins. Clones are never photocopies of originals because cell replication isn't perfect—even identical twins can differ genetically because of lost chromosomes, gene mutations, or glitches in gene expression. So if a Lance Armstrong clone were created, he might be a good cyclist, but maybe not a great one. Moreover, the right environment is also needed to nurture extraordinary talent. The Lance Armstrong clone might have great cycling potential, even better than his father, but if cycling weren't popular in his generation he might try other sports and cycle only occasionally. We might then conclude—erroneously—that the child didn't measure up to the dad.

Cloned children and their parents would most likely show some similarities (some could be quite striking), but their degree of resemblance would vary from trait to trait. Thus in some ways clones and donors could be as alike, more alike, or less alike than identical twins. They might both like weird movies (like George and Brent), have the same birth weights (unlike most identical twins), or think about history differently (like Jack and Oskar).

Perhaps people's greatest fear is that cloning would take away a child's individuality and sense of self. Again, we can turn to identical twins for help with this debate: If identical twins (who are born into the same generation at the same time) don't feel that their selfhood is under attack, then we should expect cloned children and their parents (who would be born into different generations) to feel the same. True, identical twins are sometimes referred to as "one"—Mark and Gerry were the "fireman twins"; Nicky, Benny, Matthew, and Michael were "The Quad Boys"; and Brenda and Linda were "Brenda-Linda." But the twins' differences were obvious to them and to their families. Surprisingly, many identical twins say that they don't look alike, probably because they see small differences between themselves that others don't see. It's wrong to think that identical twins' nearly identical looks and behaviors mean that they have identical selves. Every identical twin interviewed in this book made this point, which is why they intrigued me, their families, and even themselves. In fact, when it comes to cloning, most identical twins wonder what all the fuss is about, given that "[identical twins] have been doing cloning all along."[14]

Studying and talking to identical twins takes the punch out of many anticloning arguments. What twins show us and tell us doesn't necessarily justify the procedure, but it can sharpen our thinking on this controversial subject. Meanwhile, I recently heard from some twins whom I suspect have been "doing cloning" all along.

Everyone likes hearing from old friends, but I also like hearing from old twins. Identical twins Dean and David Kopsell from Hebron, Illinois, were in my first twin study when they were nine years old. They loved putting puzzles together, and they worked quickly and efficiently as a team. The pudgy twin children I remember are now handsome tall blonds in their thirties. Dean recalls that he and David "spent virtually every waking moment together from birth to high school." After that, the twins studied horticulture in the same college and graduate school. Dean continued, "Graduate school is a stressful undertaking, and having your brother and best friend there, facing the same challenges, made life a whole lot easier for the two of us." Dean and David beat the academic odds by becoming professors in the same department at the University of New Hampshire, at the same time. Most married couples can't do that—hiring committees worry that work-related rivalries might drive them apart. But twins like Dean and David say that twin professors are a safer bet than married ones. "We can't get divorced," said one of them.

Today, Dean and David are both married and living in different states. Dean is at the University of Tennessee, in Knoxville, and David is at Vidalia Labs, in Collins, Georgia. One is a father and the other hopes to be. Dean wrote, "It will be hard to be apart, but we'll make time to see each other and stay in contact for collaborations." The twins are intimate, but independent—complete individuals, but indivisible by two.

Notes

INTRODUCTION

1. Oliver Sacks, *The Man Who Mistook His Wife for a Hat and Other Clinical Tales* (New York: HarperCollins, 1985), p. viii.

PART I: SEPARATED AT BIRTH

1. William Shakespeare, *Twelfth Night*, 1600 or 1601.

2. Titus Maccius Plautus, *Menaechmi*.

3. Paul Popenoe, "Twins Reared Apart," *Journal of Heredity*, 5 (1922): 142–144. A more detailed report on these twins appeared later; see Hermann J. Mueller, "Mental Traits and Heredity," *Journal of Heredity*, 16 (1925): 443–448.

4. The Minnesota Study of Twins Reared Apart gathered data on separated sets of twins between 1979 and 1999. Twin type (identical or fraternal) was confirmed by extensive blood group analyses. I was formally associated with the project between 1982 and 1991.

5. Reunion registries consist of the names of individuals searching for their twins and other relatives. People send in their names and staff members try to connect them with their missing family members.

6. Triplets restaurant closed its doors several years ago. Sadly, one of the triplets committed suicide and the remaining two are pursuing different careers.

7. "In the Name of Research," *Newsday*, October 12, 1997, pp. A5, A48.

8. All reared-apart twin studies before and since Neubauer's study have included separated twins who were mostly reunited as adults. See Nancy L. Segal, "Spotlights (Reared Apart Twin Researchers)," *Twin Research*, 6 (2003): 72–81.

9. Interview with Dr. Lawrence Perlman, January 14, 2002. Dr. Perlman was a clinical psychology graduate student when he was associated with the Neubauer study.

10. Peter B. Neubauer and Alexander Neubauer, *Nature's Thumbprint: The New Genetics of Personality* (Reading, Mass.: Addison-Wesley, 1990); Samuel Abrams, "Disposition and the Environment," in Peter B. Neubauer and Albert J. Solnit, eds., *Psychoanalytic Study of the Child*, vol. 41 (New Haven: Yale University Press, 1986), pp. 41–60. For recent critical appraisal of the Child Development Center Twin Study see Lawrence M. Perlman, "Memories of the Child Development Center Study of Adopted Monozygotic Twins Reared Apart: An Unfulfilled Promise," *Twin Research and Human Genetics*, 8 (2005): 271–275; Nancy L. Segal, "More Thoughts on the Child Development Center Twin Study," *Twin Research and Human Genetics*, 8 (2005): 276–281.

11. With the exception of the twin study materials, Viola Bernard's papers were made available to the public in January 2004. See "Past Acquisitions: Papers of Viola W. Bernard Opened," Columbia University Health Sciences Archives and Special Collections, December 13, 2004: *http://library.cpmc. columbia.edu/hsl/archives/pastacq.html*.

12. Robert Plomin et al., *Behavioral Genetics*, 4th ed. (New York: Worth Publishers, 2001); Nancy L. Segal, "Twin Research at Auschwitz-Birkenau: Implications for the Use of Nazi Data Today," in Arthur L. Caplan, ed., *When Medicine Went Mad* (Totowa, N.J.: Humana Press, 1992), pp. 281–299.

13. Sandra Scarr-Salapatek, "Unknowns in the IQ Equation," *Science*, 174 (1971): 1223–1228.

14. Steven G. Vandenberg, "Contributions of Twin Research to Psychology," in Martin Manosevitz, Gardner Lindzey, and Delbert D. Thiessen, eds., *Behavioral Genetics: Method and Research* (New York: Appleton-Century-Crofts, 1969), pp. 145–164.

15. Leslie S. Hearnshaw, *Cyril Burt: Psychologist* (New York: Vintage Books, 1979).

16. Robert B. Joynson, *The Burt Affair* (London: Routledge, 1989); Ronald Fletcher, *Science, Ideology and the Media: The Cyril Burt Scandal* (New Brunswick, N.J.: Transaction Books, 1991).

17. Reared-apart twin studies show that about 70 percent of individual differences in intelligence are influenced by genes. However, other studies have given somewhat lower estimates—so the answer probably lies in the 50–70 percent range; see Scarr-Salapatek, "Unknowns in the IQ Equation."

18. Nancy L. Segal, *Entwined Lives: Twins and What They Tell Us about Human Behavior* (New York: Plume, 2000).

19. Thomas J. Bouchard, Jr., "IQ Similarity in Twins Reared Apart: Findings and Responses to Critics," in Robert J. Sternberg and Elena L. Grigorenko, eds., *Intelligence, Heredity and Environment* (New York: Cambridge University Press, 1997), pp. 126–160.

1. BEER CANS AND KEY RINGS

1. *Late Show with David Letterman*, New York, N.Y., 1986.
2. *Oprah Winfrey Show*, Chicago, Ill., 1988.
3. Some portions of the dialogue quoted here come from my work on the "Twin Film" with Greer & Associates, in Minneapolis, Minn., 1987. This film was never completed.
4. A slang expression for raising a beer.
5. Twin studies show that drinking tendencies are genetically influenced. Carol A. Prescott et al., "Is Risk for Alcoholism Mediated by Individual Differences in Drinking Motivations?" *Alcoholism, Clinical Experimental Research*, 28 (2004): 29–39.
6. Sandra Scarr, "Developmental Theories for the 1990's: Development and Individual Differences," *Child Development*, 63 (1992): 1–19.
7. Auke Tellegen et al., "Personality Similarity in Twins Reared Apart and Together," *Journal of Personality and Social Psychology*, 54 (1988): 1031–1039.
8. Reared-together identical twins are slightly more similar in IQ than reared-apart identical twins. This finding is largely based on comparison between young reared-together twins and adult reared-apart twins. This is not really a fair comparison because shared family environments do influence intelligence somewhat during childhood. Comparing adult identical twins reared apart and together would probably yield minimal differences in IQ similarity.
9. F. V. Rijsdijk et al., "Genetic and Environmental Influences on Psychological Distress in the Population: General Health Questionnaire Analyses in UK Twins," *Psychological Medicine*, 33 (2003): 793–801.
10. Gerry had to leave Brazil when he got sick.
11. Gerry was married on August 25, 2002.

2. SWITCHED AT BIRTH

1. Unusual pregnancy events sometimes cause twins to be born on different days. In 1996, a Pennsylvania mother delivered fraternal twins eighty-four days apart. "Twin Born, 84 Days after First," *New York Daily News*, February 9, 1996.
2. I learned about these twins and their families from the television special "My Three Sons," which aired on ABC's *Primetime Live* on April 7, 1994.

3. Nancy L. Segal, "Virtual Twins: New Findings on Within-Family Environmental Influences on Intelligence," *Journal of Educational Psychology,* 92 (2000): 442–448. I have now studied behavioral development in more than one hundred virtual twin pairs.

4. The Holmes family—Laura, a social worker, and Randy, a land administrator—declined further interviews because, according to Randy, "they didn't want to revive old hurts."

5. This information was given to me by Arthur Cogan, an attorney hired by the families to argue their case against the Children's Aid Society of Ottawa.

6. Geoffrey A. Machin and Louis G. Keith, *An Atlas of Multiple Pregnancy: Biology and Pathology* (New York: Parthenon Publishing Group, 1999). I did not inspect the twins' birth records, but the source of the misdiagnosis was the likely presence of two placentae, something many people, even health professionals, consider proof of fraternal twinning. However, all fraternal twins *and* one-third of identical twins (those resulting when the fertilized egg divides before the second post-conceptional day) have two placentae and two sets of fetal membranes (chorion and amnion). The placentae may be separate or fused. Later division of the fertilized egg produces a single nonfused placenta with a single chorion and two amnions (about days 2 to 8 post-conception) or a single nonfused placenta with one chorion and one amnion (about days 8 to 13 post-conception). Only about 5 percent of identical pairs have a single chorion and single amnion.

7. In my first twin study, published in 1984, I found that as many as one-third of the pairs had been misclassified by physicians. See Nancy L. Segal, "Zygosity Diagnosis: Laboratory and Investigator's Judgment," *Acta Geneticae Medicae et Gemellologiae,* 33 (1984): 515–520.

8. The British investigator of twins reared apart, Dr. James Shields, was reputed for his skill in assessing twin type by twins' physical resemblance—his judgments nearly always matched results from extensive blood-typing. See Robert R. Race and Ruth Sanger, *Blood Groups in Man* (Oxford: Blackwell, 1975). However, DNA or blood type analyses are required for scientific certainty. Brent and George's case demanded no less. Dr. James lacked experience with twins and twin research, but he found their strong physical resemblance compelling.

9. David T. Lykken, "The Diagnosis of Zygosity in Twins," *Behavior Genetics,* 8 (1978): 437–463. Twin typing requires comparison of about eighteen different blood group factors. For known twins, any differences prove fraternal twinning, while perfect matches indicate identical twinning but can't prove it (this is because fraternal twins can inherit the same blood groups

from their parents, although this is rare). Additional twin comparisons of physical measures improve the accuracy of twin typing based on blood tests.

10. DNA analysis is more accurate than blood tests for determining twin type. It compares individuals across seven to ten DNA segments for which complete matches would be virtually impossible unless the two were identical twins.

11. Interview on "My Three Sons."

12. The case against the Children's Aid Society lasted from 1993 until 2000.

13. Nancy L. Segal, *Entwined Lives: Twins and What They Tell Us about Human Behavior* (New York: Plume, 2000); Nancy L. Segal, Scott L. Hershberger, and Sara Arad, "Meeting One's Twin: Perceived Social Closeness and Familiarity," *Evolutionary Psychology*, 1 (2003): 70–95.

14. George reviews ministerial correspondence and records for the federal government of Canada.

3. OSKAR AND JACK

1. The Sudentenland was annexed by the Nazis in 1938 and returned to the Czechs in 1945.

2. Sharon Begley and Martin Kasindorf, "Twins: Nazi and Jew," *Newsweek*, December 3, 1979, p. 139; "The Twins: Identical Brothers Who Grew Up Apart, One Raised as a Nazi, One as a Jew," *Washington Post*, December 10, 1979, p. B1.

3. Liesel only had enough money to buy a ticket for herself and one child. The officer on board was a German who wore a swastika. Liesel told him she was German and returning to her homeland. He waived the third fee.

4. "Oskar and Jack," *St. Louis Jewish Light*, July 16, 1997, p. 7.

5. Oskar's sons think their father's family "hid" him among the Hitler Youth because of his Jewish roots.

6. When Jack's father's marriage to the beauty queen ended, other young, attractive brides followed. Miss Trinidad and Josef had a daughter, Natasha, whom Jack recalls fondly as a childhood companion, but she has not responded to his recent contacts. When Liesel was in Italy she periodically sent money and goods to her family in Germany.

7. Jack had a similar experience in Trinidad. When lined up with other (mostly black) boys, he was asked his name. "Yufe," he replied. "It's French."

8. According to Jack, who met Uncle Max on a visit to Germany, "he was a lovely guy, a chubby little fellow."

9. *Commandos Strike at Dawn*, scripted by Irwin Shaw, was based on a story by C. S. Forester.

10. Jack's failure to mention his Catholic mother to Ona might be explained by the fact that Jewish law does not consider children Jewish unless their mother is Jewish as well. Perhaps he was afraid that she would not marry him if she had known. The Third Reich did not make this distinction.

11. "Oskar and Jack," radio interview with Jack Yufe, KPBS, San Diego, Calif., March 1997.

12. Jack and Oskar were the same height, but Oskar was about twenty pounds heavier.

13. Oskar kept the luggage tags and returned them to Jack years later during one of his visits to California.

14. Liesel and her new husband had two children, Peter and Paula, Jack and Oskar's half-brother and half-sister. Liesel's husband had been a lawyer and an "Obergefreiter," a soldier of the second lowest rank.

15. The store, which Jack still owns and manages, sells everything from T-shirts to cameras to kitchen utensils.

16. Ruth and Jack also had a daughter, Lisa, who died of cancer when she was seven years old. Jack was especially proud of this girl, and her death was devastating to him. She was their eldest child.

17. Christel said that Oskar sent the Christmas cards because she could not write or read English. Ona, however, claims that the contact was between the wives.

18. Jack's father, Josef, also had the habit of wearing rubber bands around his wrist. Jack always thought he had copied this from his father—until he saw Oskar doing the same thing.

19. Jack carried a British passport, as well as an American one. Trinidad was under British rule when Jack lived there.

20. Frauke Sandig, *Oskar and Jack*, 1995. This film was the source of several quotations from both twins.

21. I visited again briefly with Peter and Adelheid in August 2004 when they came to California.

22. Peter helped me question many family members, but I spoke directly to Ingo and to Ingo's children, Anna and Kathi. Ingo translated my questions for his mother, Christel.

23. Peter also worried about his own reaction to the film because it showed scenes of his mother (Liesel). When he attended Oskar's funeral, he experienced his first asthma attack.

24. Rolf said that he attended the premiere of the film with Oskar and

Christel, in Duisberg, when it was released in 1995. Ingo had indicated that no one in the family had seen it.

25. Nancy L. Segal, "Holocaust Twins: Their Special Bond," *Psychology Today*, 19 (1985): 52–58.

26. Twins were not identified in the cities; instead, Nazi officers at Auschwitz would identify the pairs by scanning the new inmates getting off the trains and shouting, "Zwillinge! Zwillinge!" (Twins! Twins!)

27. Jack was circumcised at age sixteen before going to Israel.

28. Nancy L. Segal, *Entwined Lives: Twins and What They Tell Us about Human Behavior* (New York; Plume, 2000). When we say that genetic or environmental influence on a trait is 50 percent, we are referring to differences among individuals, not to the gene-environment balance of individuals. Genetic and environmental effects are inseparable in individuals.

29. Germany is more tolerant of homosexuality today.

30. Oskar was diagnosed with narcolepsy during his research visit to the University of Minnesota. He may have shown signs of the disorder as a young man. Jack didn't show any signs of this disorder, but he worried when Oskar referred to them as "our symptoms."

31. In August 2004 Jack invited me to a party celebrating Trinidad's Independence Day.

32. Peter and Oskar had never been close, even though they had lived together for a while when they were young.

PART II: VARIATIONS ON COMMON THEMES

1. Nancy L. Segal and David B. Allison, "Twins and Virtual Twins: Bases of Relative Body Weight Revisited," *International Journal of Obesity*, 26 (2002): 437–441; D. Hanisch, M. Dottmar, and K. W. Alt, "Contribution of Genetic and Environmental Factors to Variation in Body Compartments—A Twin Study in Adults," *Anthropologischer Anzeiger*, 62 (2004): 51–60.

4. SELECTIVELY MUTE

1. "Private Speech" (videotape), Inside Psych Series, TR Productions (Needham Heights, Mass.: Allyn and Bacon).

2. Martin T. Stein, "Selective Mutism," *Journal of Developmental and Behavioral Pediatrics*, 20 (1999): 38–41.

3. Hanne Kristensen, "Selective Mutism and Comorbidity with Developmental Disorder/Delay, Anxiety Disorder, and Elimination Disorder," *Journal of the American Academy of Child and Adolescent Psychiatry*, 39 (2000): 249–256.

4. I had known of other selectively mute twins when Donna called me in spring 2000. Marjorie Wallace's book *The Silent Twins* (New York: Prentice Hall, 1986) was the first work to draw widespread attention to the condition. She chronicled the tortured lives of June and Jennifer Gibbons, identical twins of West Indian descent raised in England. Their story ended sadly—in 1982, when they were nineteen, burglary and arson led the twins to Broadmoor, a high-security hospital east of London. Eleven years later they were transferred to the Caswell Clinic, a minimum-security hospital in southwest Wales. Jennifer died that day from a weakened heart; June was released from Caswell one year later and is living in a halfway house. See Hilton Als, "We Two Made One," *The New Yorker*, December 4, 2000, 72–83, p. 75. Little was subsequently written about twins with selective mutism, perhaps because an affected twin should occur in only about 1 in every 30,000 to 40,000 births; see Nancy L. Segal, *Entwined Lives: Twins and What They Tell Us about Human Behavior* (New York: Plume, 2000). But families suffer. In 1988 I received a note from a mother of fourteen-year-old identical twin girls that captured the gravity of the situation: "Time is running out and we are desperate . . ."

5. In her book, *The Silent Twins*, Marjorie Wallace wondered whether June might have followed her twin sister's lead.

6. Nancy L. Segal, "'Two' Quiet: Monozygotic Female Twins with Selective Mutism," *Clinical Child Psychology and Psychiatry*, 8 (2003): 473–488.

7. The identical Gibbons twins had also enjoyed a "tremendous sort of novelty value," according to Tim Thomas, one of their therapists. "But that interest quickly turned to anger." June and Jennifer's minority status and behavioral outbursts (they hit and scratched each other when Thomas proposed separating them) did not endear them to others; see Als, "We Two Made One," p. 75.

8. Harry H. Wright and Michael L. Cuccaro, "Selective Mutism Continued," *Journal of the American Academy of Child and Adolescent Psychiatry*, 33 (1994): 593–594; Karin Anstendig, "Selective Mutism: A Review of the Treatment Literature by Modality from 1980–1996." *Psychotherapy*, 35 (1998): 381–391.

9. Peter Bakker, "Autonomous Languages in Twins," *Acta Geneticae Medicae et Gemellologiae*, 36 (1987): 233–238; Karen Thorpe et al., "Prevalence and Developmental Course of 'Secret Language,'" *International Journal of Language and Communication Disorders*, 36 (2001): 43–62; Segal, *Entwined Lives*. Thorpe et al. found two types of unusual communication among young twins: *shared understanding* (speech directed to the twin and to oth-

ers, but intelligible only to the twin); and *private language* (speech used exclusively within the twin pair and unintelligible to others). Shared understanding occurred among 50 percent of twenty-month-old twins and 19.7 percent of thirty-six-month-old twins. Private language occurred among 11.8 percent of twenty-month-old twins and 2.5 percent of thirty-six-month-old twins. The findings were not reported separately for identical and fraternal twins. Unusual communication can also occur between siblings who are close in age.

10. Michael Tomasello, Sarah Mannle, and Ann C. Kruger, "Linguistic Environment of One- to Two-Year-Old Twins," *Developmental Psychology,* 22 (1986): 169–176.

11. E. Steven Dummit III et al., "Fluoxetine Treatment of Children with Selective Mutism: An Open Trial," *Journal of the American Academy of Child and Adolescent Psychiatry,* 35 (1996): 615–621; Anstendig, "Selective Mutism."

12. Judee K. Burgoon and Gregory D. Hoobler, "Nonverbal Signals," in *Handbook of Interpersonal Communication,* ed. Mark L. Knapp and John A. Daly (Thousand Oaks, Calif.: Sage Publications, Inc., 2002), pp. 240–299.

5. STRAIGHT, GAY, AND STRAIGHT

1. M. A. Reynolds et al., "Trends in Multiple Births Conceived Using Assisted Reproductive Technology, United States, 1997–2000," *Pediatrics,* 111 (2003): 1159–1162. Owen, Tom, and Frank were found to be identical on the basis of extensive blood group analyses.

2. Eric Jaffe, "Biology and Behavior," *Observer,* 17 (2004): 25–27; Ray Blanchard, Kenneth J. Zucker, and Caitlin S. Hume, "Birth Order and Sibling Sex Ratio in Homosexual Male Adolescents and Probably Prehomosexual Feminine Boys," *Developmental Psychology,* 31 (1995): 22–30; J. Michael Bailey, Michael P. Dunne, and Nicholas G. Martin, "Genetic Influences on Sexual Orientation and Its [sic] Correlates in an Australian Sample," *Journal of Personality and Social Psychology,* 78 (2000): 524–536; Brian S. Mustanski, Meredith L. Chivers, and J. Michael Bailey, "A Critical Review of Recent Biological Research on Human Sexual Orientation," *Annual Review of Sex Research,* 13 (2002): 89–140; J. Michael Bailey and Richard C. Pillard, "A Genetic Study of Male Sexual Orientation," *Archives of General Psychiatry,* 48 (1991): 1089–1096; Franz J. Kallman, "Twin and Sibship Study of Overt Male Homosexuality," *American Journal of Human Genetics,* 4 (1952): 136–146.

Kallman's 1952 study suggested 100 percent genetic influence on male homosexuality, but this work has been criticized on methodological grounds. Bailey and Pillard (1991) found that genetic influence on sexual orientation ranged from 31 percent to 74 percent. More recently, Bailey et al. (2000), using a population-based sample, found evidence consistent with genetic influence on sexual orientation, but noted that larger twin and nontwin samples were needed to confirm the findings. Recently, some researchers have looked for specific genes associated with sexual orientation. Their finding that pairs of gay brothers tend to share a gene on their X chromosome is interesting, but it has not been consistently replicated. See Dean Hamer et al., "A Linkage between DNA Markers on the X Chromosome and Male Sexual Orientation," *Science*, 261 (1993): 321–327. Italian investigators have also found evidence of genetic influence that increases both male homosexuality and female fertility. Andrea Camperio-Ciani, Francesca Corna, and Claudio Capiluppi, "Evidence for Maternally Inherited Factors Favouring Male Homosexuality and Promoting Female Fecundity," *Proceedings of the Royal Society of London* (B Biological Sciences), 7 (2004): 2217–2221.

There are also a number of biological theories of sexual orientation. One is the birth-order explanation, which suggests that women bearing sons manufacture antibodies to testosterone or other sex hormones, which affect the brain development of later-born sons. Psychological theories variously propose that later-born homosexual males were overprotected by their mothers or received insufficient attention from their fathers. Both theories support the finding that male homosexuals tend to be later-born children with a higher-than-average proportion of male siblings. Both theories fit the Marks triplets, though both require further study.

Another explanation considers prenatal "developmental disruptions" that cause deviations from typical growth. We know that two divisions of the fertilized egg gave rise to Owen, Tom, and Frank; thus we can speculate that Owen and Tom resulted from the initial split and Owen and Frank resulted from the second. This might have sent Tom down a different developmental pathway from his co-triplets. However, such explanations are tentative. For example, non-right-handedness (which could be tied to early developmental instability) has been associated with homosexuality. Owen, who was heterosexual, was the only left-handed triplet. See Scott L. Hershberger and Nancy L. Segal, "The Cognitive, Behavioral and Personality Profiles of a Male Monozygotic Triplet Set Discordant for Sexual Orientation," *Archives of Sexual Behavior*, 33 (2004): 497–514.

3. I met with each of the triplets and their mother in June 2003. I also spoke

by telephone with the triplets' older brother, Bob, and with Owen's wife, Lisa. Their father, Dan, declined to speak with me.

4. Multiple sclerosis (MS) is most likely to strike people in young and middle adulthood. The myelin sheath that surrounds nerves in the brain and spinal cord becomes damaged, affecting nerve function. Between 30 and 50 percent of identical twins with MS have affected twin siblings, compared with only 5 percent of fraternal twins. Thus, genetic factors play a role, but they are not the whole story. Apparently, an unknown environmental trigger is required to launch the disease in a susceptible individual. See Peter Riskind, "Multiple Sclerosis: The Immune System's Terrible Mistake," *Harvard Mahoney Neuroscience Institute Letter*, 5 (1996); http://www.med.harvard.edu/publications/On_The_Brain/Volume5/Number4/.

5. Hershberger and Segal, "Cognitive, Behavioral and Personality Profiles."

6. A Kinsey scale score of "5" indicates strong endorsement of an item. However, Owen had circled "1" for sexual orientation, meaning complete heterosexuality.

6. AGNES TO ANDRU

1. The identical twinship of Andru and Audrey was confirmed by DNA tests.

2. Mason Funk, from Film Garden Entertainment in Studio City, California, was producing a segment on scientific understanding of transsexualism for the Discovery Channel.

3. Andru, the firstborn twin by forty-seven minutes, weighed 5 pounds at birth. Audrey, the secondborn twin, weighed 5 pounds 8 ounces. Andru was lighter by about 10 pounds throughout childhood and early adulthood, when he weighed 130 pounds. Andru is now heavier, however, owing to his testosterone treatments and exercise regimen; he now weighs 170 pounds and is five feet seven inches tall, whereas Audrey weighs 155 pounds and is five feet five inches tall. (Audrey weighed 145 pounds when she conceived but gained 55 pounds during her pregnancy.) Both twins are right-handed.

4. Audrey began menstruating at age thirteen, whereas Andru was fourteen.

5. A. Michel et al., "A Psycho-Endocrinological Overview of Transsexualism," *European Journal of Endocrinology*, 145 (2001): 365–376. The different theories concern unusual prenatal hormonal effects, altered brain structures, atypical parent-child relations, and disordered personality development. In the case of identical twins like Andru and Audrey, it may be that some differences in gene expression, associated with when the fertilized egg di-

vides, explain their differences in sexual behavior and gender identity. Dr. Harvey Kliman (personal communication, February 25, 2005). It is unclear which genes are involved, but they could affect prenatal brain development and/or hormone production; see Dick F. Swaab, Wilson C. J. Chung, Frank P. M. Kruijver, Michel A. Hofman, and Tatjana A. Ishunina, "Structural and Functional Sex Differences in the Human Hypothalamus," *Hormones and Behavior,* 40 (2001): 93–98.

6. The first sex change operations, performed on two male transvestites, occurred in 1931, in Germany; see F. Abraham, cited in P. T. Chen-Kettenis and L. J. G. Gooren, "Transsexualism: A Review of Etiology, Diagnosis and Treatment," *Journal of Psychosomatic Research,* 46 (1999): 315–333. The first complete surgical sex change operation involved a male to female transsexual. It was reported in the medical literature in the early 1950s; see Christian Hamburger, Georg K. Stürup, and Herstedvester E. Dahl-Iversen, "Transvestism: Hormonal, Psychiatric, and Surgical Treatment," *Journal of the American Medical Association,* 152 (1953): 391–396. After treating their patient, however, these doctors discovered an analogous case reported in Germany in 1949, though the surgery was performed in 1943.

7. Audrey was also a runner-up in the local Miss Valentine competition during her senior year of high school.

8. Michel et al., "A Psycho-Endocrinological Overview of Transsexualism"; Majid Sadeghi and Ali Fakhrai, "Transsexualism in Female Monozygotic Twins: A Case Report," *Australian and New Zealand Journal of Psychiatry,* 34 (2000): 862–864. The prevalence of gender identity disorders is unknown. The estimated female-to-male ratio is between 1 to 6 and 1 to 30.

9. This two-stage process constitutes care standards for prospective transsexuals, established by the Harry Benjamin International Gender Dysphoria Association (HBIGDA), in Minneapolis, Minn.; see W. Meyer et al., "The Harry Benjamin Gender Dysphoria Association's Standards of Care for Gender Identity Disorders," sixth version, *Journal of Psychology and Human Sexuality,* 13 (2001): 1–30.

10. San Francisco employers now pay for their employees' sex reassignment surgeries.

11. "Changing Sexes: Female to Male," Discovery Health Channel, May 11, 2003. Agnes's pre- and post-operative procedures were taped and televised.

12. Agnes and Audrey are among the few identical female pairs in which one twin voluntarily chose sex reassignment. However, it is difficult to obtain

accurate statistics because some cases have not been reported in the scientific literature. A recent autobiography documents the transition of a female twin from Great Britain; see Paul Hewitt, with Jane Warren, *A Self-Made Man* (London: Headline, 1995). Paul, formerly Martine, claims that he and his twin sister, Karen, are fraternal twins, but I suspect that they are identical twins because their pictures (taken before Paul's transition) look so similar. In May 2003 I was contacted by a third pair, Juan and Liana; see note 14. In October 2004 I appeared on ABC's *Good Morning America* program with these twins.

Two additional cases have been reported: G. M. F. Garden and D. J. Rothery, "A Female Monozygotic Twin Pair Discordant for Transsexualism: Some Theoretical Implications," *British Journal of Psychiatry,* 161 (1992): 852–854; and R. Green and R. J. Stoller, "Two Monozygotic (Identical) Twin Pairs Discordant for Gender Identity," *Archives of Sexual Behavior,* 1 (1971): 321–327. I am also aware that some of my colleagues are identifying other such cases.

One published report tells the story of an identical female twin pair who both requested sex reassignment surgery, though the investigators lost track of this pair; see Sadeghi and Fakhrai, "Transsexualism in Female Monozygotic Twins." And in the 1960s, an identical male twin infant was reassigned as a female, following penile ablation during circumcision; see John Colapinto, *As Nature Made Him: The Boy Who Was Raised as a Girl* (New York: Perennial, 2001). This was *not,* however, a case of transsexualism; this individual changed back to being a male when, as an adult, he learned the truth about his situation. He committed suicide in May 2004.

13. "Changing Sexes: Female to Male," September 10, 2003.
14. As a result of my interview on the Discovery program "Changing Sexes: Female to Male," I was contacted by Juan (formerly Juanita), an identical twin who changed sex about one year before Andru. His thoughts and feelings growing up were very similar to Andru's. His twin sister, Liana, was married and had seven children; she has since delivered her eighth child.
15. Children born from Audrey's eggs would be as closely related to Andru as if he had had the children himself.
16. http://freerepublic.com/focus/f-news/1080555/posts. In addition to controversies surrounding same-sex marriages, a recent Florida ruling has banned marriages by transsexual individuals wishing to marry as their new

sex. "Transgender People Can't Wed as New Sex, Court Says," *Los Angeles Times,* July 24, 2004, p. A16.

17. http://www.lakotaarchives.com/lakritualtxt.html.

PART III: EXTRAORDINARY CIRCUMSTANCES

1. "China Redefines Extra Offspring as Burden Rather Than Offense," *Los Angeles Times,* August 23, 2002, pp. A1, A10. The Central Committee of the Chinese Communist Party formalized the One-Child Policy in an open letter dated September 1980. Karin Evans, *The Lost Daughters of China: Abandoned Girls, Their Journey to America, and the Search for a Missing Past* (New York: J. P. Tarcher/Putnam, 2000). Other sources indicate that the policy began in 1979; see, for example, "China's One Child Policy," www.overpopulation.com/faq/population_control/one_child.html.

   Chinese officials are now expected to implement corrective measures, such as criminalizing selective abortion of girls, to reverse the male-female imbalance associated with the One-Child Policy. Currently, 119 boys are born for every 100 girls; the difference is as high as 133 to 100 in rural areas. Interestingly, some parents say they are used to the policy and prefer to have only one child. Ching-Ching Ni, "China Confronts Its Daunting Gender Gap," *Los Angeles Times,* January 21, 2005, p. A6; Don Lee, "China Fears a Baby Bust," *Los Angeles Times,* December 6, 2004, pp. A1, A14.

2. "A Chinese Hotel Full of Proud American Parents," *New York Times,* March 31, 2003, p. A40.

3. "China, Land of the Only Child, Honors Twins," *Washington Post,* October 3, 2004, p. A32.

7. TWO BODIES AND ONE SOUL

1. Theresienstadt began as a ghetto work camp in 1941 and operated until 1945. Many Jews were transported from there to concentration camps such as Auschwitz. During a 1943 camp inspection by the International Red Cross, fake stores, schools, and other buildings were set up to give the impression of a model society. This sham was exposed in the 1944 film *Paradise Camp.* Stepha and Annetta were at Theresienstadt from 1942 to 1943.

2. Gerald L. Posner and John Ware, *Mengele: The Complete Story* (New York: McGraw-Hill, 1986).

3. Dr. Ella Lingens-Reiner was an Austrian-born physician at Auschwitz, sent there because she had helped Jewish people escape persecution. But as a doctor she maintained a privileged position at Auschwitz. At the public

hearing in Jerusalem she testified that though she did not assist Mengele in his research, he occasionally discussed it with her. He was worried that his material would fall into the wrong hands. (Testimony given at the Jerusalem hearing on Mengele's war crimes, February 1985.) Dr. Lingens-Reiner's concentration camp experiences are documented in her book *Prisoners of Fear* (London: Victor Gollancz, 1948).

4. It is estimated that there were three thousand Mengele twins, or fifteen hundred twin pairs. See Nancy L. Segal, "Holocaust Twins: Their Special Bond," *Psychology Today*, 19 (1985): 52–58.

5. Yad Vashem means "Memorial Monument and Name" in Hebrew.

6. Philips Island is about one hundred miles from North Balwyn.

7. The opera *Brundibár* was written and performed 55 times in Theresienstadt. Krása and the musicians were eventually executed (www.oswegoopera.com; www.classical-composers.org/cgi-bin/ccd.cgi?comp=krasa).

8. Yehuda Koren, "Saved by the Devil," *Good Weekend*, May 1, 1999.

9. Unlike most twins, Stepha and Annetta did not have consecutive tattoo numbers (Stepha's was 72919; Annetta's was 72890). Stepha's original number (72515) had been assigned to another inmate, so she received a new one. Furthermore, they entered Auschwitz with different last names— Kunewalder (Stephanie) and Heilbrunn (Annette).

10. The document requisitioning blood from the twins was sent to Stepha by the Panstwowe Museum, in Auschwitz, Poland.

11. Stephanie Heller and Annetta Able, "We Were Only Guinea Pigs," *Centre News*, 24 (2003): 11–12.

12. In 1941 or 1942, when Stepha and Annetta were still in Prague, they received a postcard from their mother, signed "widow Therese Heilbrunn"; people were ordered to write to their families from the Lodz ghetto. But it was only ten years ago that the twins learned from a ghetto archive that their mother and little sister had been transported to Chelmno, where they perished in the gas chambers. Chelmno was the first Nazi concentration camp, located fifty miles west of Lodz.

13. Apparently, Egon was covered with a blanket so he would not be able to identify the person beating him. His exact cause of death is unclear because he was hidden.

14. Letter from Stepha Heller to Rudolph Heller, Prague, March 1, 1946.

15. Stephanie Heller and Annetta Able, "We Were Only Guinea Pigs."

16. Annetta Able, "What You Saw and How You Felt at the Birth of a Baby," unpublished manuscript, 1969.

17. Robert R. Heller, "My Life in 32,044 Words," unpublished manuscript, 1996.

18. Relatives can share single copies of harmful recessive genes. If they each transmit this same gene to a child, the child will be affected with the disorder.

19. Stephanie Heller and Annetta Able, "Why We Testified against Dr. Mengele in Jerusalem," unpublished manuscript, 1988.

20. Stephanie D. Heller, "Kaleidoscope of Memories," unpublished manuscript, 2001.

21. This information was indicated on a survey the twins completed in 1995 as part of a twin study. DNA analysis confirmed that they are identical.

8. TWIN TOWERS

1. The twins' mother, Edith, later worked for Zales Jewelers before becoming a pastor.

2. According to a standard physical resemblance questionnaire that Linda completed, the twins were identical. This outcome is not surprising, given that Linda and Brenda looked very similar in childhood pictures. Most recently, Brenda was forty pounds heavier than Linda, partly because of a knee injury that kept her inactive, so they were easy to tell apart. But Linda said that the twins were the same weight when they were living together. However, they looked different enough as adults that their twin type is questionable.

3. The program, *Berman & Berman: For Women Only,* is shown weekly on Discovery Health. The twins program aired on May 24, 2002.

4. Jeffrey W. Greenberg, "September 11, 2001: A CEO's Story," *Harvard Business Review* (October 2002): 3–8. Marsh and McLennan Co., Inc., is a global professional services firm.

5. Some of Linda's remarks are from the *Berman & Berman* twins show.

6. "Doubled Loss," *Newsday,* March 1, 2002, p. A6. The twins' support group was organized by Aline Hoffman, Director of the Family Violence Unit of the Federation and Employment Guidance Service (FEGS), and the wife of 9/11 twin survivor Greg Hoffman. The group, led by a female psychologist whose twin brother had died in an accident, was funded by FEGS and by the Robert R. McCormick Tribune Foundation. Sixteen weekly group sessions were offered. Eighteen twins came to the first meeting, although five twins, three males and two females, met regularly.

7. "Doubled Loss." This article indicates that "at least 37" twins lost their lives on 9/11. Various other sources have indicated that there may have been forty to forty-five deceased twins.

8. Nancy L. Segal, "Twin Research Perspective on Human Development," in

Nancy L. Segal, Glenn E. Weisfeld, and Carol C. Weisfeld, eds., *Uniting Psychology and Biology: Integrative Perspectives on Human Development* (Washington, D.C.: APA Press, 1997), pp. 145–173.

9. I have conducted a large-scale study on the nature and consequences of twin loss. The study was started at the University of Minnesota in 1983, and has continued at California State University, Fullerton, since 1991. Over 500 bereaved twins have completed a survey asking about their twin relationship, their loss experience, and their coping skills. Grief intensity ratings were generally higher for identical than for fraternal twin survivors. About 60 percent of the participants are identical twins—since approximately two-thirds of twins in the population are fraternal, the over-representation of identicals in my study also shows that twin loss may be somewhat more devastating for them than for fraternals. Nancy L. Segal and Sarah L. Ream, "Decrease in Grief Intensity for Deceased Twin and Non-Twin Relatives: An Evoluntionary Perspective," *Personality and Individual Differences*, 25 (1998): 317–325, and references therein.

10. *B Is for Brenda* was published in 2004 by BookSurge.

11. By late February 2005 efforts to identify victims' remains were exhausted (Associated Press, "DNA Fails to Find 1,100 9/11 Victims," *Los Angeles Times*, February 24, 2005, p. A9).

12. Danielle Conway, "Family Tribute," www.mmc.com (April 2002).

13. "Posner's Shining Stars," *Hype Hair* (March 2004), pp. 128–130.

9. A GOOD-NEWS STORY

1. Some studies show a slightly higher frequency of *truncus arteriosus* in males, but this finding has not been confirmed (www.emedicine.com/ped/topic2316.htm).

2. Chance and luck reunited several sets of separately adopted Chinese twins. In one case, fraternal girls Rachel and Madison looked so similar that their adoptive mothers suspected they were related—and they were. In another case, a couple had adopted a daughter whom they named Abbi, not knowing that she had an identical twin. Five days later, the Chinese foster family that had been caring for both twins found the couple and showed them Abbi's twin sister. The babies had been found in different places, so they were not officially listed as twins. A private meeting, including the adoptive American family, the Chinese foster family, and the Chinese adoption coordinator, followed. After several days of waiting the American couple was allowed to adopt Abbi's twin sister, whom they named Grace. See Karin Evans, *The Lost Daughters of China* (New York: Jeremy P. Tarcher/Putnam,

2000); Cory Barron, "'Dropped from Heaven': Twins Reunited," http://childrenshopeint.org/Barrons.htm.

Another case of reunited twins was publicly announced in October 2004, when three-year-old twin brother and sister Tao Tao and XiMei met for the first time in Tucson, Arizona. XiMei's mother, Rose Veneklasen, knew that her daughter had had a cribmate in a Changsha orphange and wanted to contact the little girl's family. An Internet search on the orphanage website produced the name Yao, Antao, but Antao was a boy's name; Antiao was the name for a girl. Assuming that this was a typo, Rose contacted the child's mother, Jutta Walters. The mothers discovered that their children, XiMei and Tao Tao, were about the same age, had been abandoned on the same day, had been taken to the same orphanage, and had the same developmental anomaly (cleft lip and palate). Their referral pictures were remarkably similar, as were their later photos, which showed the same round face. DNA tests indicated with 98 percent certainty that the little boy and girl shared at least one parent, probably their mother. "Chinese Babies Adopted by American Couples Are Likely Twins," *Associated Press*, October 9, 2004; Interview with Rose Veneklasen, October 27, 2004. The Changsha First Social Welfare Institution is an orphanage for Chinese children. A website for families with children adopted from this orphanage was created in the United States in 2000; see http://groups.yahoo.com/group/changshakids/.

In April 2004, Jim and Susan Rittenhouse (who had adopted one Chinese twin girl from a fraternal pair) set up an Internet forum (http://groups.yahoo.com/group/sisterfar/). This group supports families who have located the twins and siblings of their adopted Chinese children. According to Susan, the group's fifty-six members represent twenty-five sets of twins and twelve sets of siblings, either confirmed or suspected. So far, DNA analysis has revealed that three pairs are identical (they include Lily and Gillian, but not Abbi and Grace, since they are being reared together) and ten pairs are fraternal; the other pairs have not yet been tested. Children in just one fraternal pair were known to be twins when they were separated, and the adoptive parents had been told of their child's multiple birth status.

There are probably other separated Chinese twins in adoptive homes who will meet at some time in the future—and others who never will.

3. See Evans, *The Lost Daughters of China*.

4. Some babies found by Americans working in China were adopted by them; see ibid.

5. Rowena Fong and Anne Wang, "Adoptive Parents and Identity Development for Chinese Children," *Journal of Human Behavior in the Social Environment*, 3 (2001): 19–33. It is estimated that 80 percent of adopted Chinese children under fourteen have siblings.

6. http://www.lorenjavier.com/toychest/asian/mulan.html.

PART IV: EVERYDAY WONDERS

1. Nancy L. Segal, *Entwined Lives: Twins and What They Tell Us about Human Behavior* (New York: Plume, 2000).

10. SELFLESS LOVE

1. Tracy and Marcy's story was aired on NBC's *Today Show* on September 26, 2002, as part of a weeklong series entitled "Overcoming Infertility."

2. My interviews included telephone conversations with Tracy and Marcy, Tracy's husband, Brian, Marcy's husband, Tom, the twins' older brother, John IV, and the twins' mother, Patti McEnery. (The twins' father chose not to be interviewed. He and his wife had divorced when the twins were five.) In July 2003, I visited Santa Cruz, California, to spend a day with the twins. I also met Marcy's two children, McKenna, and Tom, Jr., and the newest addition to the family, Tracy's daughter, Ella. A standard physical-similarity questionnaire showed that the twins are identical.

3. In vitro fertilization (IVF) is a costly and painful procedure with uncertain outcomes; each treatment cycle (IVF and embryo transfer) can cost as much as $10,000, and only about one-third of egg retrievals lead to a live birth. IVF success rates for 2002 are available at www.cdc.gov/reproductivehealth/ART02/section2c.htm.

4. Tracy had a laparoscopy, a procedure in which a tiny scope is inserted into the abdomen through a small incision. It is often used to diagnose diseases of the fallopian tubes and pelvic cavity.

5. Valley Fever has been traced to a fungal spore that becomes airborne as a result of winds, construction, or farming. The spore enlarges if inhaled by susceptible individuals (for example, individuals working with infected animals or visiting places with outbreaks), causing Valley Fever within three weeks of exposure. Approximately 60 percent of affected individuals show no symptoms.

6. IUI is artificial insemination using sperm washed free of seminal fluid. It

was performed in the landmark case of Baby M in the mid-1980s, in New Jersey. A woman was inseminated with the sperm of a man whose wife was infertile. But when the baby was born she wanted to keep the child and refused the $10,000 fee to which she had agreed; the courts awarded the baby to the biological father four months later. Ayse G. Yesilyurt, "Book: Sacred Bond: The Legacy of Baby M," *Anadolu*, 5 (1995) (*www.wakeup.org/anadolu/05/4/book.html*).

7. "Overcoming Infertility," the *Today Show*.

11. MARITAL MATH

1. The Sanders twins' marriage proposal website is available at *http://www.twinstuff.com/sanders/default.html*.

2. Craig and Diane and Mark and Darlene's situation differs from Lawrence Casler's definition of quaternary marriage: "Quaternary marriages include two married couples and their children living together, with the goals of companionship, division of labor, and increasing the number of adult role models available to the children." See Lawrence Casler, "Permissive Matrimony: Proposals for the Future," *The Humanist*, 34 (1974): 4–8.

3. The only published study of twins married to twins included fifty couples, but there were probably more. Charlotte C. Taylor, "Marriages of Twins to Twins," *Acta Geneticae Medicae et Gemellologie*, 20 (1971): 96–113.

4. Paul Lichtenstein and A. J. Bengt Kallen, "Twin Births in Mothers Who Are Twins: A Registry Based Study," *British Medical Journal*, 312 (1996): 879–881; Paolo Parisi et al., "Familial Incidence of Twinning," *Nature*, 304 (1983): 626–628. DNA tests showed that Craig and Mark, Diane and Darlene, and Colby and Brady are identical twins.

5. Twinstuff Outreach is a non-profit corporation that provides information and assistance to multiple birth families. The Texas Twins Round-Up is an annual event that celebrates having and being twins. The first round-up was held in 2002.

6. Former president Ronald Reagan; former Dallas Cowboys coach Tom Landry, former CIA director William Colby, and former White House press secretary James Brady.

7. Craig and Mark both studied history in college.

8. Gordon Claridge, Sandra Canter, and W. I. Hume, *Personality Differences and Biological Variations* (Oxford: Pergamon Press, 1973); James Shields, *Monozygotic Twins: Brought Up Apart and Together* (London: Oxford University Press, 1962). Identical twins reared apart (or living apart for more

than five years) showed greater similarity in extraversion than identical twins reared together (or living apart for less than five years).

9. Jacob F. Orlebeke et al., "Left-Handedness in Twins: Genes or Environment," *Cortex*, 32 (1996): 479–490; Sarah E. Medland et al., "Special Twin Environments, Genetic Influences and Their Effects on the Handedness of Twins and Their Siblings," *Twin Research*, 6 (2003): 119–130.

10. See www.twinsdays.org for information about Twinsburg, Ohio's, annual Twins Days Festival.

11. All four twins appeared on the *Debra Duncan Show*, in Houston, Texas. The show is no longer on the air.

12. The twins appeared on the *Oprah Winfrey Show* on March 10, 2003, and the *Montel Williams Show* on March 4, 2004.

13. David T. Lykken and Auke Tellegen, "Is Human Mating Adventitious or the Result of Lawful Choice? A Twin Study of Mate Selection," *Journal of Personality and Social Psychology*, 65 (1993): 56–68. Only 13 percent of 131 men married to an identical twin and 7 percent of 102 women married to an identical twin were attracted to their spouse's co-twin.

14. Twins and non-twins generally choose spouses similar to themselves in attitudes and values. In contrast, personality similarity is much less pronounced. See Robert Plomin et al., *Behavioral Genetics*, 4th ed. (New York: Worth Publishers, 2001).

12. QUAD BOYS ARE FINE . . .

1. Elizabeth M. Bryan, *The Nature and Nurture of Twins* (London: Baillière Tindall, 1983).

2. The figures reported here are based on U.S. births. Since the early 1970s multiple birth rates have also increased dramatically in Canada; Multiple Births Canada, "Incidence of Multiple Births" (Newsletter), 2001.

3. Joyce A. Martin et al., "Births: Final Data for 2001," *National Vital Statistics Reports*, 51 (2002): 1–103. The count is based on liveborn individuals within multiple-birth sets; thus, one triplet set yields three births.

4. Joyce A. Martin and Melissa M. Park, "Trends in Twin and Triplet Births: 1980–97," *National Vital Statistics Reports*, 47 (1999): 1–16.

5. *Go Magazine* (2001): 1.

6. Paul Lichtenstein and A. J. Bengt Kallen, "Twin Births in Mothers Who Are Twins: A Registry Based Study," *British Medical Journal*, 312 (1996): 879–881; Paolo Parisi et al., "Familial Incidence of Twinning," *Nature*, 304 (1983): 626–628.

7. Cathryn M. Lewis, Sue C. Healey, and Nicholas G. Martin, "Genetic Contribution to DZ Twinning," *American Journal of Medical Genetics*, 61 (1996): 237–246.

8. Cerebral palsy (CP) is a disability resulting from damage to the brain before, during, or shortly after birth and outwardly manifested by muscular incoordination and speech disturbances. CP may be linked to oxygen insufficiency, infections, bleeding, and other factors. Nicky's birth situation clearly differed from his brothers.' Mandy recalled that he "moved around a lot in utero and was agitated from birth."

9. I did not plan to conduct a formal study of the quad boys. My intention was to observe their daily life over the course of a few days, to understand the delights and difficulties of higher-order multiple birth families.

10. DNA testing of the quads was conducted in November 2003. As expected, the two matched pairs—Nicky and Benny and Matt and Mike—each turned out to be identical twins with 99 percent certainty.

11. A "rule" in the biology of twinning is that a single chorion (outer membrane of the developing embryo) indicates identical twinning. However, a recent report described a pair of fraternal twins with one chorion between them. The twins in question were conceived by in vitro fertilization. Vivienne L. Souter et al., "A Report of Dizygous Monochorionic Twins," *New England Journal of Medicine*, 349 (2003): 154–158.

12. Charles E. Boklage, "On the Distribution of Nonrighthandedness among Twins and Their Families," *Acta Geneticae Medicae et Gemellologiae*, 30 (1981): 167–187.

13. Implantation occurs approximately six to eight days after ovulation in human females.

14. Mandy held Benny when he was three days old, but just for a moment while nurses weighed him. She felt that she really held him for the first time when he was nearly a month old.

15. M. C. Williams and W. F. O'Brien, "Low Weight/Length Ratio to Assess Risk of Cerebral Palsy and Perinatal Mortality in Twins," *American Journal of Perinatology*, 15 (1998): 225–228.

16. E. Fuller Torrey et al., *Schizophrenia and Manic-Depressive Disorder: The Biological Roots of Mental Illness as Revealed by the Landmark Study of Identical Twins* (New York: Basic Books, 1994).

17. The higher frequency of left-handedness among twins and other multiples has been associated with delayed zygotic splitting (identicals only), birth trauma, and other factors. Birth trauma could include fetal crowding and reduced oxygen supply at birth. I. E. C. Sommer et al., "Language Lateral-

ization in Monozygotic Twin Pairs Concordant and Discordant for Handedness," *Brain*, 125 (2002): 2710–2718.

18. Nancy L. Segal, Scott L. Hershberger, and Sara Arad, "Meeting One's Twin: Perceived Social Closeness and Familiarity," *Evolutionary Psychology*, 1: 70–95 (2003).

AFTERWORD

1. "Genome Analysis Shows Humans Survive on Low Number of Genes," *New York Times* (online), February 11, 2001. This figure was later revised downward to between 20,000 and 25,000; International Human Genome Sequencing Consortium, "Finishing the Euchromatic Sequence of the Human Genome," *Nature*, 431 (2004): 931–945.

2. Ian Wilmut et al., "Viable Offspring Derived from Fetal and Adult Mammalian Cells," *Nature*, 385 (1997): 810.

3. Leon R. Kass, "Preventing a Brave New World; Why We Should Ban Human Cloning Now," *New Republic*, 224 (2000): 30–39; Nancy Gibbs, "Where Do You Draw the Line?" *Time*, August 13, 2001, pp. 18–21. There have even been wild claims that cloned children were in the works; see "A Desire to Duplicate," *New York Times Magazine*, February 4, 2001, pp. 40–45, 67–68.

4. "Perpetual Pets, Via Cloning," *Los Angeles Times* (online), March 16, 2001; T. Shi et al., "A Cat Cloned by Nuclear Transplantation," *Nature*, 415 (2002): 859.

5. http://savingsandclone.com (2004); "Cloned Felines Are the Cat's Meow at NY Show," *Los Angeles Times*, October 10, 2004, p. A24. The two cloned cats were displayed at New York's annual cat show at Madison Square Garden. Then, in April 2005, Italian scientists announced the first birth of a cloned champion racehorse. Pieraz 2, born in February, is only the second cloned horse. See Laura Smith, "Scientists Clone a Champion, *The Guardian* (London), April 15, 2005.

6. National Bioethics Advisory Commission, *Cloning Human Beings* (Rockville, Md.: NBAC, 1997).

7. Nancy L. Segal, "Human Cloning: A Twin-Research Perspective," *Hastings Law Journal*, 53 (2002): 1073–1084, and references therein; Kenan Malik, "The Moral Clone," *Prospect*, 63 (May 2001): 10–11; Leon R. Kass and Daniel Callahan, "Cloning's Big Test: Ban Stand," *New Republic*, August 6, 2001, pp. 10, 12; Martha C. Nussbaum and Cass R. Sunstein, eds., *Clones and Clones: Facts and Fantasies about Human Cloning* (New York: Norton, 1998).

8. Lee Silver, "Public Policy Crafted in Response to Public Ignorance Is Bad Public Policy," *Hastings Law Journal*, 53 (2002): 1037–1047.

9. Nancy L. Segal, "Behavioral Aspects of Intergenerational Cloning: What Twins Tell Us," *Jurimetrics*, 38 (1997): 57–67.

10. "The Ties That Bind," *Dateline NBC*, March 30, 1999.

11. Cokie Roberts, "Like Mother, Like Daughter," *Life Magazine*, May 1999, pp. 46–61.

12. Stephen E. Levick, *Clone Being: Exploring the Psychological and Social Dimensions* (New York: Rowman and Littlefield, 2004). This volume includes discussions of several kinship-based models that can inform thinking about human cloning.

13. "Conceiving a Code for Creation: The Legal Debate Surrounding Human Cloning," Hastings Law School Symposium, San Francisco, Calif., January 26, 2002.

14. Comment from an identical twin.

Acknowledgments

I owe so much to a special group of people. My editor at Harvard University Press, Elizabeth Knoll, was simply the best. Her comments, intuitions—even her cryptic handwritten notes—were always insightful and accurate. She continued to push me to write the best book that I possibly could. The staff of Harvard University Press was the finest group of people with whom to work. My manuscript editor (and mother of twins), Christine Thorsteinsson, added polish and style to the finished manuscript. Publicists Rose Ann Miller and Mary Kate Maco offered invaluable guidance and support throughout. And the comments of two anonymous reviewers sharpened my thoughts on some of the twins I wrote about.

My agent, Angela Rinaldi, believed that I had another book in me, and she did everything possible to make sure that I wrote it. Phyllis Raphael helped me find the right literary voice in her non-fiction creative writing workshop at Columbia University in summer 2002. My assistant, Lauren Gonzalez, reviewed early versions of the chapters and always came back with the finest constructive criticism possible.

My dad, Al Segal, was my best supporter, as he always has been. He has a great habit of sending me every twin-related article he reads in newspapers and magazines. My twin sister, Anne, was the reason I got into twin research in the first place—and one of many reasons that I stayed there. My mom, Esther Segal, celebrated with me in summer

2002 when Harvard University Press offered me a book contract. She passed away in January 2003 during the early stages of the writing. She would have loved seeing the finished project, and I wish so badly that she could have.

The American Association for University Women awarded me a 2003–2004 American Fellowship, allowing me the wonderful freedom to travel, research, and write. Steven Pinker invited me to spend part of my sabbatical in the Psychology Department at Harvard University, where I could work closely with my editor as the book was nearing completion. Wayne Furman arranged a quiet carrel for me in one of the special reading rooms of the New York Public Library. The faculty, staff, and administrators at California State University gave me the time and resources to see this project through. Kelly Donovan, graphic artist (and identical twin), prepared the twins' photographs for publication.

The twins, triplets, and quads and their families were generous with their time and their materials, making the interview process a sheer delight. Most important, they tolerated my many "last questions" with patience and good humor.

I also want to thank my swing dance partner: You followed me to Melbourne, San Francisco, Boston, New York, and elsewhere as I followed the twins. Because of you we danced in beautiful, magical places.

ACKNOWLEDGMENTS